More Praise for *Women We Buried, Women We Burned*

"How do you write a book about overcoming extreme hardship, about the singular people who convince you to take a chance on yourself, about finding the big world after a childhood that prepared you for a tiny one, about discovering that you love the people who failed to love you—and manage not to strike a single trite note? How do you remember every detail and make the reader feel like they saw, heard, and felt each moment? I have no idea, actually, but Rachel Louise Snyder has done it." —Masha Gessen, National Book Award–winning author of *The Future Is History* and *Surviving Autocracy*

"Bravery and honesty are the cornerstones of the memoir, but Snyder adds to this—generosity. This is a compassionate telling of a sometimes brutal story. *Women We Buried, Women We Burned* reminds me of opera, with its beautiful sadness and artistic triumph. The hope contained on these pages is hard won, and all the more precious due to the struggles from which it emerges." —Tayari Jones, *New York Times* bestselling author of *An American Marriage*

"With a journalist's keen eye and a novelist's elegant prose, Rachel Louise Snyder delivers an unsentimental and bone-deep observational memoir of death and family, class and history, East and West, and politics and travel; at the center of each story is a reaffirmation of human survival as an art of triumph." —Suki Kim, *New York Times* bestselling author of *Without You, There Is No Us*

"With wonderfully evocative prose, Rachel Louise Snyder captures here the stark horror of a child losing her mother and half her roots as she's then swept into her evangelical father's second family and has to either flee or be erased. As nakedly honest as it is fair, what is so remarkable about *Women We Buried, Women We Burned* is that Ms. Snyder does flee, and her lone voyage to her very self is the voyage of so many girls and women around the world who have been uprooted and cast aside and must find their own way back. This is an important and profoundly moving memoir, and I cannot recommend it highly enough." —Andre Dubus III, *New York Times* bestselling author of *Townie* and *Such Kindness*

"A propulsive, clear-eyed, and stunning memoir about transformation, self-discovery, and the journey we go on when we decide that yes, we want to do more than simply survive; we want to thrive. *Women We Buried, Women We Burned* is a revelation." —Chelsea Bieker, author of *Heartbroke* and *Godshot*

"A gorgeous and radiantly honest book, brilliant in its ability to capture the way grief reverberates across a lifetime. Rather than force trauma into a false closure, Snyder transforms it into a radical openness and ability to connect." —Danielle Evans, author of *The Office of Historical Corrections*

"As stunning as it is powerful, *Women We Buried, Women We Burned* is a tour-de-force memoir of family, faith, love, loss, resilience, and, ultimately, redemption. With deftness and grace, Snyder navigates the complicated terrain of childhood trauma and presents a model for how to reconcile with the ghosts of your past." —Monica West, author of *Revival Season*

"A profoundly moving and layered memoir. Snyder's story connects on so many levels because she writes honestly about traumas, forgiveness, and the hard work it takes to build a life. A truly stunning book that will broaden hearts and minds, and also educate and inspire." —Loung Ung, author of *First They Killed My Father*

WOMEN WE BURIED, WOMEN WE BURNED

WOMEN WE BURIED, WOMEN WE BURNED

a memoir

RACHEL LOUISE SNYDER

BLOOMSBURY PUBLISHING

NEW YORK · LONDON · OXFORD · NEW DELHI · SYDNEY

AUTHOR'S NOTE

Although this is a work of nonfiction, the names and identifying characteristics of certain individuals have been changed to protect their privacy, and dialogue has been reconstructed to the best of the author's recollection. The following are pseudonyms: Aaron, Bruce, Charlie, Chazz, Donna, Eddie, El Dorado, Greta, Holly, Jackie, Jackson, Jessica, and Troy.

BLOOMSBURY PUBLISHING
Bloomsbury Publishing Inc.
1385 Broadway, New York, NY 10018, USA

BLOOMSBURY, BLOOMSBURY PUBLISHING, and the Diana logo are
trademarks of Bloomsbury Publishing Plc

First published in the United States 2023

ISBN: HB: 978-1-63557-912-3; EBOOK: 978-1-63557-913-0

LIBRARY OF CONGRESS CATALOGING-IN-PUBLICATION DATA IS AVAILABLE

2 4 6 8 10 9 7 5 3 1

Typeset by Westchester Publishing Services
Printed and bound in the U.S.A.

To find out more about our authors and books visit www.bloomsbury.com and
sign up for our newsletters.

Bloomsbury books may be purchased for business or promotional use.
For information on bulk purchases please contact Macmillan Corporate and
Premium Sales Department at specialmarkets@macmillan.com.

For Eliana Jazz, forever and always (and for Khmow, of course)

Jazz and Khmow, Phnom Penh, Cambodia, 2008

There is also, in any history, the buried, the wasted, and the lost.

—MURIEL RUKEYSER

However did they worm their way in?
Clever chaps, they didn't have to! They
Were there the very moment spark and clay
Ignited, always underneath the skin.

—DR. CHARLES LEE

The author's mother, Gail Margery Lee, late 1950s.

PROLOGUE

I traveled twenty-six thousand miles, around the world by ship, looping around continents and islands, across the international date line and the equator, the world made both bigger and smaller at once by this journey. My imagination could never have conjured such a voyage. If I thought of the world beyond my life at all, I thought of danger. I thought of loss. Loss of bodily autonomy, loss of all one might need to survive. I did not picture myself, mile after mile, foreign landscapes layered by more foreign landscapes where even the color of the earth and the shape of the trees were revelations to me. Where language itself meant more than simply communicating; it could mean life or death, freedom or prison. One night, I lay on the deck of the ship, on a pillow I had carried from my cabin, huddling with a small group of new friends, to watch the stars, to sleep under moonlight. By day, the sea was a deep indigo blue all the way to the horizon. I knew because I spent hours in a crevice on the starboard side of an upper deck, swinging my legs over the side of the ship, watching the water ribbon as we sliced through it. But at night, it was a black, broiling thing, alive and terrifying and beautiful.

The stars were so bright our faces appeared as if spotlighted on the deck. Days earlier, when we had sailed from Kenya to South Africa, the ship's loudspeakers had boomed "Southern Cross" by Crosby, Stills & Nash as we passed over the equator and we hugged everyone in our midst, knowing that to travel such distances meant the people we were becoming were not the same ones who'd be returning home. We held a ceremony like the navy's, transforming from pollywogs to shellbacks (meaning to cross the equator by ship). One man wore a wig of seaweed and carried a trident. Our metamorphosis was complete when we kissed the body of a dead fish.

On this night, though, close to the end of our journey, we wanted to stay up and watch the stars. My friends and I lay on our backs talking, telling stories, promising as one does in her youth to never lose touch. We watched the sky, no light pollution from land for thousands of miles around us, and the stars were as voluminous as raindrops, in enormous, garish swaths of cottony white. So many they appeared like clouds stitched with silver sparkles. We were sailors. We were explorers. We were navigators, cruising by celestial bodies, wanting to hold onto the ancient belief that stars were fixed and only people moved.

I had left my home months earlier. Or, rather, my most recent apartment. But home? The last stable place I'd lived had been during my childhood, back when everything and everyone was still intact, back when my mother was still alive. Since then, how many times had I moved? Thirty? Forty? So many years when I held everything I owned in the trunk of my car, digging for my work uniform from a trash bag, covering the beloved stereo I had nowhere to plug in. Couches and floors, motel beds and car seats. I had been out in the world then, too, on those nights, but it hadn't been *this* world. It hadn't been a world that held any promise at all. I knew, because I had been terrified to board this ship—built for the Korean War but repurposed for passengers—yet made myself do it anyway, knew that however vague my future looked—and it looked plenty vague, still—it was this idea of *promise* that I'd hold. This sense of *possibility*.

As we lay on our backs, light began to break along the horizon, and the overhead sky appeared to cleave in half. Night on one side, dawn on the other. It was like a perfect seam down the sky. We couldn't believe what was in front of us. We whispered, *Are you seeing what I'm seeing? Can this really be happening?* Because even the visual evidence didn't seem enough. Day and night so clearly sharing the sky. A vertical vein from horizon to horizon threading right down the middle. Even as I watched it, it seemed impossible that it was real. Dozens of us witnessed the sky slowly, almost imperceptibly, folding itself in half, then in half again, the dark side eventually giving way to the light, the ocean rushing loudly as it carried us along. This night, this moment would come to me over and over through the years and then the decades. I would question my memory, think *it couldn't have been as I recall it. An artery down the sky.* But the vision was so clear in my mind, so unshakable.

I know now that science has a name for that line—dawn in half the sky, darkness in the other. The Terminator. Sometimes it's also called the Gray Area, or even the Twilight Zone. It's a fuzzy line, because sunlight bends around the earth. I like to think *to* the earth now. But it does not exist in equal proportion to the darkness. That is to say, that the world is not half in dark, half in light. It's because of that bend, the earth's diameter. It turns out that sunlight covers a greater area of earth than darkness.

Science explained the celestial vision I saw that night, but memory makes it a miracle. I wouldn't understand for years still, but that line was a kind of beginning, a reset. A visual demarcation of my own metamorphosis. That line is my origin story.

Part I

SPARK AND CLAY

Pittsburgh, PA

One

The author's mother, pregnant with David in 1967.

My brother, David, and I came home from school on a Friday in October to an ambulance in the driveway. David was a year older than me, in fourth grade. The ambulance was not in itself cause for alarm. We'd seen them before, coming or going, with our mother or without. It took up nearly the girth of our driveway, and we sidled past it, skipping up the stairs to our front door.

It was October 1977, but my mother had been sick for much of my life. Recently, a gray oxygen tank four feet tall had been installed in her bedroom, and she had been in bed pretty much ever since. In fact, she had been in and out of bed for years. The memories that dominate my time with my mother nearly all involve her sickness: pulling over our green Pontiac station wagon so she could vomit on the shoulder of the road, my father and grandfather helping her to the dinner table so she could sit with us for a few minutes at Passover, David and me making Get Well cards for her many hospital stays. I helped her pick out wigs and scarves. "What about this one, Rachel?" she asked, as she emerged from the bathroom with a Jaclyn Smith wig, long loose curls to her shoulders. "Or this one?"—short, with dark spiky tips. She tried to make it seem light, fun. At age eight it hadn't occurred to me to ask what was wrong.

We had lived in the shadow of her illness for so long that neither David nor I had ever imagined she could die. We thought she would be suspended in her forever illness. Her death staggered us, left us dazed and thunderstruck.

We lived, then, in a suburb called Moon Township in the west hills of Pittsburgh. Our house was under a flight path. A new Kmart opened just down the hill and my father took us on excursions for their blue-light specials, when we'd race across the store to find pruning shears on sale, or Fiddle Faddle, or Armor All. The blue-light specials made shopping a thrill. You never knew what you'd come away with. A new Barbie outfit. A jumble of little green army men for David. Cans of WD-40, which my father stocked up on, a new welcome mat, or tubs of popcorn; we had a cat that I'd named ABC and she loved popcorn. At Christmas one year, my mother and I strung cranberries and popcorn along fishing wire, feeding ABC a puffed kernel every few minutes until she vomited on the floor.

My father collected bargains and he collected opportunities. This was his word: opportunities. Multilevel marketing schemes that promised wild economic returns. Our garage, in those days, was filled with Bestline, a line of cleaning products whose logo was a crown with bubbled jewels atop each spike. One summer my dad convinced David and me to fill our red wagon and wheel around a stash of Bestline car wash to the neighbors using the pitch that it took "only a capful to wash a whole car." He suggested we throw in a freebie car wash with each sale. We spent most of that afternoon elbow deep in water, the return on our investment hobbled by overcommitting our labor forces. My father's entire workforce resigning en masse. Bestline was the first in a never-ending assemblage of such "opportunities" that took up residence in our garage.

That the ambulance was *parked* on this day was new. Usually they had their lights going, sirens off, engine running, strapping my mother on a thin gurney. But today it was like they'd stopped in for coffee. Popped in to see how Gail was doing, her split-level brick house a regular stop on their route. Like the mail. Like the milkman who put gallons in a silver box outside our door. Mail. Milk. Mother.

I wore pants. White jeans with the name *Benedict Arnold* in bubbly orange letters all over them. Casual Friday. The sardonic seventies. My mother only let me wear pants to school one day a week, and never jeans. *Benedict Arnold* had made the cut because the pants were white and orange and thus did not qualify as jeans. Back then, only pants that were blue qualified as jeans, even if they had rivets and five pockets and side seams and were made from cotton. I wanted the freedom of movement that boys had, the freedom to dive for a base or do a layup into a basket. The freedom to climb a tree. My mom dressed me in Mary Janes and white tights, pleated skirts, and blousy tops most days, but once a week I chose my white and orange *Benedict Arnolds.* The adults laughed at them, which I did not understand. *Benedict Arnold*, ha ha! Get it? Traitor.

I didn't get it. I heard *trader.* Thought of Daniel Boone and Davy Crockett.

An EMT stood in our blue-carpeted living room, at the bay window where my mother kept alive spider plants and a Christmas cactus and ferns. He nodded when I came up the stairs from the front-door landing. A radio crackled at his waist. I went to the large white settee—it had been designed by my great-grandmother, Florence Carp, who established Boston's first female-owned interior design shop right in the heart of Newbury Street; the settee was the size of a twin bed and had been a wedding present to my parents. I shrugged off my book bag, looked down at my white-clad legs for a second or two. *Benedict Arnold. Benedict Arnold. Benedict Arnold.*

Why wasn't he doing anything, the EMT? Why wasn't he taking her away on a stretcher? I glared at his dark blue back for a minute.

The details mattered. *Parked* ambulance. *Immobile* EMT. *Not* taking her away. *Not* the wheeled stretcher. I remember the EMT looking out the picture window, a tangle of plants waist high. In my memory, he is headless. The radio's crackling fills my house.

I ran down the hallway. My mother was propped up by one of those bed rest pillows that look like the sliced-off upper half of a BarcaLounger. Her macramé belt, unfinished, splayed on the bed beside her. Her metal tank on the floor beside her bed, tubes snaking around her ears, up her nose. A second EMT stood beside the oxygen tank. Also doing nothing. Also radio crackling. That radio ate into my brain, the noise. Drill-into-cranium. And his blue uniform, a darker version of the carpet that ran across our upper floor. My grandmother Erma, my mother's mother in from Boston, was on her hands and knees on the bed, puma-style. My aunt Greta, from several towns over, wife of my father's brother, was standing in the bedroom. I don't know where. Just there. In there. We have different memories about that day, she and I, about who said what, and who was there, and what happened when. The two of them, Grandma Erma and Aunt Greta, often took turns at my house, but this was the only time I remember them there together. People say children are intuitive, that nothing gets past them. I picked up all the tiny cues this day—parked ambulance, gathering of relatives, men in blue—but missed the primary event.

The sequence is where I'm unclear. I ran down the hallway. My mother's bedroom door was cracked an inch.

She wouldn't have wanted me to look. But I did. Of course I did. One eye, peering through the crack. Was it betrayal? Or an intimacy? This glance. This thievery.

My room was across the hall from my parents'. I skidded to my knees at my bedside, white-knuckled my hands in a coal-to-diamonds grasp. I prayed. I prayed like a desperate child. I prayed with an earnestness rising from me like boiling water. I prayed to the Christian God because He was the one who offered miracles, the one who said if you have enough faith. Jesus was the God of the future; El Shaddai, Yahweh, the God of the past. My father always told me my fate was up to me, up to the level of my belief, and I felt I finally understood that day. It was up to me, my prayer. The power of my own belief. I had, for years, prayed for an actual working car that would appear in my garage, child-sized, and ready to speed down the sidewalk. Red, if possible. I was flexible on the color. My father had sat with me through dozens of iterations of this particular bedtime prayer, and I thought of the car now as I prayed for my mother, assured God—in case it wasn't clear to him—that *those* prayers were nothing compared to the faith involved in *this* one. The car didn't matter at all. That's why it never appeared. I understood that now. But for my mom, I had more faith exponentially.

My mother was Jewish. Synagogue did not teach us to pray with faith, but my father was Christian and his church did, so I mashed the two together. Eyes squeezed shut. Radios crackling. Stationary EMTs. Parked dead ambulance. My grandmother in a freeze frame, hovering toward my mother as if she could suck the disease right out of her. I made the usual entreaties: *I'll never ask you God for another thing. I'll believe and serve. I'll spread your word around the whole school. Forget the car. The car was stupid. The car was a child's dream.*

My mother seemed old to me then. Thirty-five. It was only the years still to come that brought her youth into sharp focus, as I myself aged toward that number.

She was old, and then she was young. I was young and then I was old.

But another part of me is frozen forever in 1977, a girl with her young mother; sometimes, as I watch the reel in my mind, I understand what any viewer would also immediately glean: that we lose them both in that moment. The woman and the girl. I read once how trauma freezes a person in time so that a part of them remains tethered to the person they were at the time of that trauma. Somewhere, inside me, I am forever eight years old.

I prayed for as long as I thought I should, as long as it would take for God to see how much I meant it, prayed until I ran out of ways to beg. The earnest integrity of kid-faith. Then I dashed back to her door, cracked an inch. I'm unsure of the sequence. Had she already died when I skidded to my knees praying? Or had she died in the minute after? Did I see her dead? Or only dying?

I remember her there, her breath ragged, like she had cut glass lodged in her throat. There is nothing profound about this kind of death. No honor or heroism. There is the quiet life and there is the absolute stillness of death and what comes between is the violence, the dying itself. We think of life and death as intrinsically binary. Here and then gone. Alive and then dead. But there is a third category, an in-between. And dying, no matter the cause, no matter the context, always contains within it a kind of violence.

It is also profoundly intimate. To watch someone die.

"Don't you do this to me, Gail," my grandma Erma said. "Don't you *dare* do this to me." My grandmother's voice had a panicked edge, a terrible hiss. Had I already prayed? Or had I not yet begun? The terror of her voice might have led me to prayer.

Don't you dare do this to me, Gail.

"I can't breathe, I can't breathe," my mother hissed, grasping for air. Pinpoint the violence to this second. Oxygen tubes impotent against the cancer. She'd had two mastectomies, a second exactly one year to the day after the first. Radiation, chemo, vomiting, hair loss, organs so burned from the chemotherapy they froze like a rusted engine. Two weeks before her death, she and my father would sit in her oncologist's office in Pittsburgh as he declared her "cancer-free." Officially in remission, he would say. I imagine him with a grin as he says this, a celebratory tone, man v. nature and man wins this round. My mother said to her doctor, "If the cancer is gone, why can't I breathe?"

My father recounted this story to me only decades later.

I can't breathe. I can't breathe. Those were her last words. Trite. Literal. Her entire focus bringing into sharp relief the failure of her autonomic nervous system: *Breathe. Breathe. Breathe.* The banality haunted me, the physicality of the moment—the failure of her own biology—her final tether to this earth. Not her future, and not her past. Not her husband or her children, or her mother on all fours yelling at her to stay in this damn world. This is what people mean, I think, when they say we die alone. *Breath. Air. Oxygen.* And then nothing.

FOR YEARS, MY father told me my mother was in heaven, looking down on me, that she'd called out to Jesus in her final seconds. That he believed she was present in all the moments that mattered in our lives, a God-like omnipotence. She was there when I came in second for the class spelling bee, a devastating loss to me. She was there when I caught the ball after a pop fly directly into the sun and won the inning for my softball team. She was there every time I creamed the neighborhood kids at four-square. She was there when the fourth graders saw the outline of a training bra under my white cotton shirt and ridiculed me until I ran and hid in the coat closet. She watched it all, a beatific, pain-free benevolence on her face, he'd imply. I believed it in the same way I believed it when my parents told me clasping your hands at a restaurant made the food come faster. She was up there all right, her dark brown hair long and shiny to her waist as it had been before the chemotherapy claimed it. Her jaw line sharp and angled as it had been before the chemo bloated it. She was sublime, at peace, communing with God and catching glimpses of her daughter as she turned nine, then ten, then eleven.

But for me, the literal translation for years in my child's mind of her watching me meant that we had buried her alive, and then she had died in her casket, and now she existed as a ghost, forever betrayed by the people who were supposed to love her the most. I would lie in bed with my eyes squeezed shut, terrified her disembodied face would suddenly hover in the corner of my room. I whispered into the darkness of my bedroom, the sound of my own voice haunting me. I begged her not to appear. I told her I was scared, too scared. I believed she could see me, believed I had no secrets from her. She was able to peer into my heart and my mind, know how my faith couldn't save her. She saw right down into the very place inside me that had learned to fear her ghost before I'd yet learned how to miss her body.

But when my father claimed she had called out to Jesus in her last moments, there was no getting around that he had been at work that day. And he and his coworkers took off early to go and play flag football and this was the age before mobile phones, so no one could get hold of him for hours, long after the immobile EMTs turned mobile again and took away her body. He hadn't been there. But I had.

Two

My dad had just turned thirty-nine when my mom died. He had come from solid, salt-of-the-earth stock in Bellevue, a working-class neighborhood of Pittsburgh, and he worked his way to the white-collar world of upward mobility, the first in his family to graduate college (my aunt Janet, his sister, would complete her teacher's certification). And he landed not just any white-collar job, but a job at IBM, home of the supercomputer. IBM *was* the future, and my father was a natural salesman, someone who could comfortably move through a party of steelworkers or stockbrokers. His father, John Wesley, had graduated high school and become a printer. His mother, my grandma Katie, never made it past third grade—one of her great regrets. His life must have felt to all of his family like a promise fulfilled. My mother's death was a wild detour in the advancement of that promise. This wasn't the way it was supposed to go. She'd been healthy, beautiful when they met, raised by strong-willed New England feminists, her grandmother and then her own mother notable interior designers. She attended private school in Boston, spoke French, and edited her high school literary magazine. She loved horses; my father loved boats. She laughed at his stories and together they threw tremendous Super Bowl parties with endless trays of French onion dip, Brie cheese, and crab balls. They had a stash of Iron City beer and my dad entertained the guests while my mom kept their plates full. There was nothing my father loved more than talking, both sharing and hearing stories, nothing she loved more than entertaining.

In one of my favorite pictures of my mom she is wearing a green flowered summer maxi dress, her hair twisted in a thick bun, her shoulders copper from the sun; she is pushing a lawn mower, laughing, one leg hitched up in a kick. As a mother she was strict, but also fun. In her healthier days, I remember having to tiptoe around the house so as not to disturb the cake she was baking; she'd melt me a handful of crayon bits in the oven to make an enormous rainbow crayon, or sit and color Shrinky Dinks, form flowers from pipe cleaners. She styled my long hair into braids and pigtails and taught me to blow bubbles with my gum.

Her death was the one story that nothing in my dad's life had prepared him for. And in that story, the loss of her, something of him—that gregarious, smiling, warm man beloved by strangers and family alike—disappeared too.

I sat in the front row at temple, my mother's silver-handled mahogany casket in front of me. I couldn't stop staring at it, trying to figure out how the tall mother I knew could fit in a box that seemed so short. Outside, it was unusually cold in Pittsburgh for early October, and over my black dress, I wore a taupe winter coat with fake brown fur and wooden toggle buttons—my mother had bought it for me at Kaufmann's. The fake fur made my neck itch.

I knew I was supposed to be sad. But I kept turning around, seeing people I hadn't seen in so long as they filtered quietly into the temple. The neighborhood kids and their parents, my cousins from Illinois—people I was happy to see, actually, and so when I saw them, I waved and smiled, and then remembered I wasn't supposed to smile.

The day before, my father had called David and me into his bedroom after we'd returned from spending the night at the neighbor's. He lifted me on one knee, David on the other, his back hunched and his face dark. We sat on the bed where just a day earlier, my mother had struggled to breathe, but now the blue print bedspread was smoothed over and tucked in, the oxygen tank and tubes removed. The stillness of the room held a sluggish density.

"Your mother"—my dad looped an arm around each of us—"went to be with the Lord . . ." Then he bowed his head and wailed and his whole body jerked from the force of his howling. My brother broke into tears. I am sure I cried, but all I remember is the embodied grief of my dad, how his physical form seemed to careen and spasm from the weight of his pain.

My dad had always been the funnier of my parents. The jokester. He told stories of fishing and road trips with his brother, Wes, and their uncle Harold. The stories always seemed to end in some sort of vaudevillian mishap, like when Harold's white suit got covered in mud after church one day when he played on a wooden, makeshift roller coaster built by Wes. Or like the time they'd remembered to pack a picnic but then stored it in the car's trunk, so fumes had infiltrated their chipped ham and cheese sandwiches, which did not prevent their consumption. My primary image of my father was a man laughing as he told a story, smiling with his white, perfect teeth (long before dentistry could bless anyone with such a smile), and his azure eyes tearing up from the hilarity. He loved nothing more than a good pun. "Drink a fifth on the fourth for the third," he'd say every July. At a flat tire, he might roll his eyes and say, "Spare me!"

I would invent my own story in years to come, of watching my mother's casket go down into the ground at the Coraopolis Cemetery and how I'd tried to fling myself toward it, atop it, but had been held back by my father. Such a cinematic moment of despair and angst. An eight-year-old girl gripped by loss and grief. A howling dog.

But here is the truth: I did not cry when they lowered the casket. I shivered from the cold, and itched my neck, and I watched it slowly sink, mesmerized. That mahogany wood, those silver handles, cranked lower and lower into the rectangle of dirt. I folded into myself. When people say they feel dead inside, I think what they really feel—what I really felt—is the opposite: volumes of pain that must be reined in, held by a dam. *That box is definitely too short to be holding her.* I did not cry later at the shiva at my house, but I took a framed picture from our piano of the four of us—mother, father, brother, me—and I offered up a few sniffles, and I heard a small group of women standing nearby say, "Oh, the poor dear. Look at that. Just look at that." Their response was the blueprint I needed for how to act.

Later, I would train myself to cry in public when I knew I stood to gain something—extra dessert, say, or a later bedtime, or a sleepover, some kind of attention—but I did not cry privately. Her death simmered inside me, an eternal gloaming.

* * *

DAVID AND I had two days off from school. Mrs. Ralston, my third-grade teacher, must have prepped the class because when I walked in the room the Wednesday after her funeral, everyone was painfully quiet, with the kind of silence that feels like you're the only one not in on the joke. Mrs. Ralston herself was red-faced, tear tracks trailing down her cheeks, and I felt a surge of anger. I wanted to scream at her that she had *no right to cry*. It had been *my mother* who'd died. Not hers. Not anyone's. Mine. Why was *she* crying? I looked at her curly brown hair, scraggly and thick, her puffy, voluminous midsection that had, until that moment, always felt matronly and warm to me. I had loved Mrs. Ralston. She spread her arms and gestured toward my desk and I didn't know if she wanted me to hug her—right there in front of the whole class—or make my way to my seat as if I didn't know where to go. I resented Mrs. Ralston for her red eyes and though she had been very kind to me, I hated her after that. Hated that she cried. Hated that I hated someone so kind to me. Hated my hate.

It was the first time the story of my mother—what would become my life's defining story—preceded me. Knowing someone's prevailing story makes them vulnerable, and I resented being vulnerable to my classmates. It took something of my mother away from me, to have to share my grief with others.

As time passed, if my mother's death came up in conversation—and it often did—the sympathy was immediate and sweeping, and suddenly no other topic of conversation mattered. In places David and I would visit where my mother's death was known—my cousin's church, for example—strangers reminded me how beautiful my mother had been, how much she had loved me, how much of a shame it was that she had been taken so young. One woman used to compare her to a Greek goddess. This was always the line: her beauty. The loss that mattered most. What else was she except a woman stolen at the pinnacle of that beauty? Whatever she was, the vast constellation of human elements that made her up, was distilled down to this loss: youth and beauty, gone. Heaven help the children who lose ugly mothers, for what does the world say in their absence?

I became aware of myself as a kind of infamous child, both watched and pitied.

I was told I would move on. Grief wallops you, then gives way to healing. A geologic miracle. Maybe a little scar tissue left, like strata. Some hairline cracks. Grief plus time. A mathematical equation, clean and neat as a set of new linens. Worse things happen to people in far greater numbers. Not that it isn't sad, of course. So terrifically sad. Young kids, losing their young mother. Young mother, losing her life.

In her absence, I often returned to the scene, tried to micromanage details. I'm walking up the driveway, sitting on the living room settee in my *Benedict Arnold* pants, running down the hallway, peering into her bedroom, then on my knees at my bedside, and back at the bedroom door and she's saying *I can't breathe, I can't breathe.* Then it's nighttime and I'm in a strange bed and I am asking the neighbor as she tucks me in when my mom will be back from the hospital this time. I can't remember the neighbor's name or face. But I remember her saying, "I don't know, sweetie." Because, of course, she already knew.

I have written it, over the years, dozens of times: ambulance, Benedict Arnold, hallway, prayer, doorway, breath, neighbor's bed. I didn't want my mother's death to define me. We will, all of us, lose our parents. We will lose our loved ones, we will lose our selves. This is what I tell myself for years. Time swoops in and fuses you back together. There is nothing special to see here, about me, about my mother, about our story.

Three

One evening after my dad came home from work, he took me to Kmart but left David at home. Normally, I loved our Kmart excursions. He had taught me to use the reference manuals in the auto section, so that I could look up any car's replacement part—air filters, windshield wipers, oil (thicker in summer, thinner in winter). He had bought a Toyota Celica, which I considered a hot rod, especially compared to the old wood-paneled green station wagon we'd had when my mom was alive. My dad taught me to check the fluids—oil, wiper, transmission, brake—and the air in the tires, and he'd eventually ask me to change the air filter when it needed doing. I knew the auto parts section better than anywhere else in the store.

But on this day, my father and I skipped it. Instead, I found myself in women's undergarments. Clouds of lace and billowing synthetic silk brushed us as we wandered through the racks. I didn't understand what we were doing or why—my face burned with shame—until he found a saleswoman, and gently pushed me between the shoulder blades in her direction. I was in the fourth grade, an early developer as they called it then. He must have stumbled through some explanation, but I don't recall it. He left me there, instructing her as to where he'd be when we were done. Then he was gone and I was standing among towers of fabric.

Both my mother and grandmother had what were called in those days *full figures*, probably D or double D cups, and I had never once given a single thought to this biological fact until the moment I stood before a Kmart sales clerk. For her part, my mother's double mastectomy didn't even register with me until many years later. I did not yet know how she had died. It would be several years before I learned she had breast cancer, and many more years before I learned it put me at risk, but on that day standing in Kmart, all I knew was that a strange woman had been enlisted to help me buy training bras, and I did not want to be a girl and I did not like girl things, and I felt trapped. Trapped by the woman herself, trapped by the racks and racks of lace and silk and cotton, but most of all trapped by my own impending anatomy. David and my dad were together on one side of the world, and I was on the other, alone.

The saleswoman took two lacy white training bras and held them to my chest, right there between the racks. I felt my whole body stiffen, my eyes get teary. I didn't want them, of course, but I also didn't know how to get out of this moment. I didn't even know the woman's name.

She took me to the changing area and deposited me behind a three-quarter-height door, the color of pool water. Over the loudspeaker, I could hear pages for various departments, or sale announcements. I imagined my father looking at spark plugs or antifreeze. I stood in the dressing room alone, holding several bras on plastic hangers, all stretchy white. I didn't try them on. I just stood there.

After a few minutes, she said, "Well?"

I told her they were fine.

AFTER THAT DAY, my father must have felt himself lacking as my sole parent, because women began to take a more active role in my life. First there was Cherry, a babysitter who came on Mondays, Tuesdays, and Wednesdays. Cherry had short dark hair and introduced me to Styx and the Little River Band and Cheap Trick. Up until then I had mostly been a Shaun Cassidy/Leif Garrett girl. Or horses. I loved horses as much as my mother had. Above my bed was a framed portrait of Man o' War, the famous racehorse. The frame had olive green velvet around it and was the only tangible element of my bedroom that linked me to my mother. The rest of my wall art was basically centerfolds of Shaun Cassidy from *Teen Beat* or *Tiger Beat* magazines.

Every few weeks, my aunt Greta had me sleep over at her house with my cousin, Amy, who was two years older. One afternoon, when she came over to pick me up, she pulled me into the bathroom I shared with David and pointed to the green Herbal Essences bottles on the rim of the bathtub. She asked me to explain my "haircare routine." I didn't know I was supposed to have a "routine" but every day, my hair hung in greasy clumps to my shoulders. I didn't know why. I'd stand in the shower, the hot water pouring over me, and I'd scrub my scalp, unable to produce the kind of frothing bubbles I saw on blissed-out women in television commercials. I was too ashamed to ask my dad what I was doing wrong. But Aunt Greta asked me for a step-by-step description of what I did when I showered. It turned out that the green bottles looked the same and I'd been using the conditioner as shampoo.

Of all these women, it was Karen Jones who mattered most to me in those days. She came into our lives shortly after the bra incident at Kmart. She and my father had met at church. Sometimes, late at night, I'd see her lying with my dad on the bed, both of them watching a movie on the small television in his room. His arm would be draped over her shoulders, though she never spent the night in the bed with him. Instead, she'd tiptoe into my room and curl up beside me.

I knew she was my dad's girlfriend, but she felt like mine, too. I'd spend the night at her house often, where she lived with her ailing father, and we'd watch *The Love Boat* and *Fantasy Island*, eating popcorn and drinking papaya juice. She knew I wasn't very girlie, but she showed me the fundamentals anyway. One Sunday before church, she pulled a pair of pantyhose from an egg-shaped plastic holder, and then did a series of pliés in her bedroom while gently rolling them up her legs, making sure her nails did not snag the fragile fabric. I sat in a chair in her bedroom and watched in the mirror as she used a metal tool to curl her eyelashes. She'd draw lipliner around her mouth, then swipe gloss across it; she'd rub crème blush into her cheeks. I had occasionally watched my mother apply lipstick, or pin her hair into a large bun atop her head, but that was the extent of it. She'd have never let me see her in her bra and underwear, most certainly not when she was sick. But with Karen, nothing seemed off limits.

She sauntered around her bedroom in her bra. She taught me that, contrary to what I'd assumed, divorce was more complicated than simply donning one's wedding clothes and walking backwards down the aisle. And she said a mother's breasts did not contain milk *and* orange juice, as

I had long assumed (because this is what mothers in TV commercials always gave their children at breakfast), but rather *both* sides had milk. Such a failure of anatomical imagination.

Karen wasn't just access to a world of women that had been slowly disappearing from my life for years, as my mother's illness progressed. She was a symbol of normalcy, of freedom even. The initial shock of that first year after my mom died had dissipated. My mother's illness was no longer the primary event that ruled our schedules. No more homemade Get Well cards. No more listening to my mother gag in the bathroom. We could take family vacations—to Myrtle Beach, Disney World, and Denver. We could scream and laugh hysterically and dance around the house without fear of waking our mother. We could play for hours, inside or out, loudly or quietly. It made my sadness confusing, laden as it was with guilt over my newfound freedom.

It was a freedom unlike any David or I had ever experienced before. We could play till nightfall in the cul-de-sac, or the woods. We could eat whatever snack we could find in the pantry, including fistfuls of Frosted Mini-Wheats and Apple Jacks, which felt deliriously lawless. We could watch television for hours at a time or have friends over without asking anyone. The adults around us did not discipline us, in part because we didn't do much that compelled discipline, but also because with my mother's death, we were treated as fragile little birds, able to get away with things other kids probably could not. For me, this freedom translated to simple things—like wearing jeans and T-shirts every single day. Like screaming and yelling in ways unbecoming to girls. Like riding my orange and yellow Schwinn around the neighborhood or playing pickup games of kickball without having to check in every few minutes to see if my mother needed anything, without having to worry about grass stains on my clothes or scabs on my knees. Other girls weren't loud the way I was becoming. Other girls didn't have boys as their best friends the way I did. Other girls didn't have dirt eternally under their fingernails.

Karen Jones quickly became part of the rhythm of our new lives. On the weekends, if I didn't sleep at her house, she'd sleep at ours. She took me to practices and games for the Condors, or to meets after I'd joined the Montour Heights Country Club swim team. I remember her being in the stands at my softball games, cheering for me as she sat with my father. I'm sure he cheered, too, though I can barely recall his presence there. Maybe all of this familiarity, all the places he'd spent years visiting with my mother, all the activities he'd loved to do with her—boating, fishing, entertaining—maybe the familiarity that saved David and me in those first years without our mom was the very thing that made his life unlivable there. Driving the streets he'd driven with my mother, sleeping in the bed he'd slept in with my mother—the bed in which she'd died. The synagogue she'd attended. The people she'd known. Maybe he couldn't live among the Wedgwood and the menorahs and the people who looked at him as a poor widower abandoned with two young children. The neighbors who'd loved her, the friends she had. All of it so entangled with her absence. Women swooped in where my mother had left off. Women cleaned for us, and cooked for us, and cared for us, but still. Those women were our women, not his. Perhaps Karen was more mine than his. And maybe it was too much. Because when the opportunity for change came, he leapt as far and as fast as he could.

Four

In the revival tent, I could feel the sweat gathering along my hairline, streaming down my temples. The adults around me sang, their bodies swaying, and they blocked a clear view of the stage, but I saw glimpses of people in prone positions or falling under the influence of God, caught by big-shouldered ushers sweating through their suits. Speaker stacks blared out what some of us might now call slow jams, while a minister—sometimes my uncle Jim, sometimes a guest pastor—prayed for diseases to be healed, for sadness and pain to be lifted, for debt to disappear. As people fell, others would rise, dazed and blinking, into the stage lights. Dozens made their way to the stage, where they fell and rose, and then made their way back to their seats, where they seemed to emit a kind of shimmer to those who sat around them. Where temple had been a staid affair, sonorous enough that I slept on my mother's lap through much of the service, this was frenetic with energy, ear-shatteringly loud.

My aunt Janet and uncle Jim had invited us to this family camp, a *revival* they called it. We'd gone the summer before, too, though nothing about the experience stood out to me, in part because our trip to Disney World was far more memorable that year. My dad had taken David and me, along with our grandma Katie. The highlight for me was getting Wonder Woman's autograph.

My father had always been a Christian, though he converted to Judaism to marry my mother. They'd wed at the New Ocean House outside of Boston, and a short time later, the New Ocean House burned to the ground. They talked about this for years, every time we visited my grandmother Erma at her house in Swampscott, on Boston's north shore.

They'd point to the bare patch of land where their lives as a couple had begun and wonder at the absence of something that had seemed so beautiful and so permanent.

As kids, my parents' solution to their mixed religion was just to drop us into each of their respective beliefs. We celebrated Hanukkah and Christmas, Passover and Easter, Rosh Hashanah and New Year's Eve. We hid matzoh and dyed hard-boiled eggs. We ate gefilte fish and left cookies out for Santa. We attended temple on Friday nights with my mother, and church on Sunday with my father. But neither of them attended the other's services. Religion was a backdrop in our lives, a social event and a chance to forge community.

My parents had been raised with a lackluster commitment to their respective religions. My grandmother Katie attended church on Sundays, and she had even remarried a pastor after the death of my father's father. But the church hadn't been the fulcrum upon which her life revolved while she was raising my father. The same was true of my grandmother Erma; she attended temple occasionally on the high holidays or maybe for the odd bar mitzvah here and there.

Before illness took away her mobility, my mother volunteered for all sorts of community gatherings through the temple. She contributed food for potlucks, visited elderly members, and wrote letters on behalf of hospitalized patients. In my mother's absence Judaism had been summarily erased from our lives. Before long, I had forgotten all the prayers I'd once been able to recite in Hebrew. I couldn't remember what Rosh Hashanah stood for, or why we had once celebrated Yom Kippur.

My aunt and uncle's Illinois church was very different from either of my parents' places of worship in Pennsylvania. At the revival, people prayed in tongues, fell under the spell of the almighty God, and preached that we must go forth and spread the word of God in order to save a world of sinners. The Bible was the ultimate authority and we believed it to be literal in every sense. The New Testament was a new covenant with God whereby Jesus's sacrifice of his own life could save us all. The congregation did not belong to any particular denomination and maintained that in order to make it to heaven, one had to become reborn, both symbolically and by claiming salvation aloud. My uncle baptized people in a nearby lake, one after another, including me. During the revival one afternoon, I stood in my bathing suit beside him as he laid one palm atop my head and prayed. He asked God to watch over me; he called me a "lamb of God." Then he covered my face with his other hand and swung me backward under the water. When I emerged, the attendees along the shore applauded. And my dad came over and hugged me and said "Hallelujah" and then he tossed me in the lake and I laughed like crazy.

These were the early days of American Evangelicalism, the movement that preached health and wealth as a birthright for the righteous and that would soon give way to the megachurches we have today. This Christian message said that we deserved riches, and if we hadn't received them, it wasn't because we deserved any less; it was because our faith and commitment simply weren't strong enough yet. It said miracles could be ours if only we would have faith. It said God wanted us to prosper and to be filled with joy. It was a message that must have had a particular resonance for my father, that all he'd lost would mean something someday, that his sacrifices as a young man would restore to him so much more in the coming years.

Now, my dad stood beside me, also sweating, his eyes closed and his arms raised in praise to God. I could smell his aftershave and I leaned toward him, away from the sweating stranger to my left. I had seen my father pray dozens of times, seen him sing along to church hymns and put envelopes of money in the brass tray every week at Wildwood Chapel. But this revival tent had a different emotional tenor. People openly wept and wailed. They fell under God's spell. "Slain in the spirit" was the name given to those falling and rising on the stage. It stood for a kind of spiritual death and rebirth. One person would spontaneously spout what sounded like gibberish into the air, and then after a few awkward moments, another person would offer an interpretation. This call and response came from God himself. Tongues was the universal language, meaning that no earthly being could understand it. It was God's language alone.

Evangelicalism also spoke to the cultural phenomenon of American exceptionalism, bred from the same roots as the Greatest Generation, and from which my father was born. People rarely speak of religion as culture. I heard so often how lucky I was to be growing up in America, that this was the greatest country in the world, that it was the chosen country. Images of children behind the Iron Curtains of Russia, Germany,

China haunted me, with their dark-rimmed eyes and itchy sweaters, or the children of Africa with their distended bellies. I *did* consider myself lucky to be in America. I *did* believe it when my father told me America was the best country in the world. And now here we were not only in the *best* country, the chosen country, but we were the chosen among *those* chosen. We were the children of God. I never questioned this privilege of geography.

My father felt loved and supported at my aunt and uncle's church, of that I am sure. But he must have also seen an opening, the chance to start over without the baggage that came from being a young, male widower in 1970s America, and without the constant reminder of all he'd lost in Pittsburgh facing him daily. Two motherless kids. The house where his wife had died. A neighborhood that maybe saw him differently than how he wanted to be seen. By the time he came home from flag football the day my mom died, her body had already been taken away, and he felt stripped of an essential ritual for widowers. One of the only regrets I ever heard him voice. How he wished he'd gotten home before they'd taken her body away.

So perhaps that August revival was a true overhaul for my father. The chance to free himself of bad memories and terrible associations. The chance, maybe, to expunge his grief.

MY DAD MET Barbara at the revival, though he always maintained that he met her at the family camp the year before. Perhaps he did. But it was in 1979 that he *noticed* Barbara. She also had two kids, Holly and Aaron. Holly was four years older than me, Aaron just five months older. Barbara was alone. My dad was alone. She was divorced, he widowed. She was a born-again Christian; he was becoming a born-again Christian. She was beautiful, shiny brown hair in waves past her shoulders. Wide green eyes, and high cheekbones with full lips.

She was a lot of things, but perhaps the most attractive was that she was everything that his former life wasn't. She wasn't educated in the way my mother had been. Her family heritage was rural Nebraska, whereas my mother's was urban, secular Jewish. She worked in a factory called Burgess-Norton that made parts for internal combustion engines; she was the only woman in her department and she carried a clipboard, which I thought was extremely interesting. She was a new geography and culture entirely. And she'd known some pain in the world: she'd gotten pregnant at sixteen, dropped out of high school, had a second child, and then got divorced. And with all of that, she was surviving, raising her two kids in a small apartment, independent without being critical or questioning. She could hold a conversation, but rarely started them. She was competent, but not showy, not outspoken. She was obedient. She was neither Gail Snyder nor Karen Jones.

I remember just one conversation with my father in the days after we returned from that family camp. I sat at the Formica table in our kitchen while he stood over me. My brother was in his room, or maybe downstairs in the family room. My father told me he'd made a decision. We were moving to Illinois, the three of us, and ABC, the cat. And because he wanted us to start the new year at my aunt and uncle's religious school, we were moving very soon.

I told him I wouldn't go. I cried. I begged. I loved my home here, my neighborhood. We'd just finished an addition on our house, two new bedrooms for David and me, and a new playroom in the basement. David's bedroom had blue and red race car wallpaper that I'd begged for in the store; mine had amber-colored Holly Hobbie. I said I'd do anything to stay in Pittsburgh. I told my dad he could go without me and I'd live with Karen Jones. I screamed and howled. It seemed I could imagine life without him more readily than I could imagine life without the infrastructure of my aunt Greta and uncle Wes, my cul-de-sac and my grandma Katie. I didn't want to leave my softball team—the Condors, or Carnot Elementary School, or the woods behind my house. I told him I'd stay behind and live in the house alone with ABC. I told him I'd take over David's paper route to support myself. I bargained and pleaded. I ran down the hallway to my room and hurled myself across my bed, burying my face in stuffed animals. Not once during that conversation did he mention Barbara.

Had my father kept Karen around only as a surrogate? Did he have any feelings at all for her, or was he using her in the ways that men have used women for time immemorial? At ten years old, the loss of Karen hit me somehow harder than the loss of my own mother. Perhaps because cancer gave my mother a reason—however painful—to be gone, whereas Karen was healthy, and seemed happy to be with my father and my brother and me. One was a choice, the other a conviction.

Soon after that conversation, my father broke it to Karen that we were moving. I was not in on this conversation, but I saw her minutes afterward, standing on our driveway, her face mottled with tears and her body bent like a scythe, frozen in a howling cry.

I'll never know why my father took the wild detour he took. I asked. A million times I asked, in ways both covert and direct. In whispers and in screams. In violence and submission. I asked for years. And others asked me, so many others. Friends I would meet throughout my life, and my relatives in Pittsburgh and Boston, and people who'd once known my real mother, or only later heard her story. They all asked. And I kept asking. The whiplash of what came next, after that revival. I only ever got one answer: *because God told us to*. Even today, with all that I know and all that I've lived, I still can't answer.

David and I moved to Illinois two weeks after family camp. Cancer took my mother. But religion would take my life.

Part II

SOME CARELESS STRENGTH

Chicago, IL

Five

The wedding at Baker Church, 1979, author in foreground.

My father walked me down to the basement of Baker Church. He slung one arm over my shoulder and I thought I could feel his tension. I wore a yellow dress with tiny white polka dots, a matching cape that snapped around my neck. I looked like a prepubescent sunflower. My father wore a light brown corduroy suit, and he had grown a mustache, unfortunately enshrined in photos from this day. In a far corner, Barbara sat in an ivory dress, pulling up pantyhose over her shapely legs. She'd put hot rollers in her hair, and it now hung in swooping curls to her shoulders. I held a purple comb shaped like a fish in my hand and squeezed the tines into my palm. They left savage little red indentations.

"Rachel," my dad said, "meet your new mother."

She looked up; her smile was equal ratio teeth to gums, but neither of us said anything. It occurred to me that I had never really spoken to Barbara. I had spoken around her, in her proximity. But *to* her? I could not recall. What did we know of each other? I knew she worked at a factory, knew about her carrying that clipboard, and I knew that she would now no longer work there. I knew she was a single mother who'd gotten pregnant at sixteen, and then married, and then divorced so somehow her sins had been forgiven. I knew she was a Christian like my father. I knew she drove a manual-shift orange Gremlin with black stripes. I knew she had shiny hair, and that her own mother lived nearby and enjoyed Scrabble.

The wedding was two months after David and I moved to Illinois. We moved in with my aunt Janet and uncle Jim and their kids. My father had stayed behind in Pittsburgh to pack up the house and put it on the market.

One afternoon, my cousin and I giggled as we snuck up the carpeted stairs until we came to her parents' bedroom. We tiptoed through the door and to their bed, where a telephone sat on the nightstand. Eavesdropping on my aunt Janet comprised one of our primary forms of entertainment since she was the de facto leader of church women and thereby spent much of every day on the phone, talking to other female members of Life in the Spirit Ministries (LISM, for short, though it would soon change to FCCF: Faith Center Christian Fellowship). Aunt Janet had described these calls as "ministering" to women. To me it didn't seem any different than any other old phone call where friends confided in and gossiped with each other, but what did I know?

We lifted the phone receiver, covering our snickering mouths, silent as we could be. We'd gotten stealthy in the weeks since I'd moved in. I held the plastic handset between us, trying to hold in my breath so I wouldn't give us away. On the phone, I heard my aunt say a single complete sentence: "He's moving here to marry Barb."

I knew immediately who she meant. I felt it in my gut, in the acid of my stomach that suddenly gurgled up into my throat. I dropped the phone and it clattered, then fell from the nightstand. I fled down the stairs in my bare feet and shorts, and out the front door, down the sidewalk. How dumb had I been? How had I missed all this? My father hadn't moved David and me to Illinois because he wanted us to start at the beginning of the new school year. He moved because he wanted to get remarried. Why hadn't he told us? Was it because he knew I'd react this way? But if he knew, then why the rush? My aunt Janet had hung up the phone and immediately run out the door to follow me. When she got to me, she pulled me to her and held me as I sobbed, frenetic energy zinging through my body. I wanted to run and run, away from her house, away from my father, away from the doom that began to settle into me.

Now, in that church basement, just weeks after learning about his impending marriage, it felt very much like a first meeting with Barb. All those times I'd been around her, I hadn't paid attention, hadn't really *noticed* her. She was just one of the adults in my new orbit. Now I was forced to wonder who she really was, this new person in my life. Something about my father's sweeping declaration—*your new mother*—seemed to want to erase everything that had come before. I would learn later that he believed in the power of positive thinking, the messages of men like Zig Ziglar. That when my mother was still alive, he had taken her to healing evangelist Kathryn Kuhlman, had asked her to accept Jesus into her heart so that she could be saved. She had refused. What must she have felt when Kuhlman herself died of cancer shortly after?

My father must have been speaking aloud what he'd been praying to come true. I felt a heave in my stomach. His hand across my shoulders heavy as dead weight. The low ceiling, the dust on old tiling, the buzzing fluorescent lights. I wanted to melt into the floor. *My new mother.* I sobbed throughout the entire ceremony, loud enough that it echoed through the cavernous sanctuary, loud enough for even the guests in back to hear.

At the wedding reception I stood in the basement hallway near the coats and my papa Chuck found me. He was my real mother's father.

Divorced from my grandmother Erma, though still a close friend. He carried golf pencils and tiny sheets of scrap paper in his shirt pocket. He had pens made with his quips: *Remember the best, Forget the rest.* Or *I'll live to be a hundred or die trying.* He sent me enormous boxes of books on my birthday that were far more advanced than anything I could capably read. Histories of the English language and linguistics, for example. Textbooks on grammar, or a reference manual of Shakespeare. I thought it was because he held a misguided notion that I was exceptionally smart. Later, I would learn that most of these were review books he'd been given by publishers and he was basically offloading them onto my brother and me. But maybe he was also sending us something aspirational. I loved opening those giant cartons of books each year, their titles impenetrable, their weight and heft practically coffee-table books in my skinny arms. Of course he must have known these books were far beyond what I could grasp (perhaps less so for my brother's fierce intellect), but as a kid, I only guessed he thought I was smart enough for them.

Papa Chuck had written a poem for my mother called "The Hunters (for Gail, 1942–1977)." In those first years after her death, and then especially after my father married Barbara, no one ever talked about my mother. Not my father, certainly not my stepmother. Not my aunt Janet or my uncle Jim. I was far away from anyone who'd known her, or known us with her. Eventually, my papa Chuck published the poem in a book called *Love, Life and Laughter*:

> *However did they worm their way in?*
> *Clever chaps, they didn't have to! They*
> *Were there the very moment spark and clay*
> *Ignited, always underneath the skin.*
> *Such patient stalkers, tracking, probing where*
> *Some weakness might be pressed, some careless strength*
> *Be ambushed, ready to attack the length*
> *Of any front, and, finding treason there,*
> *Move surely to the kill. And yet that spark*
> *That gave those clever chaps their Trojan Horse*
> *May set their victims on a different course:*
> *Can one know light who doesn't know the dark?*

In that last cell where doughty minds retreat
May stretch a blazing road beyond defeat.

When we'd visit my grandmother Erma in Boston, papa Chuck would drive up from Philadelphia with a friend—or with one of the many women he dated over the years—and visit with all of us. He had a velvety voice, which had earned him the honorary title of one of Philadelphia's most beloved arts critics on WFLN, when it was still a classical station. He'd changed his name from Levy to Lee in order to be a reporter during

The author with her grandfather Papa Chuck,
around 1973.

World War II. He'd had a one-night stand with Marlene Dietrich, published a book blurbed by Milton Berle, and enjoyed a lifelong friendship with Robert Alda, the father of Alan. I knew the basic contours of his public life, but I also knew he'd been disowned by his own father after he cheated on my grandmother—a source of lifelong pain for him. He'd gone years without my mother speaking to him, but after David and I were born, they reconciled. Whatever sins he'd committed in his life before I came along, I endured none of them. To me, he was soft, funny, generous. His voice could calm me. He taught me to always carry a pencil and paper. He said if I had problems in life that I should compartmentalize them, so they seemed less big. I asked him once what the difference was between poetry and journalism, and he said journalism was just a form of poetry that lasted only a day, whereas poetry lasted forever. But they both captured something about how we live today.

In the basement hallway, he found me. I had stopped crying but spent most of the reception hiding near the coat rack, ashamed that I'd embarrassed my father and new stepmother by sobbing through the wedding, embarrassed at who we were expected to be, this new family, in our glorified symmetry. I was afraid I'd be in trouble with my dad. I didn't want to talk to anyone.

What could anyone say, anyway? There was no way out of this for me. It was a miracle that my papa Chuck had come to this wedding at all, two years after the death of his own daughter. I felt my grandfather's hand on my head. He didn't say anything. He just held his hand there on me, in stillness.

Six

After they were married, my father and Barb took a month-long honeymoon to Israel, with a short stopover in Rome. They had a teacher from the school stay with us who had wide hips and dandruff and the back of her hair was always flat as if she'd just arisen from a cross-country flight.

Aaron and I fought immediately. He'd snap his fingers and thwack me on the shoulder and in retaliation I'd chase him through the house, dodging furniture, trying to get him back (he was stronger, quicker, always ready to fight). Our backyard was a deep forest with a creek at the bottom of the hill. You could sled the hill provided you steered carefully through the thicket of trees. One afternoon during the first winter we all lived together, I was on a sled, preparing myself to go down, when Aaron suddenly pushed me. I careened down the hill diagonally, out of control, screaming in terror, and flew full speed into a tree. It knocked me out cold for a couple of seconds. When I shook off my dizziness, I stood defiantly and went wailing into the house.

Aaron ridiculed my father's nickname: Dick. Both Aaron and Holly called my father Richard, but whenever my dad and Barb weren't around, Aaron would shout out *Dick* in a singsong tease. I screamed at him to stop and he'd laugh and sing more loudly, skipping around the furniture. He'd throw his head back in a full-throated howl. He'd swing his elbows and march around the living room making lewd rhymes with the name. *Dick. Slick. Thick.*

David and I had been told to call Barb "Mom," but the word had become so foreign to me that I never called her anything to her face.

(The logic behind the naming was that Aaron and Holly's father was still alive, so technically my father couldn't be their "dad," whereas my mom was dead.) Even outside of her presence, it seemed too adult to refer to her as "Barb" but factually inaccurate to refer to her as "Mom." It was as if I were frozen between languages. If I needed her for some reason, I learned to stalk the house, up and down the stairs, to the laundry room and back up to the kitchen, sometimes outside, until I found her. Then I'd pretend I'd just stumbled into her and ask my question. I managed to keep up this charade for the better part of a year.

WE LIVED, THAT first year, in a damp rental home in a Chicago suburb called Woodridge. Our street was mostly blue collar, parents who smoked in their BarcaLoungers and didn't much care what their kids were up to so long as they were left alone. The kids called Holly "Jugs" on account of her ample bosom. They also sometimes called her Big Red, because she loved the Nebraska Cornhuskers. Her extended family lived in Nebraska and so Nebraska was to her what Boston was to me. Holly and I shared a room with twin beds, and I copied her every move. If she put a throw pillow on her bed, so did I. If she folded her blanket a certain way at the foot of her bed, so did I. As one might expect, this drove her bananas. She complained about it to me and to our parents, who asked me to stop, but I did not. Holly was nice, as far as strangers went, and as a teenager she had access to a whole world of knowledge that I was not privy to. It was Holly who would eventually explain terms like "give head" and "blow job."

David and Aaron had separate rooms. Aaron was everything that David was not. Aaron was loud and obnoxious. He ridiculed everyone; he'd snap at kids and then run away cackling. He was neither obedient nor disobedient; it was more like he just lived in a world inside his own head, where his actions and consequences were eternally separate from one another. He might have been diagnosed with ADHD (Attention Deficit Hyperactivity Disorder) had such testing been around back then.

The only thing Aaron and I bonded over was collective ridicule of David. We ridiculed how he dressed, how terrible he was at sports, how nerdy and smart he was. We ridiculed his wavy hair and his floods. We

ridiculed how much the adults fawned over him—because of his bril-
liance, his ability to preach like an adult, to memorize long passages of
Biblical text. On occasional Sundays, David would prepare a sermon
and be called up to give it in front of the church. He would stand, in
suit and tie, as a twelve- or thirteen-year-old, his well-read Bible flipped
open in one palm, a microphone in the other. And he would offer up
interpretations of Biblical passages that seemed to me as nuanced and
intelligent as my uncle Jim's. David was the model child. He took to
Christianity with fervor. He prayed and read and spent hours on his
own, studying and meditating on the Bible. Still, when the time came,
none of this would save him.

I WONDER SOMETIMES why the changes were so hard, why I had such
an incredibly difficult time adjusting. For years all I could do to explain
it was make comparisons, talk about the little things: the unfamiliar food,
the endless church services, my mother's furniture in that strange place.
My mother and Grandmother Erma and even my step-grandfather were
gourmands, their tables set with extravagant flavors. I was eating hummus
and Brie in 1974, when most of America had never heard of such items.
My stepmother, on the other hand, would crack a dozen eggs into a
casserole dish, stick in a handful of cocktail weenies, and call it dinner.
Pasta with a can of tomato sauce, roast with mushy carrots and grainy
potatoes: these were our new cuisine. And our house wasn't unusual. It
was standard fare for many American midwestern homes in 1980; what
was different was me, my Boston relatives, the food at the Jewish tables
of my mother and grandmother, abundant, freely available, something
to celebrate, to connect us. Now my stepmother counted out pretzel sticks
and duplex creme cookies (two each) after school; we had Special K instead
of Apple Jacks, and liverwurst instead of chipped ham. We used
Hellmann's instead of Miracle Whip. Mustard took new prominence.
I found myself unable to voice all that was happening around me, the
emotional earthquake of a brand-new family in a brand-new place, so I
pointed to things like bologna sandwiches to express my discontent. My
father would shake his head in disappointment, tell me to get over it. It
was only a sandwich, after all.

I was fortunate. I had enough to eat, even if boxed potatoes now replaced real ones, or paper plates replaced porcelain. We used powdered milk because we couldn't afford bottled milk, and the smell was so bad I held my breath as I ate cereal. We bought generic everything: noodles, soup, bread, toilet paper, peanut butter. My father still wore a literal white collar to work, but our middle-class status plummeted: in addition to rent in Illinois, my father was still paying the mortgage on the house in Moon Township, and it would take four long years to sell. Off and on for several years I saw my father or stepmother use food stamps, though they tried to hide it.

For Barb, Holly, and Aaron, though, much the opposite had happened in their lives. In her apartment, Barb had slept on the couch while the kids each took a bedroom. When she married my father, they both declared him head of the household per Biblical edict, and her working outside the home was forbidden. But she lived now in a house with her own bedroom. A house with four bedrooms. My mother's furniture that once had sat in our house in Pittsburgh now furnished our rental house, with its drafty windows, its peeling siding, its ubiquitous spiderwebs. The furniture was white, oversized, art deco. The time capsule of an elegant past life. The settee where I'd shrugged off my book bag the day I wore my *Benedict Arnold* pants to school. The cherrywood dining room table with hand-carved legs where we now ate our egg-and-cocktail-weenie casserole. It was as if McDonald's had suddenly furnished its restaurants with Herman Miller. When Aaron sat on the white settee, I screamed at him to get off it. Sometimes he'd walk around just touching things that had moved from Pittsburgh with us. "Cut it out," I'd yell. "That's not yours!" He'd cackle and keep on, putting his fingertips on one thing after another, then skipping away.

For my part, I made sure to only use that which I recognized from Pittsburgh, the white plastic bowls that had moved with us for my morning cereal, rather than the yellow plastic bowls that Barb had brought. I dug through our conjoined silverware drawer, the shelf for our glassware, making sure to touch only what was familiar. I situated my toothbrush so it did not touch anyone else's in our shared bathroom.

I considered myself morally superior to Aaron and Holly because my mother was dead, but their father was alive and was choosing not to be in their lives. It was cruel and it must have hurt, but they never let on. Aaron would always just return to the insult of my father's name: Dick, Dick, Dick. And I felt powerless against the anger that began to boil in me.

On their honeymoon, meanwhile, my dad and Barbara visited Jesus's grave, the Garden of Gethsemane, the Dead Sea, and the Wailing Wall. They must have believed this month without them would bring the four of us closer. But when they returned, the lines had been drawn. And instead of pulling the four of us out of our fighting, my dad and Barb seemed to get dragged right into it. We fought together, and then we'd hear my dad and Barb late into the night, in their bedroom, screaming at each other. Occasionally, I heard Barb crying. This gave me a sliver of hope: maybe they'd get divorced.

In fact, if we kids prayed for anything in those years, it was that our parents, this whole new experimental family, would split up. I had no loyalty to David over our shared trauma, no sense of wanting to protect him, stand up for him. We four kids could have been a life raft for each other, a secret club surviving through our shared enmity for the adults. Or at least, David and I could have been this. Instead, we turned on each other. David and I never spoke of our mother, never spoke of what we'd lost or the foreign place we'd landed. He turned inside himself, in some ways forever. He lived life inside his capacious mind, keeping his feelings in. I was the opposite. Once I began to scream, I never stopped.

Seven

My new school, Faith Center Christian Academy (FCCA), rented the first floor of a former school building in Downers Grove. My aunt Janet and uncle Jim had started FCCA just a year or two before Holly, David, Aaron, and I arrived. To contain costs, they had enlisted the help of the small congregation to build us bespoke cubicles. I faced a burlap wall, with two particleboard dividers painted forest green on either side of me, like a horse with giant blinders. The dividers could be removed, and the desk had hinges in the back that allowed it to be folded up, like a lockbox. My cube was about two feet by two feet. FCCA used a pedagogical system called Personal Accelerated Christian Education (PACE) that allowed students to progress in school at our own speed through individual subject booklets, primarily English, math, social studies, science, and theology. I pinned index cards on the padded burlap where I wrote my daily goals in each subject. And indeed, I was soon working several years ahead of my grade level in English and social studies. But I also began to fall woefully behind in math and science. Math was particularly difficult and I struggled to stay awake reading through equations in my PACE booklet.

Since we worked on our own, the primary orchestra was silence. We had two flags with which to summon the teacher (my aunt in this case): the American flag meant you had a curricular question, the white flag with a blue cross on it meant you had an administrative question, like getting permission to test and move on to the next PACE booklet. Or going to the bathroom. I thought of it as the white flag of surrender.

I raised a tiny American flag and placed it into its hole at the top of my cube. This was at least the third or fourth time I'd called for help with fractions. My aunt was preternaturally patient. She spoke in a kind of whisper even in her regular life outside of our silent school. Her kitchen was perpetually supplied with homemade cookies in a cow-shaped jar, and hot chocolate, and sometimes she'd make macaroni and cheese from scratch. She seemed to me religious, but not overbearing. She was kind, and although I couldn't make sense of the upheaval my life had taken, she felt like a soft landing for me. I didn't know then how much of my life had been orchestrated by her and my uncle Jim, how in thrall my father was to their advice and suggestions. I didn't talk to her about the chaos in my new house, but I jumped at every chance I got to be at her house, with its endless snacks and its padded quiet.

She took her pencil and showed me again how to multiply quarters and thirds, and then went into square footages and circumferences, which I'd skipped over. She slowed it down, drew arrows on the page. I just could not grasp it. And I couldn't explain why I couldn't grasp it. Often in my flowered pink diary, I would write things like: "I love Allen, but hate math." Or "I love Jeff, but hate math." Or "Aaron spit milk out his nose today and I cried in math." My parents, boys, and math all took up more or less equal real estate in my diary. Today, I would surely be tested for dyscalculia, but such testing wasn't common in the 1980s. And because I could not articulate what I did not understand, I nodded when my aunt asked me if I understood it this time. She went back to her desk, and my eyes filled with tears.

It was further evidence of how I felt about myself, that whatever elements cobbled together created the whole of a person, they were somehow lacking in me. I couldn't understand basic math or science. I couldn't abide the many changes in my life. My feathered hair was too short and stuck out like fish gills from my face. My front teeth were too big. I had a face full of pimples. And I was taller than all the other middle-schoolers. My aunt had chosen green plaid jumpers for the fifth- and sixth-grade girls, along with yellow shirts that had Peter Pan collars. The jumper came to just above my bony knees. It was worse than anything my mother had ever put me in.

I think now that the silence of FCCA may have prepared me for a life of writing. I learned to sit inside my own imagination in those cubicles, my mind wandering. I'd imagine Karen Jones showing up and rescuing me. I'd imagine running out the door, into the parking lot, and then beyond, into the school's Downers Grove neighborhood. I imagined standing on one of our gold-padded desk chairs and suddenly shouting into the silence. I also imagined going upstairs.

Upstairs held mysteries, darkened shrouds of storied rebellions. There was another school above us, a school that could not have been more different from ours if it had come from middle earth. Called SASED—I no longer remember what the acronym stood for, if I ever knew—it was a school for troubled teens. For every sibilant whisper from the two teachers at FCCA, there were howls, thumps, and wicked, deep-throated laughter from the students who occupied the upstairs floor. They'd been booted from public high schools for behavioral problems or drugs. Sometimes we'd see the police pull up outside our windows in the parking lot, followed by an unfortunate SASED student led out in handcuffs. To see them in human form walked to a waiting squad car was paradoxically to diminish them and to expand the power of their scandalous lore. They terrified and entranced us, their rumblings upstairs a constant reminder of the polarity. We imagined them as monsters, as crime bosses, as murderers-in-the-making. Rumors circulated that the SASEDs had cages in their classrooms, and restraints, that some of them were Satan worshippers. That they brought knives and nunchakus to school.

FCCA and SASED staggered their schedules so that we would never so much as cross paths. We even used different entrances and exits and they did not have recess like us. We were told that any interaction at all with a SASED would result in immediate detention and possible expulsion. The SASEDs haunted our minds: fascination and fear in equal measure.

Lately, the SASEDs had taken to calling out to us from their second-story windows as we wandered the playground during recess. I hung around with a couple of girls either a grade above or below me. The older girls were set apart by their freedom to wear plaid skirts instead of the sheath-like jumpers. The two-year window of freedom I'd had with clothing was heady, if short-lived. I could run, jump, kick my legs. I could move my body as I wanted without fear of my underpants peeking from under a hemline. Once, in kindergarten, for show-and-tell, I'd gone to the front of the classroom and done a headstand. It was only after I was fully in position and the laughter blitzed my upside-down ears that I thought of the pull of gravity on the blue dress that now pooled around my head, the full-on display of my flowered underpants.

To taste the freedom of jeans for two years at Carnot Elementary in Coraopolis, and then be forced not merely into a dress, but into a jumper, *with pleats*, felt like a degradation not merely of fashion, but of movement itself. It's no wonder girls' sports has taken generations to catch up to boys. Our clothing banished us to the sidelines, limbs caught up in stiff postures in order to protect our feminine vulnerabilities.

The SASEDs hollered out the window to us girls as we chatted by the swings or paced the parking lot. One girl named Sheri was often singled out with some version of "Blondie. Hey, Blondie!" and a whistle. She would turn to the second-floor windows and smile coyly when the teacher's aide wasn't looking. This intrusion into our otherwise silent days was both thrilling and terrifying. We conjured the crimes they'd committed to have landed at SASED. Stolen cars. Sacked convenience stores. Our imaginations could blossom from the safety of the ground floor after one classmate pointed out that they weren't likely to kill us from their second-story window in broad daylight.

For weeks they hollered at us during recess. There weren't many of us to keep track of—I had five students total in my fifth-grade class. And as their voices gained a familiarity, we, slowly, responded in the tiniest of ways. An upturned glance, a wave behind our back. They'd hoot and bellow and we'd smile to ourselves, among our own little group. When the aide noticed, she'd shush them and the windows would close, but *we* could hardly be blamed for what *they* did or did not do and the thrill of it was heady. I both loved and feared the attention. I'd been told that everyone in the secular world was searching for God in their empty, meaningless lives. And this meaninglessness, this absolute sadness I assumed they all carried, made them dangerous and untrustworthy, but also exciting.

In my new life, I was taught that if people in the world only heard the good news, that Jesus offered salvation and fulfillment to those who followed him, then their lives would have purpose. They would stop feeling empty, they would stop chasing after material things that could never fill their souls. They would no longer even *want* fancy cars and big houses. I didn't know what the SASEDs might have wanted, but I believed they were empty and searching and this had to account in some measure for their fascination with us.

Under this new version of God, rock and roll was banned. Television shows that my brother and I had loved, like *The Monkees* or *The Partridge Family*, were also off limits. No secular movies without permission. No music unless it was Christian. Books were less of an issue since no one in the house bought them, but we were encouraged to read *The Pilgrim's Progress* or anything by C. S. Lewis. We were told that if we befriended nonbelievers, like the SASEDs, then we might "backslide," which is to say we might become non-Christians. "Lead us not into temptation," the Bible warned, temptation being the secular world. Sports were still allowed and, somewhat inexplicably, country music was also allowed, because this is what Holly and Aaron and Barb had listened to in their house.

We read from a daily devotional at dinnertime now, one child reading the day's passage aloud for the rest of the family. We had Saturday morning chores that included cleaning our bedrooms, cleaning the bathrooms, vacuuming, dusting, weeding, window washing, and mopping the floor (which Barb insisted we do on our hands and knees and which I would tell my friends made me a real-life Cinderella). Cleanliness, orderliness. Now, we came home and did homework or chores. Only later did I understand how the SASEDs symbolized so much of what had once made up my daily life, which is to say that they symbolized freedom.

ONE FALL DAY at school, after a morning spent struggling through math, I watched during recess as a scrap of paper pirouetted from the window. Trash? Were they tossing trash at us?

But then came another one. And another.

We inched our way over as the scraps fell, careful to avoid the aide's glances in our direction. Someone picked one up. It had a name, written in pencil. A *boy's* name. With a phone number. We picked up another. And another. Glen, Jackson, Bill. The SASEDs had names. Normal boys' names. I folded one up and put it under my heel inside my shoe. It was only after school in my bedroom that I dared take it out and unfold it.

Bill Tepper, it said. With a phone number underneath.

Eight

One Friday night, I sat with my classmates and some of the other kids from church in a spare classroom. We regularly attended Sunday mornings, Sunday nights, and Wednesday nights. But this was a special night, a movie that we kids were told would "make believers out of men." We had popcorn, and we sat in the same metal folding chairs with green and gold padding that we used for school. The movie, *A Thief in the Night*, follows the story of a woman named Patty who wakes up and finds that her husband has been airlifted into the sky, raptured with millions of others. In the opening sequence, Patty runs to the bathroom calling her husband's name, but she finds only his electric razor, plugged in and still buzzing in the sink. She lets out a curdling scream. We see full grocery carts abandoned in aisles, cars left running and sitting on highways, planes zooming through the sky unpiloted. A global government put together by the United Nations forces those left behind to tattoo their body with something like a QR code; it's meant to be the mark of the beast spoken about in Revelations, during Jesus's second coming.

The movie terrified me. In my diary, I wrote that I was going to believe in Jesus from now on, and soon after that, during one Sunday morning service, I recorded being "slain in the spirit." I noted that I had feared the ushers wouldn't catch me, but they did, and I declared the entire experience "okay."

For several years, the movie's theme song, "I Wish We'd All Been Ready," became an anthem in the evangelical world: "Children died, the days grew cold/a piece of bread could buy a bag of gold." In our house, the song became shorthand for any of our sinful actions. Not doing

Saturday chores, for example, which was the sin of disobedience, made questionable our status vis-à-vis the rapture. If it came in the hour of our disobedience we wouldn't be "ready" and might well get left behind. Having been left behind by one parent already, the thought of being left behind by an entire family—even a family I didn't particularly like—overwhelmed me with fear.

The Bible was presented as literal in my life. God creating the earth in seven days was not a metaphor. Isaac really did take his son to the altar to kill him. Moses spoke to a bush while it burned in front of him. Noah built a boat big enough for every animal in the world, including cockroaches, hippos, sloths, and snakes, because they were all part of God's creation. Lot's wife had been turned into a pillar of salt for her disobedience (though Lot offering his daughters to be raped went unmentioned; I was an adult before I learned about this Biblical anecdote).

My aunt and uncle kept a poster board at the entrance to the building on Sunday mornings that had a science beaker drawn onto it with red marker filling in our slow progress toward the building of a new church and school. They asked for weekly tithes, and this fund, dollar by dollar, was someday going to free us so that we didn't have to meet in the mildewing gym of our decrepit school building. The congregation consisted of those same families whose kids I attended school with, along with a couple of ushers and a smattering of other families. After a few years, my aunt and uncle were able to buy land on which they hoped to build this church, and we gathered and walked around it seven times in order to sanctify it, the kids trudging behind the adults in a straggly, disinterested line. (My aunt and uncle also once walked around a condo in Colorado seven times, which was their way of claiming it "in the name of the Lord.")

We kids watched as Patty scurried on the screen from place to place, trying to figure out what to do now that she had missed the call of Jesus. She had thought herself a Christian because she went to church and sometimes read the Bible, but then she discovered when the rapture came that she had not been Christian after all. This deeply unsettled me. If I said out loud that I accepted Jesus into my heart, as was commanded in John 3:16 (*For God so loved the world that he gave his one and only Son, that whoever believes in him shall not perish but have eternal life*), wouldn't that do it? Or what if you lived a life of earthly pleasures, a life full of sin, but then just made sure you accepted Jesus on your deathbed? Murder? Rape? Robbery? I had been told all would be forgiven. How had Patty believed herself to be saved, but then not actually been saved at the critical moment? Or what if you were a young Jewish woman on your deathbed and you'd never claimed Jesus, but then with your last breath, you whispered his name? I created an image in my mind, my mother with her laughter, sitting with a group of reborn ancestors—which I imagined as her new neighbors, each of them in a mansion of their own. She was happy. Life—or whatever life was called after mortal death—moved slowly and without ruptures like terminal illness. But in that image, I was also missing. What did it mean that she could be so happy without me? And was I selfish then for wishing her to be in my world still, with all its pain and suffering and emptiness?

For my father, the power of language was paramount. He never dared speak aloud what he feared lest he give power to it and make it come to pass. But this also meant he never spoke anything aloud that was unpleasant. If we were sick, or scared, or hurt, he would tell us "not to claim it." I once attended school with strep throat for a whole week, discovered only after Barb accidentally brushed up against me in the kitchen and declared her shock at my "burning up." If we worried about a test at school my father would say "not to claim it." Any negative thought would be dismissed as something for us not to claim.

I tried to talk to my father about all this on the way home from *A Thief in the Night*. If Patty, who'd actually read the Bible and gone to church, turned out not to be a Christian after all, what did that mean for my mother? Was she in hell? My Jewish relatives in Boston, grandmother Erma and papa Sam, and my papa Chuck in Philly, were they all destined for hell? We four kids sat in the brown conversion van that my father had recently purchased in order to fit our new family.

"Jesus can read your heart, Rachel," my father said. God would know if we meant it when we accepted him.

"What about . . . our relatives?" I asked. I said "relatives," but I meant my mom. I wouldn't dare say this with Barb and her kids in the car. We never spoke of my mother now that we had a new family. No one ever said we couldn't; it just seemed like the expectation.

"They'll all be in heaven," he said. "If they accept Jesus."

This unsettled me even more. My dad maintained that my mother had accepted Jesus into her heart before she died, and she was now looking down on me from heaven. But I knew what her last words had been. *I can't breathe.*

"All of them?" I asked. "I mean, even the distant ones?" By distant, I meant dead, but he did not pick up on this.

"Knock it off, Rachel," he said. He seemed to think I was goading him. Usually, I was. But on this night, I had that movie playing in my head; the people I loved would be left behind on a cold and sunless earth and then sent to hell. I saw that buzzing razor in the sink over and over, heard Patty's chilling scream. It would keep me awake for many nights. And what of me? The church told us nonbelievers were unsettled, constantly searching, wandering like the SASEDs. How would I survive in such a world? How would I eat? Where would I sleep? Would some lonely secular guy kill me in a dark alley?

"I mean Grandma Erma and them?" I said.

He told me he prayed for them all the time.

THAT SUMMER, I took it upon myself to alert my grandmother Erma about her unfortunate destiny. It was during David's and my annual visit to Swampscott, where we'd spend most of July with her, complaining about the sand at the beach and the boredom at the house, but also happy to be free. Or a little freer anyway. We could listen to record albums, watch TV, read books. She took us to museums and to the theater and to historical sites I never tired of, like the House of the Seven Gables or the Salem Witch Museum. I spent long afternoons in her attic studio listening to Phil Collins, the Bee Gees, and Pink Floyd. Sometimes I maneuvered the plywood boards she propped against the walls over top of the carpet and danced to the music. Other times, I painted faces on rocks I'd collected from the beach, and I would later try to hawk to her friends.

She had pulled out one of her cushioned, oversized gold dining room chairs—the table was big enough to comfortably sit sixteen—and motioned me to hop onto her lap. I began to tell her about Patty, and the grocery carts, the unpiloted airplanes full of doomed people. She gasped when I told her how Patty had lost her husband and all her friends who had been raptured "in their clothes" (the movie at least clarified this one longstanding question I'd had). Then I got to the main point: Grandma Erma was Jewish and did not believe Christ was the son of God, so unfortunately, I told her, she was going to go to hell. It was my duty to inform her that she could avoid this crushing fate. I cried as I broke this news to her. The stakes felt utterly catastrophic to me. In one corner of her dining room sat two large wooden sculptures in ebony that came from somewhere in Africa. They had exaggerated, long faces and I had to look away from them because they always scared me. In another corner was a turquoise-blue Korean screen hiding an impressive number of spirits: bourbon, scotch, gin, vodka, rum. Probably two dozen bottles or more. This was in addition to the card room next door that had a wet bar in it, and the three-season screened porch with its wheeled cart of cocktail makings. Liquor, forbidden by God, surrounded me in Boston. I could drown in the overflow stash of alcohol in the dining room alone.

My grandmother stopped me. "I am certainly not going to hell."

I reminded her that she was a "nonbeliever." My grandmother was stern and strong-willed, but I doubted even *she* could stand up to God. "All you have to do is accept Jesus," I said.

I mentioned that the rest of her life could be exactly the same, though I suspected she'd have to give up all the booze (though stocked, she only drank a single martini at five o'clock each night). "Or you don't even have to say that whole sentence. You can just say 'Jesus' like my mom did."

"Your mother"—she spoke through her nose, like an angry horse— "did *not* call out to Jesus."

"I know," I told her. "But also, she sort of did, because she's in heaven now watching me." It made zero sense, but I felt the weight of my grand-mother's eternal soul on my shoulders. If I failed at this task she'd scream in a lake of fire and forever remember this moment.

My grandmother woke every day of her life, washed off the night's Pond's Cold Cream, and put on full makeup: pink blush, blue eye shadow, black liner, and mascara. Her eyes were the color of the ocean far across the horizon, a deep blue. In pictures I have of her from the 1940s and '50s she is often hamming it up for the camera, smiling hugely, kicking up a high-heeled shoe like a Rockette. Before she took over her mother's interior design firm, she'd been a professional dancer in New York during the Depression, a Chester Hale Girl, known for their tap dancing. She is dazzling, her makeup always perfect, her outfits tailored and polished. Her home looked straight out of a 1930s movie set. One enormous red silk Chinese screen with white painted storks sat behind the oversized white couch. You could imagine Katharine Hepburn speed walking through the doorway. I think losing her daughter broke something in her. After my mother's death, she never laughed.

My grandma said she didn't want to talk to me anymore about this Jesus business and she asked me to bring her the phone. I didn't know if I was crying because she wouldn't go to heaven, or because I was scared about Jesus looking into my heart.

My grandmother held the phone to her ear, the cord dangling in knots beside her. I had pulled out another dining room chair and sat slumped over the glass table. What if the rapture happened while I was in my grandmother's house, surrounded by nonbelievers and liquor? I would definitely be abandoned in the rapture's airlift.

"Richard!" She had dialed my house in Illinois and yelled my father's name. I mean *yelled*. As if he were a child. She was the only one I ever heard call him Richard. Everyone else called him Dick.

"How. Dare. You!" She was so angry I could see her short gray hair shaking. Her lips—outlined and filled in with red lipstick—were pursed.

I had never in my life heard anyone talk to my father the way my grandma Erma was talking to him now. What we heard in church, that *women are subservient*, would not ever apply to her. "You will not fill my granddaughter with this kind of nonsense," she said. Her cheeks and neck were red. She'd punch the devil in his smug evil face if need be, but no one would order my grandmother Erma anywhere, she said, dead or alive, in this life or the next.

She was the only person I ever saw stand up to my father like that. But that one time was enough. I held on to the memory, not because it entirely relieved my fears of heaven and hell, but because I saw her truly understand—from that day forward and in a way I was still too young to be able to articulate—that my father was no longer the same man who'd married my mother.

Nine

I held on to Bill Tepper's phone number for weeks. I'd tucked it away in a desk drawer, checking every now and again to make sure it was still there. I had developed the belief that because my mother was dead, certain knowledge eluded me and boys topped this list, along with wearing makeup; coordinating outfits; how to walk, talk, and sit like a girl; what to carry in a purse; curling iron and hair dryer operations; the exact nature and use of Stayfree maxi pads; and how to walk in heels. In fourth grade, my dad had given me a ten-dollar bill once to get a haircut at the beauty salon in the strip mall on Beaver Grade Road, which was on the other side of the woods behind our house. Up until that day, my dad had always taken me to his barber. I remember going by myself to the salon, stopping at the front desk, and asking could I please get a haircut and here was my money. I didn't know an appointment was required, but they fit me in and a hairdresser not only cut my hair, but she blew it dry and curled it, then sprayed it all with hair spray. I left that salon feeling like the most drop-dead gorgeous human alive. My hair bounced around my face, the stray frizzes disciplined down from the styling and hair spray, and I felt the sunlight hitting my scalp in a way that made me want to skip through the woods singing like a cartoon. I'd been trying to return to that coiffed halcyon afternoon ever since.

I'd never seen Bill Tepper and knew nothing about him, not his age, not what he'd done to arrive at the SASED school, not even where he lived. I pictured him looking like Leif Garrett, light brown hair down to his shoulders in thick waves, overly pronounced Adam's apple, pale eyes, freckles.

Since the day they'd fluttered phone numbers down to us, the SASEDs had grown emboldened with their hoots and hollers until their teachers must have forced them to close their windows during our recess. Still, some of my classmates had called those phone numbers, which seemed courageous to me. We'd sneak looks during recess, and on days it wasn't too sunny, we could sometimes make out the shadows of their faces looking down at us. What were they thinking, stuck behind their closed windows? What might have happened if they'd just broken free, run down the stairs, and met us on the playground?

One evening, my father came to my room as soon as he got home from work. I knew what this was about. After school, I'd lied to Barb about having done my science homework. (Science was only marginally less painful for me than math.) When Barb discovered my lie, she'd had me bite down on a bar of soap. Then she'd pulled it out and made me read the Bible aloud to her for twenty minutes with chunks of soap stuck to the backs of my teeth. It tasted sharp and poisonous. Bubbly saliva dripped down my chin and neck.

Now, my father came to confront me about the lie. But I had my own agenda. Surely once he discovered what she'd done, he'd be appalled. He'd forget all about the soap and *she'd* be the one in trouble. Maybe she'd have to apologize to me with a mouth full of soap.

My father stood over me, still in a suit and tie, his blond hair parted on the side and greased back, as neatly as when he'd left that morning. I stood next to my bed. Lying, he reminded me, was a sin against God and any sin against God was a sin against him, the head of our household. "I know," I told him, "but wait—"

"Wait, nothing," he interrupted. "Thou shalt not lie. You know the Ten Commandments." He often went into Biblical syntax when he was angry. *Thou shalt.* Like he was a religious Shakespeare. His blue eyes seemed to have a shiny overlay to them, and I found myself looking down toward the edge of my bed, rather than directly at him. His suit was beige, his tie a deep maroon. Barb ironed his shirts for him now.

"She made me eat soap!" I cried. For good measure, I added, "And soap is poisonous!" I did not know if this was technically true.

My father stopped for a moment and studied me. Something in him shifted, and I wasn't sure how to read the shift. Did he get it now?

"She, who?" he said.

His voice lowered to an eerie quiet.

"You know," I said. I felt myself growing unsteady, losing control of the conversation.

"Who?" he said.

I understood now where we were headed. He was on to me. For more than a year, I had scurried around the house, searching for her when I needed her, and avoiding that word. *Mom*. Sometimes when I was alone, I would try to mouth it—*mom, mom, mom*—but it felt like a foreign language on my tongue.

"Your wife," I told him.

He stared hard at my face. She'd made me *eat soap*, I wanted to holler at him. *And read the Bible out loud!* Somewhere in there must have been the father who'd sat around the table during Passover reading from the Torah and who loved herring in wine sauce, and boats, and sledding, and an Iron City beer during the Super Bowl.

"What's. Her. Name," he growled.

"The woman you married," I yelled.

The thought of saying it made me go dark like it would poison me, put clots of dirt in my belly. It was a betrayal, though I don't think I would have used the word then. It was more that the word itself was so wildly foreign that it demanded a new way to think and move through the world when I was finally getting used to the world in which I did not say it.

"What Is Her Name?" His voice boomed. David had conceded early on, obedient son that he was. It wasn't a rebellion so much as what felt like a physical inability. God had instructed it. And God, it seemed, only spoke to adults, never children.

Finally, I screamed: "*Barbara!*"

Up until that moment, my father had left corporal punishment to my mother, who occasionally spanked us with a wooden spoon. This was not uncommon in the 1970s. Lots of kids were spanked. Probably most kids. And wooden spoons, for whatever reason, had become the implement of choice. Back then, my father didn't demand, didn't holler, didn't discipline.

But he was so different now. There was static in the air, my father with a look on his face that I'd never seen. Surely, I could make him understand, I thought. I just had to say it again. *Soap!*

His hand reared back, open-palmed, and he slapped me hard across the face. His eyes blazed. I held my face and wailed, looking up at him.

But he said nothing. This man, standing in front of me while my cheek burned. This man was not my father.

He looked at me for another second, then turned and left the room. My cheek held his handprint. I felt something inside me, some volcanic mass, start to form; this other loss. My mother had had no choice in her own fate. She died wanting desperately to live. But my dad? He had done all this willingly.

THAT NIGHT, I waited until everyone was asleep. ABC was doing her feline patrol around the house, and I made my way to the kitchen phone. ABC followed and did figure eights around my ankles, which normally I hated, but tonight I reached down to pet her, listening for any other human sound in the house. It was near ten o'clock. ABC purred. I sat on the carpet and waited.

Nothing. No sound of any type, just the furnace blowing out tepid air.

Slowly, I stood up. I held in my clammy palm the tiny paper with Bill Tepper's name and number on it. My heart thundered. I didn't know if I was more terrified of getting caught by my parents, or of calling Bill. I couldn't have articulated what I wanted from him really, or why I was even doing this, apart from the fact that this phone number was the single tangible link I had to the world outside the church.

I lifted the receiver and heard the dial tone. Slowly, one clear number at a time, I dialed. A man answered on the first ring. ABC's fur was staticky on my legs. The man's voice was harsh, and sounded angry. Ten o'clock was *just* on the edge of being too late, I knew. In my house, no one was allowed on the phone after nine. I considered hanging up, but then I didn't. It must have been some tiny impulse I had held on to, some measure of self-salvation. Was anyone out there in the geography beyond my own shrinking life? My cheek burned.

Then I heard my own voice, somewhere just above a whisper. "Is Bill there, please?"

"Hold on," he said, not even asking for my name.

And then the voice of a boy, "Hello?" He sounded so much younger than I imagined.

"I'm Rachel," I told him, "from the school downstairs."

Ten

My new baby brother, John-John, arrived three weeks late, on a hot summer dawn ten months after the wedding. The four of us older kids had sat in the waiting room of the hospital all night, sometimes stretching out on the vinyl green couches to sleep, other times running through the hallways until we were shushed by an exhausted nurse. Until that night, I had no idea it took so long to have a baby. One hour had turned into a dozen, and after that I stopped counting. At one point, my dad came down and gave David a five-dollar bill to buy snacks for us from the vending machine (David being the most responsible). We three waited until David fell asleep, face down on a couch, then we pickpocketed him and spent all the money, leaving him with nothing.

Culinary sabotage was not new. We took turns making lunches for the week: girls one week, boys the next. We'd smear hot sauce on the boys' bologna, swipe mustard in their peanut butter and jelly, leave the wrapper on the American cheese slice inside the sandwich. We were a riot.

By now, we had moved from the Mildew House in Woodridge to the Mirror House in Lisle on Old Tavern Road. This time, Aaron and David shared a room and Holly and I each had our own bedrooms in the basement. The Mirror House was a slight improvement over the Mildew House. For starters, it did not smell of mildew. It did not have drafty windows and ubiquitous spiderwebs. It was two stories, with rust-colored shag carpeting and blocky mirrored wallpaper. The house sat across the street from a park and playground, which we were mostly too old for by now.

My dad came to get the four of us just as morning broke. He wanted to introduce us to our "new sister" which was his idea of a joke since we all knew it was a boy. We peered through the window at him as he lay sleeping in the hospital crib, more or less a clear plastic bucket. John-John was crinkled, with white paste all over him, and looked more like an old man than a brand-new baby.

"What's wrong with him?" I asked.

My dad said that's how babies looked when they came into the world, and John would look better in a day or two. My dad wore a blue hospital gown, tied at the waist, which I thought was hysterical.

The next year of my life with John would wind up putting me very much in demand as a babysitter. I learned to change diapers, clean up puke, rock a colicky baby to sleep. I fed and burped him, lay next to him as he stared at the rhythm of a slow-churning ceiling fan, took him in the backyard on blankets to look for squirrels. I rolled balls to him once he could sit up, and I read board books to him. In time, I could slip his squirmy limbs inside a snowsuit in seconds. I knew to cut his grapes in half and played choo-choo with his dinner. I loved his wispy blond hair, the way his mouth always had a gurgly shine. Babysitting got me more money than most twelve-year-olds were likely to have, even at the going rate of two dollars an hour. But more importantly, it got me out of my house, out of what my father had taken to calling our continual family "strife." I could put a child to sleep and then go watch TV, or turn on the radio. It was a lifeline to a forbidden world. Shows that were banned from my house were available to me. I watched *Diff'rent Strokes* and *The Facts of Life*. I loved *The Dukes of Hazzard* and *The Love Boat* and *The Jeffersons*. I listened quietly to the Loop or WBBM, careful to always keep an ear on the driveway in case the family's car pulled in. I danced to the Rolling Stones' "Start Me Up" and whisper-wailed along with Steve Perry when he asked, "who's crying now." I gravitated toward the kind of music that I knew should be played loud, so listening to it at a whisper felt strangely thwarted, like seeing only half your shadow on a sunny day.

ONE MORNING AFTER our daily school devotions, my uncle Jim announced that producers from a television show were visiting the school. They aired a program on Channel 38—the religious channel in Chicago—called Bible Baffle. It was a game show for adults, but the producers were planning to run a weeklong special with kids. Anyone over the age of twelve was invited to try out.

Apparently, the producers were having trouble finding female candidates willing to brave humiliation. I was as insecure as the next girl, but I was also boisterous. Plus, I could memorize things fairly easily and it was impossible to be in my social circles now without learning a lot of the exact kind of thing this game required. In fact, I'd learned the Bible in spite of actively wanting to *not* learn it.

So one snowy afternoon I found myself excused from school as I drove into downtown Chicago in our brown van with Barbara and John-John. Channel 38 aired preachers like Kenneth Copeland, Jimmy Swaggart, James Dobson, and Pat Robertson. My dad and stepmom were warriors in the army of Morris Cerullo thanks to Channel 38. And Bible Baffle, the station's signature game show, gave surprisingly exotic prizes to their winners—most notably, cruises.

I remembered well the cruises I'd been on when my mother was still alive. My uncle Robert, from New York, footed the bill. He was my grandmother Erma's brother and he'd become a jeweler after World World II, then invested the majority of his money in Coca-Cola and McDonald's. Since he had no children of his own, he had become a kind of surrogate to my mother. We'd traveled to the Caribbean: Bermuda, Martinique, Antigua. I still had a tin drum my mother had bought me on one excursion. I'd tried frog legs and snails, declaring them delectable. My mother dressed me for dinner in a floor-length pink satin and white lace dress. Aboard the *Maxim Gorki*, I befriended our cabin steward and one evening, as I played Ping-Pong in the smoky employee lounge deep in the bowels of the ship in my fancy dress, the captain put out a mayday to the entire crew and they spent a frantic half hour looking for me. My terrified mother didn't know whether to hug me or spank me when I finally turned up.

Maybe winning this game show could be a turning point in our new home. Maybe being the person responsible for all of us going on a cruise would change the trajectory of our hatred, not to mention my own personal standing in the family. Perhaps then they'd be indebted to me,

The author with her family and her Uncle Robert on a cruise to the Caribbean, circa 1975.

somehow. It was the kind of dream kids often have that involves them saving babies from burning buildings, and dogs from frozen lakes. A fantasy in which a bad kid does a great thing and reinvents herself forever. I had no blueprint for how to save myself from the anguish I felt in my everyday life, so in its absence, any fantasy would do—even one as short-lived as a cruise.

My stepmom had taken me shopping and purchased a royal blue terry-cloth V-neck dress, and the second prettiest girl in school, Lisa Mirabelli, styled my hair so that it feathered in two large curls running down either side of my face. At the studio, a makeup artist put foundation and mascara on me. I wasn't allowed to wear makeup, so this felt slightly seditious. My stepmother took a photo of me holding John-John just before the start of the game. I look relaxed, happy even. And confident.

The author holding her baby brother on the set of "The New Bible Baffle."

The set was surprisingly flimsy, aluminum foil backing the three player's stations, and our buzzers were made of a strip of unsanded wood, like kindling. I played against two boys, a total of three rounds, and after each round, the winner unscrambled a Bible verse on a magnetic board. On television, it looked so sleek, so professional, but in real life, the scrambled words were just white Styrofoam with black lettering.

The first question came, and I knew it. Then another, and another. I hit the buzzer again and again. The questions were ridiculously easy: which disciple betrays Jesus? What is the shortest verse in the Bible? What is the primary subject of First Corinthians? Name the boy king who slew the giant. I'd been nervous, practically shaking on the drive down the Eisenhower Expressway into the city, but once I got the first answer right, my anxiety melted away. I *knew* this stuff. Knew it in my sleep. *Judas betrayed Jesus*, and *Jesus Wept* is the shortest verse, and *First Corinthians is about love* and *David slew Goliath*. The studio was freezing cold, and goose bumps broke out on my arms, but even shivering didn't stop me from hitting the buzzer again and again. After I won the first round, I began to dream of the cruise I might win. It'd be small. This wasn't *The Price Is Right*, after all. I knew that much. Maybe Florida? Possibly it wouldn't be a cruise at all, but some other sort of vacation. The Wisconsin Dells? The Ozarks?

I lost the second round by a point. Only one of the boys—tall, curly black hair—was any competition at all. The boy to my left, brown shiny hair, a full foot shorter than me, answered just a handful of the questions. When the third round came, I forced myself to concentrate, to study the lips of the host and try to glean the words before they even left his mouth. I hit my splintery buzzer again, and then again. I was on autopilot, answering every question, trying to stay laser-focused on the next one. If they asked an Old Testament question, I guessed a New Testament one would come next. If they asked something from the Gospels, I suspected they might try to trip us up with Deuteronomy or Psalms.

I won the third round easily. The final test in order for me to be named the grand prize winner required me to unscramble an extended Bible verse on the magnetic board in under a minute. The verse was from Ephesians. And I had it solved before I'd even taken the few steps required to cross the set. My mind worked faster than my hands, but I finished quickly enough that the host had to fill in some extra time. He made his way over to me. He held a long, skinny silver mic, like an oversized pen. We shook hands. He was talking to me, but looking into the camera, and the makeup line across his chin gave him the appearance of unbaked clay.

Those seconds felt the longest to me in the whole game, the time between my solving the verse and the grand prize announcement. He motioned for me to go back to my pedestal, and slowly the disembodied voice of the announcer began to list the day's prizes: a New International Version of the Bible, an annual calendar of daily devotions, and then, finally, the grand prize. The voice got deeper and slower, the drama unfolding slowly. I braced to hear the words: an all-expense-paid trip.

But instead, I heard *Panasonic*.

I heard *state-of-the-art*.

The announcer cited the highlights: dual cassette, turntable, hi-fi, built-in equalizer, Dolby speakers.

I held in my anguish. Of course, I thought, as I stood there with a smile plastered on my face—I knew the cameras were on me—*of course* they wouldn't have the same prize for adults and kids. How could I be so stupid? How could I have believed someone like me—twelve years old—could win an entire vacation for a family of seven? I'd been an idiot. Shame coursed through me, embarrassment flooding my cheeks.

I had won a stereo.

I knew my father wasn't happy. He didn't want me to have that stereo any more than he wanted me to have a subscription to *Seventeen*, or a set of drums. But what could he do? He and my stepmom had encouraged me to try out for the game show in the first place. We set the stereo up on top of my dresser, my father plugging in the speakers, testing out the decibels. He warned me not to play it above three on the volume control. He reminded me again of the rules: no rock and roll. I could lose this as easily as I had won it.

I was only allowed to listen to Christian rock, so at home we played Keith Green, Amy Grant, Petra, Stryper. One song, by Petra, called "For Annie," was about a young girl ignored by her family until the day she swallows a jar of pills and kills herself. I took my dad out to his car one afternoon and popped the Petra tape in his tape deck, asking him to listen. When the song ended, he shut off the ignition. "Kind of a bummer, isn't it, Rachel?" he said. And then he climbed out of the car and went back into the house.

THAT NIGHT, AFTER everyone went to bed, I snuck out to my father's desk in the family room, quietly dialing the number that I'd long ago memorized. I called often, two or three times a week, always after ten o'clock, and always he was there, answering on the first ring, ready to talk. Bill Tepper. My SASED. He rattled off his favorite bands: AC/DC, Black Sabbath, Led Zeppelin. I took notes furiously. The first album I bought was Tom Petty and the Heartbreakers. ("*Oh you don't have to live like a refugee . . .*")

Bill Tepper and I talked for years. But we would never meet in real life.

Eleven

Inside the gymnasium, the congregation sang, the two dozen or so families filling the airy space. We were, as usual, late for church. I hadn't wanted to come, and my father had dragged me by the ankle from bed. I'd flopped onto the floor pulling pillows, sheets, and blankets along with me, and he'd kept pulling me across the carpet until I'd gotten rug burn on my stomach and finally hollered, okay, I'd go. Now, still irritated and resentful, I stopped immediately inside the double doors, beside an usher named Big Bob, who was morbidly obese and perpetually sweating, and incredibly kind to me. The service was still in the early stages, the small congregation on their feet. My father signaled me to follow him. I shook my head and stepped closer to Bob. Being in public was a measure of safety.

The rest of the family found seats in one of the back rows, but I hung back by Big Bob as the song ended, and my uncle Jim began to pray. Then my dad and stepmom were stuck awkwardly in the middle of the gym, forced to close their eyes and bow their heads. I bowed my head, too, tucked away behind Bob. The prayer took forever. I could feel Bob's heat like a mist. My uncle's voice boomed through the microphone, interrupted every few seconds by a creak in the floor, a chair leg, a sniffle, a cough, someone clearing their throat.

The prayer ended. My dad mouthed: "Get up there."

I shook my head.

"She's okay here," Big Bob said.

But I wasn't okay there. My father's word was God's word. Power structures had to be maintained. Appearances, too.

My uncle told the congregation to be seated, and there was a general commotion while folks got comfortable. This allowed my dad and stepmom to each grab an arm and escort me out the double doors. We made our way down the same hallway I walked for school, and out onto the playground. The rubber-seated swings stirred in the breeze.

"What's wrong with you, Rachel?" my stepmother demanded. "What is *wrong* with you?"

I refused to talk.

Maybe she slapped me first. Or maybe I balled my fist and punched her. Both those things happened, but I can't be sure of the order. I'm guessing it was me. Partly because I want to absolve her somewhat. I understand now how young and overwhelmed she was, how she was herself being commanded in much the same way I was being commanded. But I comprehended none of that then. She was easier to fight, easier to hate, easier to blame than my father. The hatred and disappointment I felt from my father devastated me, but he was still my only living parent.

I knew enough not to fight like a girl. I didn't slap her or pull her hair, as she did to me. I punched square on her cheek. And I punched again. A rusting metal merry-go-round and monkey bars surrounded us. A slide. A seesaw. It was gray outside, chilly. Her slaps stung, but they were nothing compared to spankings. I wanted to hurt her. I wanted her to understand she could not overpower me, not like my father could. That we were outside, in a public space, did not stop me. I didn't care who saw us. I remember her tiny, breathy screams. Her shock at the manner of my fight.

It lasted only seconds, but it was long enough. My father got between us, pulled us apart. We took a breath in our standoff. Physical violence is always a shock, even if it only lasts a second, even if it happens often. An unspoken agreement betrayed. A social contract, ruptured. But the thunderbolt of it, the adrenaline, lingers long afterward. Something changed for the three of us that day. This violence could no longer be rationalized as "discipline." And the confines of our own home no longer hid our rage, this dark secret of our family.

MY FATHER ASKED the neighbors who lived behind us to come and get me, to let me stay with them for a few days. These neighbors were secular, which speaks to how desperate my father must have felt. There were a dozen families just steps away in the congregation who might have taken me in for a time. But he couldn't ask any of them. It would have humiliated him to show them the spectacle of his failure.

I spent a week sleeping on a mattress in my neighbor's laundry room. All that week, their daughter and I snuck up to her parents' bedroom where her mother kept an impressive collection of Harlequin romances. I'd pick one, and then I'd go back downstairs, curl up on the mattress with the hum of the dryer, and read.

Writers always have origin stories of reading, of hours spent in the company of the classics. They'd found their way to Madeleine L'Engle, maybe, or Judy Blume. *The Call of the Wild* or *A Tree Grows in Brooklyn*. I read those Harlequin romances. Every woman was beautiful, quiet, uninterested in a relationship until one dropped into her life. They were always somehow alone but not lonely, and unaware of their own romantic need. They seemed whole to me, independent, self-determining. I didn't care about, or even notice, the uniform plots, how the man and woman would wind up together, after some period of time in which they appeared to despise one another but were somehow forced together. Maybe the electricity went out, or they were stuck in a cabin during a blizzard, maybe their helicopter crashed and they, relatively unscathed, had to scale down a mountain. The particulars didn't matter. It was the women I studied, the women who seemed like mysteries to me. How had they become so autonomous? How had they materialized as adults without the messiness of other people? Even after I left their house and returned to my own home, their daughter would let me borrow books from her mother's voluminous stash, provided I always returned them. Maybe that week was the start of something that shook loose in me, something that told me the secular world wasn't entirely how the church portrayed it to be, which is to say that maybe it wasn't all lost.

And maybe we weren't the chosen. Even the kids in my school weren't immune to their own sinful nature. Once, on a sleepover at my friend Donna's house, her oldest brother, Charlie, came into the room where we were sleeping and put his hand up my pajama top and felt my breast. I'd never have known if he hadn't confessed to me later. He was seventeen or eighteen years old, his lanky body drooped in shame as he told me. I was twelve.

I told my parents, and my aunt and uncle, and their response was to have us dance together at a Friday night square dance at the church. I was humiliated, enraged. Instead of feeling like Charlie deserved forgiveness for touching me, I wished he'd never said a thing. I was disgusted by him now, his palms sweaty as he twirled me around, careful to avoid eye contact, or physical contact of any kind except when we were forced to lock elbows or hold hands. He was tall and skinny, with brown curly hair and a voice that cracked when he spoke, as if it had begun to change but then had gotten stuck. He was as ignorant as I was. No instruction on sexuality. I should have blamed the adults for their refusal to acknowledge the biological nature of adolescence itself. In the absence of questions and answers, actions fill the void of knowledge.

One afternoon in the spring after my twelfth birthday, while my dad was still at work and my stepmom was upstairs with John-John, I took out my blue flowered suitcase and packed some underwear, a few T-shirts, and my jeans. I got my toothbrush and hairbrush and journal, then I slid open my window and tossed the suitcase out onto the side yard. I threw out my roller skates—orange wheels with brown suede tops. They'd been my Christmas present that year. To climb out my window, I simply had to get up on my dresser and maneuver out onto the grass. It was bright afternoon still, and I didn't want to take a chance on my stepmother seeing me, so I carried my suitcase and roller skates to the side of our neighbor's house and sat on the grass while I put on my skates.

I skated off in the direction of a friend in the neighborhood. I didn't know her well but I'd been to her house once or twice and remembered it as soft and warm, with plush carpeting and a television right off the kitchen in the sunken family room. The sofa and love seat were so fluffy they enveloped you.

I rang the doorbell. Her mother answered. I stood in my skates and told her I didn't want to live with my parents anymore. I didn't quite know how to ask her to let me live there, but I hoped she would just make the offer. She invited me in and I took off my skates, made my way in socks to those soft couches. She left for a few minutes and I sat there, trying to picture my new life in this house. Maybe I'd vacuum and do chores around the house. I'd get good grades and always clean up after myself. They'd wonder how they ever had lived without me. I'd clean their toilets and iron their blouses. I'd be a wholly different person here than whatever creature I had been in my own house.

But even as I imagined this, I understood it wouldn't work. I knew them no better than I'd known Barb when my dad married her. This house was no less strange than my own.

She came back to where I was sitting and offered me a soda and some cookies. I nibbled away, trying to tell her what my house was like, how everyone yelled at everyone else all the time. I told her how I hated my stepmother and my stepbrother, and how all we were allowed to do was church day and night. I did not tell her about the spanking; it was too humiliating. As I talked, she listened, nodding every once in a while. I remember her eyes welling up with tears at one point. But something about the story eluded me. I couldn't capture what it all really felt like, how my insides were in a constant churn at home. How I had begun to hate God, and hate the Bible, and this made me afraid that I was destined for hell. And I feared my mother was already in hell, and my Jewish relatives would also go to hell, and however bad this current life was, it was only a precursor to an eternity that would be so much worse.

She told me she was sure my parents loved me. She said all parents loved their kids.

"Mine don't," I assured her.

She touched my knee. "They do. I know they do," she said. I rubbed my feet in her soft carpet, my socks getting tiny electric shocks.

I knew I couldn't live with these strangers, but I couldn't go home either. I imagined the spanking I'd get for running away. But it became clear that my time had run out at the neighbor's. We'd talked and talked, and I'd used the necessary words: raging, screaming, fighting. But at the end I felt like I'd said nothing. I'd failed to capture the despair. I thanked her for the cookies and the soda. I went back to the front door with my blue flowered suitcase, and I laced up my skates again.

My father's car still wasn't in the driveway. I slipped off my skates and went around the house, to the back deck. The afternoon light waned; I'd been gone two or three hours. We kept the back door mostly unlocked, and I thought maybe there was a chance that Barb hadn't missed me. Maybe she'd been so busy with the other kids, my absence hadn't even been noted.

I walked up the back steps in my socks and put my skates and my suitcase on the deck outside the door, figuring I'd come back and get them after bedtime. My skates being outside was not in itself unusual. I spent hours and hours after school nearly every day skating on my driveway, aware only of the sound of the wind and the clicking of my plastic wheels on the cement.

I opened the back door and there was Barb, waiting for me, her gaze fixed on the back door. Then she held out her arms and said, "God told me you ran away."

I went to her and I hugged her. Was this how God worked? Had he made the neighbor call, or had my stepmother really received a divine message?

We hugged, and then she let go, and she kept her arms on my shoulders and looked me straight in the eye and said, "Don't do it again, okay, Rache?"

She never told my father.

Twelve

One night not long after Bible Baffle, I waited on the edge of my bed for my father to come home. I knew I was in trouble. Maybe the biggest trouble I'd ever been in. I'd been caught by the principal of the school—a woman who had taken over for my uncle Jim. Her name was Candy Klein. She was a tiny woman with frizzy hair and what we'd now term mild vocal fry. She'd caught me smoking behind a dumpster with the entire pep squad, and every one of the four of them had told her the truth: I was the ringleader.

I snuck my pack of Salems with me everywhere, though I never brought them out. It was far too dangerous. I'd smoke down by the creek hidden by trees when we lived in Woodridge, or across the street at the playground after we moved to Lisle. The older sister of a church friend bought them for me. But on this blustery day, I pronounced to the pep squad—all five of us had more or less been conscripted onto the team—that I had learned to blow smoke rings, and whatever practice we were supposed to be doing was quickly upended by this astonishing claim. Evidence was needed.

So we marched outside in our green T-shirts and our painter's pants—the squad uniform. I carried a single cigarette in my palm. It took three or four matches to get the cigarette lit, but once it was going, I inhaled a deep drag of smoke, then formed my lips into an O and snapped my jaw as my friend's older sister had taught me. A series of smoke rings dissipated into the wintry air. The pep squad, impressed, wooted quietly, and we passed the cigarette around. I do not believe I am overstating it to say that my smoke rings elicited as much enthusiasm as the pep squad had demonstrated that entire year. We were crouched by the side of the dumpster, the smoke visible as it rode into the sky.

One by one, we were called into the office with Principal Klein and my uncle Jim, still the de facto person in charge. My uncle spanked me right in the office. They kicked me off the pep squad and then disbanded us for the rest of the year.

But none of that concerned me. I can't even remember now if my uncle spanked me with his bare hand or with a ruler or a belt or something else entirely. It was my father I feared. Since remarrying, he and my stepmother had created new protocols for punishment, under advisement from my uncle Jim and aunt Janet. Spankings were now a regular part of our lives, with a paddle from Sigma Delta Tau, the (Jewish) Greek sorority house my real mother had pledged at the University of Pennsylvania. The paddle was half an inch thick, blond wood, maybe eighteen inches long, the Greek letters carved into it and painted black.

MY FATHER'S CAR pulled into the driveway and I felt my limbs start to buzz, a nausea creeping up my throat. I heard the front door open then close, heard his voice, muffled. Heard my stepmother. Heard the floor creak under the weight of his steps. Every second stretched out. I dreaded it as much as I wanted to just go upstairs and get it over with. The spanking was only the finale. Discipline in this new house involved a long, drawn-out conversation in which my parents—my father and Barb—lay on their bed, propped against the wall as my father read passages from the Bible, interspersed with lectures on the sin of the infraction. The guilty party, most often me, would sit in an olive-green vinyl chair across from the bed having to answer questions: *So you understand why we've called you up here tonight? You understand what you've done wrong? Do you repent for your sin?*

It didn't take long to hear him call my name. My siblings were squirreled away in their own rooms, apart from whichever one of them had been charged with entertaining John-John out of earshot—which meant outside. I could picture him at the park across the street, hurling his little body down the metal slide, or giggle-screaming as he pumped his legs on the swings.

I sat down in the chair. My dad had taken off his tie and jacket, but he still wore his suit pants and white button-down. He asked me if I knew why I'd been called to their room. I nodded. He asked me if I knew I'd sinned. I did not nod to this. Instead, I told him that nowhere in the Bible did it specify that smoking was forbidden. Not the Old Testament and certainly not the New. My father raised his hand to stop me. "There are God's laws," he said, "and there are laws of the land." The former commanded we obey the latter, provided it was not in conflict with God's law. To press my case would have been a hopeless endeavor, and so I sat, my jaw clenched, my body frozen in dread. On and on he talked. In hurting my own body, he said, I hurt his body and in hurting his body, I hurt God's body. We were all temples to the Lord. How could I defile my temple?

My stepmother didn't say a word, a silent witness. His personal squad.

My father ended, as he always did, by reading Ephesians 6:1. *Children, obey your parents in the Lord, for this is right.* He reminded me of how all of this—the lecture, the reading, the spanking—hurt him much more than it hurt me. This never felt right to me. How could it? Spanking with a thick wooden paddle hurt like a motherfucker. My father, according to the tenets of FCCF, subscribed to the *spare the rod, spoil the child* philosophy—an erroneous reading of a ubiquitous misquote in the evangelical culture that enables parents to justify physical abuse. The actual verse is Proverbs 13:24: *He that spareth his rod hateth his son: but he that loveth him chasteneth him betimes.* Interestingly, the more commonly cited "spare the rod, spoil the child" isn't anywhere in the Bible. It comes from a mid-seventeenth century bawdy poem called "Hudibras" by Samuel Butler.

My father instructed me to stand at the foot of the bed and lean over. The formality itself was humiliating. He told me to put my palms on the bed. I didn't cry at the first thwack. Not the first, but every one thereafter. My hands instinctively moved to offset the blows aimed at my rear, and I felt the hard wood of the paddle on the side of my wrist, and on my palm, and my father said if I couldn't keep my hands on the bed, it would go on longer. It was up to me. I howled, I brayed, and I hated myself for giving my father the satisfaction of knowing how much it hurt. He'd hit us ten times, a dozen, however many it took until he felt he'd broken us down enough to be truly repentant.

And then we three would pray together and repent for my sins. We'd hug. Cry, because at the end of the day, it was necessary to see how all of this was done out of love. God's love and my parents' love. And surely I could understand that. Surely I could feel the love. Feel *their* pain. I hugged them both, sobbing, apologizing, and hating them all the while.

Afterward, I walked gingerly to my basement bedroom, peeled off my painter's pants, and studied the vast web of welts and red splotches in my dresser mirror. For several days, sitting would be uncomfortable and I would sleep on my stomach. That night, I lay diagonally across my bed, fuming with an unspoken rage. They'd hoped the punishment was enough to set me back on the right path, where I'd read my daily devotions, call Barbara "Mom," pray to Jesus, and not smoke cigarettes. But the spankings never had this effect on me; all they ever did was fuel my anger.

THE ONLY THING worse than being the object of punishment was having to listen as my siblings were spanked. Their screams, like my own, resounded through the entire house. It was impossible not to hear. We brayed savagely, like animals in deep wilderness. We shook the window-panes with our howls. The sound stays with me even today. I loved my brother, David. He was spanked least of any of us, but when it happened, I would crawl into my closet and bury myself in shoes and clothes and stuffed animals, trying to muffle his cries. On a number of occasions, the behavior of the four of us older kids resulted in collective punish-ment. Our parents would line us up over my late mother's oversized settee in the living room, the same one where I shrugged off my backpack, looked down at *Benedict Arnold*. We'd assume the position—leaning over, palms flat. And we'd be spanked in an assembly line. I never remember what we had done to earn this punishment, only the punishment itself. The anger that swelled like a contagion, from one of us to the next, with each blow. Palpable as mud under your toes. It snaked its way inside me, curled itself around my stomach and into my cells, molded itself into a permanent occupant that I carried like an invisible sarsen.

Aaron was as angry as I was now. He'd bump me hard in the shoulder as we passed in the hallway. Once, on the landing by the front door, he tackled me to the ground and sat on top of me with his hands around my neck. I fought back, but he was bigger and stronger. He banged my head against the floor and Barb heard us and came running down the hall from her room. She screamed at him to stop, to get off me, but he didn't. I was choking, sucking at air, clawing at his hands. She ran down the steps to the landing and grabbed him by the shoulders, yanking him backward and off of me.

All of us were spanked with my mother's paddle regularly, well into our teens. Finally, one night, when it was once again my turn in the vinyl chair, I decided I'd had enough. I was fifteen by then. My stepmother was heavily pregnant with another baby who would be born less than two months later. We'd name him Joshua and he would be the sixth and final kid in our makeshift brood.

I no longer remember what I was even in trouble for on this night. I'd gotten so used to my own anger that I'd become venomous, calloused by hatred. I didn't pretend to listen. I didn't return their hugs afterward or try to understand why they had to do it. What did it matter if I bent over or didn't? What did it matter if I had anything to say or not?

I leaned over the bed when my father told me to. As usual, my reflexes tried to deflect the blows, my hands moving to protect my rear before I even knew it was happening. This only served to anger my father more, my self-protective reflex a sign of rebellion.

"Move your hands," he bellowed. "Move them."

I did.

And then I didn't.

Fuck you, I thought. *And fuck this.* I turned around and stood up, facing him. If he was going to hit me, he was going to have to look in my face. I was just a few inches shorter than him by now and the same height as my stepmother. She got up off their bed and stood behind me. My father looked stunned for a second. His face reddened. Then he swung. If he couldn't hit my rear end, he'd hit where he could. The paddle thwacked into my thigh. I reared back and kicked him. He stumbled. He began to swing wildly, the paddle everywhere at once. I felt it on a rib, on my hip, against my forearm. My stepmother was screaming. "Stop! Stop it! Stop it!"

I didn't know who she was talking to. Perhaps both of us.

I kicked at him again, then lost my balance, and I was on my back, like a beetle, and I pedaled my legs, kicking madly. My father was on my right side, swinging with what felt like his entire body. My stepmom was trying to grab one of my legs. I was half under the vinyl chair.

We must have heard it at the same time because we all froze instantly at the sound. A sharp crack. It took me a few seconds to understand where it had come from. My father was holding the handle of the paddle, and from there the rest of it dangled from one thin fracture of wood as sharp as a knife. He had broken the paddle on me.

And then my body was not my own. It was a beast, a weapon. I kicked again and again, because now I understood that he was powerless against me. He tried to grab one foot, but I was fast, and static with rage and by the belief that I had nothing to lose. I kicked with abandon, adrenaline like fireworks in my body, and then I heard my stepmom scream. She fell back, holding her stomach where the baby was curled up inside her. I'd kicked her. I'd kicked my unborn baby brother.

Part III

PATIENT STALKERS

Thirteen

Joshua was born in early winter that year, and they rushed him immediately into emergency surgery. None of the four of us was at the hospital this time and we waited for hours to see if he would be okay. He had a condition called bladder exstrophy, whereby his bladder and kidneys had been outside his little body, the umbilical cord wrapped around them. Urine was leaching poison into his body and the toxins could kill him. All at once, the image came to me, the sharp crack of the paddle, my stepmother's scream as she stumbled backward from my inadvertent kick. My body froze, the guilt like acid in my throat. I was sure that what was wrong with him had been my fault. I'd been trying to save myself, but the God of my world knew where and how to enact revenge. Was he trying to compel me to pray to him so that my baby brother would live? Was this one of those mysterious ways God worked? If God wanted revenge, I thought, why couldn't he come for me directly?

I spent the whole of that day unable to complete a thought. I went between tearing up and squeezing my palms together as tightly as I could. What if it *had* been my fault? What could I do? I wasn't a doctor. I wasn't a parent. I was no one, nothing. I was a kid with an anger problem.

Joshua spent several days in the hospital. He would have many surgeries in his young life, and he would lack muscle control over his bladder until he was well into middle school. My stepmother homeschooled him until high school to save him from the meanness of kids who might find out about his condition. We older kids would learn to change his bandages after each surgery, to check his wounds for infection, to rub antibiotic cream along the seam of his body as he healed. We carried him like crystal. And he hurled himself into furniture, walls, people with gleeful, baby-boy abandon.

By now, FCCA was visibly failing. The school couldn't compete in pedagogy or extracurriculars, so unless you were a family who felt theology was your entire future, it was a mighty gamble on your child's education. One after another, families pulled out their kids. My aunt and uncle declared they were going to close the school. Eighth grade was my final year at FCCA. Holly was in the last high school graduating class of FCCA, one of three seniors. We held graduation in the back room of a restaurant.

There had been rumors of mishandled money, and the building fund never grew enough to break ground on a new church or do much more than move beyond the land my aunt and uncle had purchased. Televangelists like Jimmy Swaggart, Morris Cerullo, and Kenneth Copeland had been my aunt and uncle's role models, men with sprawling empires. They all preached about health and wealth as an American birthright, but my aunt Janet and uncle Jim never could seem to get beyond that gymnasium, that decrepit old rental building.

My aunt and uncle had moved into a brand new, state-of-the-art modern house that they'd built themselves—my father saw it as a reward for their faithfulness to God. My father tithed 10 percent of his income to my uncle's church. And tithing was pitched as an investment for which the faithful would be blessed someday by God. And those blessings inevitably came in the form of material goods. Like a new church. Like bigger houses and better cars. My aunt and uncle had a picture on their refrigerator of a Buick they desired. When they eventually got that Buick, another picture of a newer Buick went up. The Christians around me all wanted material things—fancy vacations, nice clothes, upscale suburbs. In the secular world, it signaled an empty life to want such things, whereas in our world it signaled faith in God.

DAVID, AARON, AND I would start at Naperville North High School in the fall and the course offerings were dizzying. Even to have a choice over what to take felt oddly subversive. Extracurriculars had the usual cheer-leading and sports, but then there was also modern dance and music and games (Dungeons & Dragons was all the rage), and chess club and language clubs. When David and I went to Swampscott for our annual July visit, I took the school catalog with me to show my Grandma Erma. She was particularly interested in the dance extracurriculars and encouraged me to try out for a dance troupe called Orchesis. I'd taken ballet and gymnastics when my mother was alive and so I thought maybe it would be in my blood, passed down from my grandmother Erma. I had memories of my mother doing yoga with a neighbor before she got sick, both of them in black tights and black leotards.

I spent that summer in a state of controlled anxiety. I could redefine who I'd be in high school. I'd be popular. Once again, I'd be able to wear jeans daily. My grandma Erma took me shopping for new school clothes, the first time I'd ever needed much of a wardrobe. We went to Marshalls and she let me pick out a periwinkle pair of Vidal Sassoon jeans, a purple plaid matching button-down shirt, and white Nikes with a red swoosh.

I'd even made a friend, named Cindy Landorf, who was starting at Naperville North too. Cindy loved roller-skating as much as I did. She'd been friends with a girl in my neighborhood and we met one night at the roller rink, and after that, we went as often as we could on weekends, often taking an old Bonne Bell bottle and filling it with a variety of liquids from her parents' liquor cabinet—vodka, gin, bourbon, vermouth. We called this masterpiece of a beverage our "suicide solution" and we'd skate around, then take breaks at the roller rink cafeteria sipping from it. She wasn't a Christian and her family didn't go to church, but they also didn't seem empty and hopeless and searching, though I sometimes wondered what someone who was empty, hopeless, and searching would even look like. Maybe I just didn't know how to recognize their anguish.

Cindy lived within walking distance from Naperville North, whereas my family was nearly four miles away and we'd go by bus. Cindy's parents had allowed her to cover her entire room with cutouts of heavy metal bands from *Hit Parader*, *Rolling Stone*, and *Circus*: Metallica, Led Zeppelin, Ozzy. Tommy Lee and David Lee Roth looked out at her, their faces shining with sweat. She had even covered her ceiling. In her room, I often wondered how she had won the parent lottery so fully. She was never grounded for months on end. She was never spanked. She was never forced to attend church. She probably never worried about spending eternity in a lake of fire.

Nature had gifted her with a perfect smile and skin so flawless that every errant pimple looked outsize to her and she took pains to cover it with concealer and foundation. She reminded me of a Cover Girl model with her professional-looking, multistep makeup routine and her tiny powder-sized mirror, which I imagined her mother bestowing on her in some extravagant mother-daughter ritual.

HOLLY HAD HER own new friend, a guy I'll call Jackson, who showed up at church one night with two other friends. All three of them were SASEDs and their appearance electrified our tiny congregation. SASEDs, right there in our little ministry.

Toward the end of the service, when my uncle Jim put out the altar call for anyone wanting to be saved, all three SASED boys rose and went forward. My uncle laid his hands on their foreheads, one by one, as they closed their eyes. The rest of us were also meant to close our eyes for this holy moment, but none of us did. We all watched as the boys repeated after my uncle, "I take Jesus into my heart, to forgive me my sins and to forgive those who would trespass against me." I didn't really know what it meant to trespass against someone, apart from wandering into a yard uninvited, but the language was so common to me by then that I never stopped to wonder about it.

Whether the SASEDs had actually been saved or had done it for show in order to get access to the FCCA girls was never clear to me, but after that Holly and Jackson were an item and he spent nearly every Sunday afternoon at our house. Jackson was tall, over six feet, with sandy hair to his shoulders and a bucktoothed smile. He and Holly would sit in the family room for a while, and then they'd go out driving around. He looked my dad in the eye when he spoke, and he shook my dad's hand, and so my dad said God was working in Jackson's life.

On weekend nights, Holly would sometimes allow me to go out with her when she met Jackson and his friends in the back parking lot of Ogden Mall. We'd sit on car hoods drinking beer from Styrofoam cups while music streamed from car stereos. My parents must have trusted Holly to keep me in line, though mostly when we went out she ignored me for people her own age. One night, as I was climbing in the passenger side of the orange Gremlin, Jackson sidled up to me. He was so tall and smelled so good I felt my breath catch and my head go fuzzy. His uniform was a T-shirt with a plaid flannel unbuttoned over it.

He invited me to a party, saying I could sneak out. He knew Holly and I had basement bedrooms. He promised to have me home before dawn. He didn't wait for me to answer, just winked and strode away.

When his knock came, at one A.M., my heart hiccupped into my throat. I slid open my window and saw Jackson crouching there in our yard with his toothy smile.

We drove in a brown Trans Am to a garage where a dozen kids sat on crates and beanbag chairs in a haze of gray smoke. Heavy metal thundered through a boom box. Two kids played Ping-Pong. Then someone passed me a joint. My hand shook a little, and Jackson put his arm around me, told me to inhale a small amount, hold it as long as I could. Then he handed me a Mickey's Big Mouth beer. I clung to his side and the circle of kids opened to make room for us. Occasionally, my thigh would bump Jackson's or we'd knock shoulders, laughing, and I felt cared for and protected.

THE FIRST WEEK of school, I stayed late one afternoon to try out for the Orchesis dance troupe. Tryouts were held in a classroom in which all the desks had been pushed to one wall. A small boom box was plugged in and sitting atop one of the desks. Girls talked quietly in small groups with their ponytails bouncing around. They wore tights and leg warmers; some even had leotards on. Others had cutoff sweatpants and oversized shirts with tanks underneath. It was as if I'd walked onto the set of *Fame*. I was wearing my school clothes. Jeans and a T-shirt with my new Nikes. I smiled nervously as I sat at one of the empty desks near the door. Why had it not occurred to me to bring a change of clothes? Why did I think I could walk in with no experience, with no idea what to bring or how to prepare, and just *dance*? It dawned on me only then that my grandmother must have trained for years, though she never spoke about lessons, about what came before you actually appeared on stage. What did I have? I had roller skating. I had rock albums played late at night at a whisper through my headphones. It seemed so obvious to me in retrospect that I should have prepared something, chosen music, at the very least asked someone who might know the general requirements, but I hadn't even thought to ask. It felt like I was one of those children raised in the wilderness by chimps and brought suddenly into civil society. When the first girl got up, her side ponytail bouncing off her shoulder, and handed her own cassette tape to another student to put into the boom box, I quietly snuck out the door.

The next morning before school, I went outside to the school smoking lounge to find Cindy. I knew about the smoking lounge, but I hadn't worked up the courage to visit yet, because the kids there intimidated me. They looked mean, and dangerous. Cindy herself wore lace-up brown moccasins and feather earrings, which seemed extremely tough to me. On this morning, with the shame still acute from my failed attempt to be what I considered one of the normal kids, I had to find her—I knew she would find a way to make us both laugh about it.

She was standing in a small group of other kids, smiling, smoking. "Finally!" she said when she saw me. "Took you long enough!"

I bummed a Marlboro Red off her and she introduced me around to this network of kids who scurried between classes to the lounge, sucking down what they could of a cigarette in the six minutes between periods. They had long hair and wore torn jeans and flannels, rock T-shirts, leather biker jackets, thick eyeliner, and black leather boots—my next uniform. Suddenly, I belonged somewhere.

Fourteen

Around anyone other than my baby brothers, I was sullen, angry, quiet. I spent long hours in my room listening to Iron Maiden and AC/DC, Journey and Fleetwood Mac. Jackson had a fake ID and I gave him money to buy me gallon jugs of Gallo wine, which I kept far back in my closet and drank at night after everyone went to bed. On weekends, I'd wait to hear Jackson's quiet tapping, and I'd race out of bed, draw back the curtains, and be off into the night. On those occasions that he didn't knock, I'd be disappointed and wonder if I'd done something wrong. Holly was still dating him, but I told her nothing of our late-night rendez-vous, and neither did he.

By the end of my first semester freshman year, I was failing nearly every one of my classes. Failure was easy. Easier than anything I'd ever done.

I fell asleep in class all the time, having drunk wine well into the night. I sniffed rush with a fellow classmate on the way to school on the bus, the world going green and warm for minutes at a time. When we could get away with it, we passed around a one-hitter in the smoking lounge outside, so I'd waltz into my classes glassy-eyed and buzzing. Once, my freshman math teacher, offended by my napping, came to my desk and squeezed my forearm harder and harder until I woke up. "What?" I said, without lifting my head, my voice filled with disdain and false bravado. He ordered me to the dean's office.

There were two deans at Naperville North and I was assigned Jim Dollinger, a ruddy-faced chain-smoker with an oval belly and thinning hair. I was one of maybe half a dozen kids who were regularly sent to his office for punishments, the most common of which was BAC room, Behavioral Adjustment Center. BAC room meant sitting all day long in an unused classroom in the far hinterlands of the school, down a hallway reserved for occasional classes, like woodworking or small engine repair. We ate our lunches alone, separate from the rest of the school, took our breaks alone. Seven hours of silence might have felled many students, but I was an FCCA veteran. Solitude was second nature to me. In BAC room I could read all day, draw, write. If I was good at anything in those days, it was sitting in silence. What was supposed to be a punishment felt like a reprieve.

At least once or twice a week, I missed the bus to school and my parents soon refused to drive me. So I would walk along Ogden Avenue, a five-lane artery that ran through my suburb—Lisle—and into Naperville and beyond. It went all the way east to Chicago, a distance of maybe thirty miles. Forty-five minutes into my walk sat a Dunkin' Donuts and one morning I stopped in to warm up, ordering a hot chocolate. My feet were wet and cold in my tennis shoes, the air biting. Gray mounds of snow piled along the side of the road meant no sidewalk. Around my ankles, my socks were damp. I'd planned to get my cocoa and keep walking, but it occurred to me that if I was late for school it hardly mattered whether I was an hour late or three hours late. No one was waiting for me. And what was my rush? Algebra? Earth Science? The worms, frogs, fetal pigs to dissect in biology, where the smell of formaldehyde brought bile to my mouth? I sat on one of the circular stools and swung back and forth, trying to warm myself up. The floor was slick and muddy with melting slush. The woman behind the counter brought me my cocoa and looked at me for a long second. I cupped my drink to warm up my frigid, pink fingers.

"Aren't you supposed to be in school, honey?"

No one had ever called me honey before. I told her how I had missed the bus and so my parents had made me walk. When she learned I lived in the next suburb over, she shook her head, closed her eyes like they were hurting, and said something that I interpreted as agreement that my parents were mean.

"You come in here anytime you need to, honey," she told me. "I mean it. Anytime." She didn't charge me for the hot chocolate.

And I did. I never purposely missed the bus, because miles were miles in a winter walk, but I at least had her to look forward to. I never cared about the classes I was missing. I had no vision for the future, no reason to believe any of it mattered. If my parents made me walk to school, then it was hardly my fault. Or not entirely my fault.

I would waltz into school sometime midmorning and go straight to Dean Dollinger's office. My situation had nuance. It was my fault for missing the bus, certainly, but was it my fault for having to walk nearly four miles? Did my parents share part of the blame? Dean Dollinger just wrote me a permission slip and I'd walk into health or English class halfway through. If it was math or science, I was likely to hang around outside until it was over, even though the biology teacher, Mr. Effinger, was everybody's favorite and I felt bad about disappointing him. Even the fundamentals of biology were lost on me, having learned only Creation Theory.

There was, though, one class in which I excelled: typing. And by "excelled" I mean that I ended the semester with a C. I got Ds in physical education and acting. The rest of my classes—biology, algebra, ancient history, world cultures—I failed. I had finished out my freshman year with more or less the unanimity of failure.

ONE SATURDAY NIGHT when I wasn't expecting it, I heard Jackson's telltale tap at my window. I'd been dead asleep, in one of my dad's old button-down pajama tops and my underpants. I switched on the lamp and climbed out of bed to draw back my curtain. There was Jackson's gummy smile as he knelt on the snow outside. I slid open my window and a burst of frigid air chilled my face. My hair was messy from sleep, and my legs had goose bumps. "Give me a sec," I told him, trying to conceal my excitement. It had been weeks since I'd last gone to a party with him.

"Can I come in?" he whispered. I could smell the beer on his breath, see the glazed look in his eyes. He'd never come in before. I'd only ever gone out. "I tried Holly's window, but she didn't answer."

So that was it. He just wanted to get to his girlfriend. I opened the window wider and motioned for him to jump inside. He was so tall he had to contort his body to fit through the window, and he stumbled over my dresser and landed on the floor, his body hiccupping with laughter.

"Shhhhhhh," I told him. My bedroom was right below my parents'. What kind of punishment would my father mete out if he found my sister's boyfriend in my bedroom at three A.M.?

"Sorry, sorry, sorry," he slurred. He got up and sat on the edge of my bed.

I shut the window and stood in front of him. I wanted to put on pajama bottoms. "Should I get Holly?"

"Shh, just wait a second," he said. "Give me a second." All of this came out as a single long word. He reached for my hand and pulled me to the bed beside him. I felt my legs start to tremble slightly, from the cold or from his touch I didn't know, but it embarrassed me. I looked around my room, unsure of what to do. He reached under my pajama top then, and leaned down. At first I thought maybe I was dreaming it. He was . . . kissing me? He had his hand under my pj's kneading my breast, which was uncomfortable. I didn't mind the kissing, but I could feel my back curving, trying to escape his fingertips. His tongue was in my mouth and his breath tasted like beer. I knew this was what adults did. What boyfriends and girlfriends did. They kissed. I had not known it involved tongues. At FCCA, we were told to abstain from "pleasures of the flesh" to keep ourselves pure for marriage, but I did not know what pleasures of the flesh meant and no one ever clarified. I knew boys were obsessed with breasts—I'd been wearing a bra since fourth grade, after all—but I had never considered their specific part in boy–girl relationships, and I definitely never knew they were conjoined with kissing.

And then Jackson's hand moved from my breast down to my underwear, and somehow everything down there was wet and I felt immediately riddled with shame. Was it urine? Had I started my period? I thought he would yank his hand away in disgust and flee out the window. But he didn't. Instead, he said, "Nice. Nice."

I didn't know what I had done that was nice, and I liked being kissed by Jackson, but I was also stiff with fear. What if my father heard us? What if Holly heard us? I didn't exactly know what was going on between Jackson's hand and my genitals and I didn't know how to extract myself. I wondered how long people did this kind of thing. Was this normal? Did

Holly do this with him? I considered how I might get him to climb back out that window. Maybe if I fake sneezed a few times? Maybe if I pretended to fall asleep? I had to be up in just a few hours for church. What if he passed out in my bedroom?

But then he pulled me to the floor and half fell on top of me. It knocked the wind out of me for a moment. He kicked off my underwear and used his knee to pry apart my legs. I wanted to say something. To tell him he should go. But what was happening with my body was so consuming, so terribly foreign and unexpected that words failed to form in my brain.

Now, he pulled his jeans and underwear down to his knees and I felt enormous, overwhelming pressure. I had no idea what this pressure was. To me, it seemed he was trying to slice my body in half. He kept pumping at me with his hips and the pressure would start up near my vagina, but then he'd slide down and the pressure would go toward my rear and his body was so heavy that he pushed the breath out of my lungs with every thrust. I was still a virgin and weighed probably a hundred pounds. He was six four, clocking in somewhere around two hundred. Again and again he rammed himself into me, but he couldn't get it in, and I clenched my teeth and closed my eyes and lay there not moving, hoping whatever he was trying to do would be over soon. My body was jerking out of my own control. It was like slipping down a mountain of ice, desperately grabbing for anything to temper the velocity. My father would never forgive me for this. I had to be silent, because however bad this was, I thought it had to be less bad than if my dad found us.

It was a different kind of hurt than any spanking I'd ever gotten. I could feel his frustration escalating. "Fuck," he said. "Goddamn it." The tip of his penis went into my anus and tears sprang to my eyes and my whole body went stiff; Jackson got the hint and readjusted himself, trying hard to break through with as much force as he could muster. I was crying now, but still I didn't tell him to stop. Would he tell all his friends I was a baby and a prude? Would I be cast out of the burnouts? I wanted Jackson to get what he wanted quickly so the pain would stop and he would leave. He was no longer giving me his toothy smile; instead he was sweating, swearing under his breath. "Help me out here," he finally said, too loudly. Jackson seemed mad at me now. I tried to move my hips to keep him from getting more frustrated, but my legs were straight out in front of me in a V because I didn't know to lift them, or wrap them around his waist or whatever, so I just lay there, trying to flop my hips up and down. He tried and tried and tried. He was sweating and I was sweating. And finally he said, "Fuck this," and he jumped up, buttoned his pants, and ran his hand through his long hair to get it out of his face. He picked up his leather jacket, took one quick look back at me, and then escaped back out into the winter night, leaving the window open after him.

I lay there for a minute. Or maybe many minutes. I was freezing. I knew "sex" involved a boy's parts and a girl's parts, but I'd never thought of the puzzle of them. I didn't even know that menstrual blood and urine did not exit the same place.

My legs were so sore they shook. Deep bruises blossomed all along my inner thighs. There was blood and white discharge all mixed together on me and on the rusty shag carpet. I could smell his skin on me, his beer breath in my own mouth.

I got up for church that morning without having to be awakened. I wore a white dress with purple flowers that had a matching jacket. In the middle of the service, I needed the bathroom, so I got up, and I could feel the soreness of my legs as I walked quietly through the gymnasium and out into the hallway. When I sat to pee, it stung so acutely I held my breath, my eyes tearing up. I wondered if this was the beginning of my death, if he had injured me in some invisible biological way that might slowly be killing me. That whole day, I kept quiet, turned inward to my own body, my own injuries, as if I were listening to it recount its experience of the night before. I hurt here and here and here, it was trying to tell me. And here and here. I barely made eye contact with anyone. When my parents asked me what was wrong, I told them I didn't feel well. I spent the rest of the day in my room, curled up under the covers, listening to heavy metal ballads, terrified that I'd fall asleep and never wake up.

I didn't see Jackson again for four years. I don't know how he and Holly ended things. I want to think it must have been some kind of shame over what he'd done that made him disappear so quickly and completely, but when I did finally run into him, whatever shame he may have once felt had calcified into something else entirely. I was seventeen by then, and he was hanging with some of his friends leaning against the door of his car. He had his arms crossed over his chest, which had filled out some. We were all on the Riverwalk in Naperville, a family-friendly commercial district surrounded by shops and restaurants.

A casual, confident lean. A torch sparked in my stomach. I marched up to him. I was a girl burned, a woman burning. He gave me his toothy smile once again, only this time it was sinister, holding our secret within it. I pulled my hand back, then slapped him as hard as I could across the face. Jackson's head snapped to the side. It took him a split second to register, and then when he looked back at me, he began to laugh.

Fifteen

My guidance counselor, Bob Martin, had a soft voice and wore a mustache that curled up at the ends like a cartoon villain's. Soft yellow lamps glowed in his office, and he kept a beanbag chair for comfort and a pillow for kids who needed something to punch. I was one of a handful of troubled teens on his roster who could show up whenever necessary without an appointment.

Ever since that day in the playground, when I had punched Barb, I had been fighting back. I wasn't strong, but my rage gave me fuel. And every day I woke up angry. It took almost nothing for me to call forth this feeling. Anger was my shadow, my ghost. Once on the bus at school, a girl hadn't moved over for my friend to share the seat with her. The next morning, when she exited the bus, I pulled her by her shoulder and began to pound on her. It wasn't even my fight. But I threw myself into it, a place to channel all I felt. It seemed like a kind of justice. Bob understood this intuitively, gave me a wide berth in which to channel the feelings I couldn't control.

One morning, early in my sophomore year, I arrived before first period. Bob was sitting at his desk and turned as I closed the door. I pushed my pants down to my knees. From knee to hip, I had multicolored bruises running the entire lengths of my thighs on both sides. It hurt to walk. To sit, to stand. Like my thighs had been tenderized.

The night before, my dad had stormed into my room right after I'd gotten out of the shower. I was still in a towel. What had I done to the medicine cabinet? he bellowed. He began to hit me, first with his hands stiff, and then with fists. I was on the edge of my bed, trying to hold my towel around me and deflect his blows at the same time. "What did you do?" he screamed. "Tell me!" He raged as I cowered, dripping wet, on my bed.

Finally, Holly burst into my room, telling him to stop, that she had broken the mirror. He took a few moments to register what she was hollering. He turned around and looked at her and then between us, perhaps to gauge if she was telling the truth.

"Dad," she said again. "It was an accident."

Bob listened without interrupting as I told him the whole story. Then he told me what his being a "mandatory reporter" meant. I nodded. He apologized, said he had no choice but to call child protective services. But I didn't need the apology; I wanted nothing more than to bring the outside world in.

I WAS PUT in a temporary foster home midway between my house and Naperville North. The foster dad was a police officer who worked the second shift, and there were a handful of us kids who stayed there temporarily, along with the police officer's teenage son. We berated this young man as a narc. A girl with a pixie haircut and black eyeliner who also lived there seduced him, had him strip down as if she were going to sleep with him, and then she stole his clothes and threw them up into a tree. He was forced to retrieve them naked. He cupped his hand over his genitals as he climbed the tree and we laughed and laughed.

It had been more than a year since Jackson's assault in my bedroom and over that time I had learned a great deal more. I learned the mechanics of sex, the burn of physical desire, but I had not learned that I could stop or say no at any given time. So if a boy kissed me—sometimes I wanted to kiss him back and sometimes I didn't—I generally went all the way and had sex with him. Sometimes I felt deep remorse afterwards and sometimes—if it was someone I liked—I felt elated. But what I never felt was that I had any choice at all, any agency over my own body.

At the foster home, there was a tall guy who was always stoned and held his face nose to nose with mine as he laughed maniacally. He wore a black leather motorcycle jacket even inside the house and he had the fine blond curls of a toddler. He'd whisper in a baby voice, "Let's fuck."

We did it on the floral couch in the basement, sometimes with other kids there and sometimes not. The TV would be on or off. There was a shared shower upstairs and a toilet in the basement, where clothes spread across the common area couch, a pile of blankets on the floor. Everyone was temporary. Kids came and went. The narc had his own bedroom. One kid cycled out after only a day. Others had seemed to be there much longer.

I would learn later that Child Protective Services opened an investigation into my family the day of Bob Martin's call. At the end of several weeks they declared that my father's violence did not rise to a level such that a child needed to be rehomed away from her natural parents. Case closed. So one Sunday I climbed into father's car to go back home.

His face looked drawn, not mean exactly, but impatient, firm. Was he defeated? Was he going to double down on his punishment now? I hated the sight of his face, the car. I didn't want to stay in this house, but I didn't want to go home either. I wanted blue carpet and a cul-de-sac. I wanted a woman in a green maxi dress, pretending to mow the lawn.

I HAD PROMISED my stepmom I'd never run away again, not after that time on my roller skates, clutching my blue-flowered suitcase. But I ran away again. And again and again. Sometimes I'd be gone for a night, sometimes more. I went to friends' houses and begged them to let me stay. I slept on couches and on floors. And then, after I returned from the foster home, I decided that what I really needed was a plan to get away permanently. Some serious money that I could fall back on. I was still babysitting. And for the past two summers, my father had had us all detasseling corn on a work crew of teenagers five days a week. We made $3.35 an hour, which felt like a fortune, and I managed to save some of what I'd earned, after buying a stock of Gallo, weed, and rock albums.

Once school started again, I got a part-time job at a burger and ice cream place in downtown Naperville called Cock Robin, part of a local chain in the western suburbs. We were famous for our malts. I was a dependable worker, and I closed late on Friday and Saturday nights. Although the legal working age was sixteen, my dad had signed a work permit for me.

This time when I ran away, I meant to be gone. By now our anger—my father's, Barb's, and mine—had broken loose in some way. In my journal, I fantasized about my stepmom dying in a fiery car crash, or asphyxiating some morning in bed.

My friend Jessica and I left on a Monday morning. Her boyfriend, Eddie, was older and said he'd rent a room for us. Eddie lived in Bellwood and carried a knife, which seemed as much protection as we'd need. Jessica had what felt like a fortune in her bank account—over a thousand dollars. We'd take the train in to the city, rent a motel room for a couple of days, find jobs, share a studio apartment, and then eventually make our way to California, where my real mother's brother lived in the Hollywood Hills. I hadn't talked to my uncle Myles in years, but I felt confident he'd take me in. The few times I'd seen him, we'd play practical jokes on each other, like take one out of every pair of shoes and hide them, or stick the toothpaste in the freezer. His life seemed hopelessly romantic to me. He was a cardiothoracic surgeon, Harvard educated, and dated lots of beautiful women. I imagined him dining with movie stars, driving a fancy convertible. You could even see the H of the Hollywood sign from his house.

JESSICA AND I rode the nearly empty Metra in silence. The world outside looked green through the tinted windows as we passed through one suburb after another. Glen Ellyn, Lombard, Villa Park, Elmhurst. We got off the train in Bellwood, one of the inner suburbs just west of Chicago. Eddie was supposed to meet us. But when we got off the train, he was nowhere to be seen. It was not quite noon, and the air was biting. Outside the station, a maroon taxi idled. We slipped inside its tobacco warmth. The driver had frizzed brown hair past his shoulders, a cigarette burning in the ashtray. We told him to take us to a motel, any motel.

He pulled into a place called the Red Lantern. The sign had a fluorescent old-timey lantern on it, like what Paul Revere might have carried through the night. We paid the driver cash and then made up a lie about a lost ID, a plan to get a replacement, and asked if he'd mind renting the room for us. No problem, he said. And maybe we could all party later, which Jessica and I were all too glad to do. The Red Lantern was a seedy place with red shag carpet, two queen beds with matching red bedspreads, and a round pressboard table in one corner, padded metal chairs pushed in around it. It smelled like damp winter and stale smoke. Jessica and I had a quarter ounce of pot with us, and several tabs of acid. We smoked a joint and called Eddie over and over. I was deep into a biography of Jim Morrison, *No One Here Gets Out Alive*, which I'd read so many times the pages had begun to fall out. Morrison was also from the suburbs—in Florida. He'd also escaped a strict father and made his way to California, where he found his poetic voice and skyrocketed to fame. His life was my beacon. Aspirational, romantic, doomed.

By that evening, four of us—Eddie, Jessica, me, the taxi driver—were in the Red Lantern motel room drinking beer, listening to the Scorpions, passing around a bowl of weed. The taxi driver snuck out sometime in the night after I was passed out. We never saw him again.

JESSICA AND EDDIE had sex in the bed beside me. I feigned sleep. In the morning, we ate Dunkin' Donuts and went out to look for work. Eddie walked us from the Red Lantern to downtown Bellwood, where we went store to store asking for applications. It was January in Chicago, a month after the holidays, but we were too young to understand market dynamics. In one women's shop, I walked through racks of women's suits and cardigans, seafoam satin shirts, and an entire wall of scarves. I asked for an application, and the woman behind the counter eyed me up and down with what even I recognized as disdain. "We're not hiring," she said.

We tried more than a dozen places before the cold finally drove us back to the Red Lantern.

The next day, we answered an ad in the paper for a room for rent. It was cheap, around a hundred dollars a month. A fat man with his shirt half unbuttoned eyed us with suspicion and walked us down a flight of rickety stairs to the basement, where a single bed sat in the middle of a tiny room. A small closet with an accordion door ran along one wall.

"Who's renting?" he asked.

"All three of us," Eddie said.

The man shook his head. He'd bend some rules, sure, but there wasn't even the slightest chance we three could sleep in that tiny room, even if we brought in another mattress. "No way," he said, pointing us back toward the stairs. "No way, no way." I didn't understand his anger until years later, when I saw what he must have seen. Eddie and two obviously underage girls.

We returned, again, to the motel. Our money was dwindling fast. We'd been gone three nights and although we'd factored in the cost of rent, we hadn't factored in the cost of restaurant food for the three of us, or how much a motel room actually cost. We hadn't known of security deposits or utility hookup fees, and furniture escaped our minds entirely. Eddie had brought no money himself, but he managed to smoke our pot, and eat the food we bought, without adding much of anything else to our plans.

We did not talk about the homes we'd left. But I thought about mine, constantly. Mostly, I thought about John-John. He was only two or three, but I was the one closest to him. He couldn't pronounce "Rachel" and what came out instead was something like "Hottoes," and the whole family had taken to calling me that. How would they explain it to him when he asked where Hottoes was? There had been afternoons when my stepmom asked me to watch him and I was exhausted, and begged him to take a nap. I understood at a young age something about love and about parenting that most people don't understand until they become parents themselves. I understood how you could be so exhausted that you'd hurt your own child. I also understood how you could love something so much that love felt alive inside you. Once in downtown Chicago at the multistory Marshall Field's department store we'd lost him, and each of us ran screaming through the many stories and sections of the store. I finally found him, standing by himself in front of a utility elevator, crying. When he saw me, he ran howling like his feet were aflame. I couldn't hold him tightly enough.

How could I leave John-John? How could I live without him? He and Joshua were the only things we all agreed on, the people we'd all protect. I wonder if they knew how much they held us together in those years. I imagined them missing me.

But I imagined my father relieved.

* * *

NO PLACE WAS hiring. No one was interested in us. We had no permanent address, and no identification. Neither of us was old enough to drive. Eddie said we could use his mother's address, which we did, but then we also had to use her phone number, which meant that if someone called we wouldn't be there to talk, and Eddie had to phone his mother every few hours to see if we had messages. She was, understandably, suspicious of the entire scenario, especially since we'd never even met her.

On Thursday, we checked out of the Red Lantern. It was bitter cold that evening, well below freezing. I didn't own a winter coat, was wearing two flannels and a jean jacket. Jessica had a down coat with a hood, and Eddie wore a black leather biker jacket. We walked to Denny's. Our plan, such as it was, was to sit in a booth all night long. We ordered slowly, first appetizers. Then coffee. Then, after an hour, we ordered more. I got pancakes. The waitress eyed us suspiciously from her coffee station. I knew what she was thinking: that we'd dine and ditch. But our needs were even simpler: to stay warm inside. She refilled coffee after coffee. We talked, we sat in silence, we shifted. We nodded off. A night had never felt so long. At one point, we were the only customers in the place. The manager walked past our table again and again, asking if he could get us anything more. Asking if we needed the check. Then, around three A.M., Eddie took out his lighter and lit the check on fire.

"That's it." The manager was at our table in seconds. "That's it. Get out. Get out before I call the police."

I wanted to punch Eddie. How idiotic could he have been? It was dead cold outside, single digits. We huddled with our backpacks, my hair frozen on my scalp. For the first time all week, I was truly terrified, dread ballooning in me. I felt sure I would vomit. We walked along the side of the road, knowing only that we could not stay outside.

Jessica had just enough money to pay for one more night at the Lantern. Eddie rented it. By now, the front desk personnel all recognized us. In the morning, Jessica and I took a Metra train back, the one that led directly into downtown Naperville. Her bank was walking distance from there. I ordered a hot cocoa at a downtown diner, where she was to meet me after she had gotten more money. Fifteen minutes, we figured. That's how long I'd have to wait.

But it wasn't fifteen minutes. It was half an hour, then an hour. And then I saw Officer Dwyer, the truant officer at the Naperville Police Station, come into the diner, look around, and lock eyes with me.

My parents did not scoop me up into their arms and tell me how glad they were that I was home. They did not tell me they had been afraid for me. They did not mention missing me at all. Instead, it was as if they were beaten down. They no longer had the energy to grapple with all that I was. They sent me to my room when I got home and told me to stay there, which I did. Once or twice, I heard John-John's little fist knocking at my door, gentle as a flapping wing, and I brought him into my room and hugged him till he squirmed from my arms. I came out that weekend only to eat. There was silence in the house now. And the silence somehow seemed more terrifying than the fighting had ever been.

All of us had had enough. All of us wanted it to be over. And very soon, it would.

Sixteen

There must have been a sense of how much my parents were losing control after my runaway with Jessica. I wouldn't admit to anyone how scary it had been, and how clearly I'd misjudged what I knew of the world. Maybe what my parents told me was true. It was dark and ugly out there. I wondered if I'd ever belong anywhere or feel less lonely than I felt all the time.

One night, shortly after I'd returned, I dropped acid with a friend but then had to get home for curfew. When we pulled up to my house there was a car in the driveway. I recognized it as belonging to my stepmother's relatives in St. Charles, a suburb to the west of us. I had expected to walk into a dark house. But when I opened the front door, I could hear them all huddled upstairs in the kitchen. I was in the full bloom of my acid trip and wanted—needed—to go straight to my bedroom. But I heard my father's voice, calling me up to the kitchen.

I knew better than to go, but I could conjure no immediate excuse. I knew my eyes would be dilated, so I told myself not to look up. Not to meet anyone's gaze. The shag-carpeted stairs roiled in front of me, and I turned my head away from the pull of the mirrored wallpaper, inching my way up the wall toward the kitchen. I found this worming movement hilarious, but tried to conceal my snickering. Do. Not. Laugh. This is not *really* funny, I told myself, as I slithered stair by stair.

The kitchen's fluorescence burned my bloodshot eyes. There was nothing my father loved more than a good road trip, and he was planning one. He'd decided that's what we needed—a family journey in the conversion van.

I mumbled a greeting to everyone, but the minute my father held the oversized atlas up to my face, I lost all semblance of control. The laughter erupted out of me. I was doubled over before my father understood what was happening, laughing so hard no sound emerged. Tears sprang from my eyes. "What's so funny?" he said. He looked around at the others, who were all equally confused. But I couldn't even form words. Tears rolled down my cheeks. My mouth was open in a silent howl.

"What's the matter with you?" he said.

I wiped at my eyes. I tried to frown, I even put my hand over my mouth in an attempt to redirect the flow of emotion, but nothing helped. The laughter was violent,

The kitchen went utterly silent apart from me howling with laughter, my body boneless and wobbling. My dad sent me to my room, his tone disgusted. Unfortunately, when I got downstairs, an errant smoke alarm sitting on a shelf by my dad's desk began to go off, an ear-shattering siren. I went over to it to try and stop it, held it in my hands like a precious shell, and then screeched along with it. I could just make out my father's voice yelling from upstairs. "Turn that thing off! Turn it off!"

And I wanted to, I really did, but it was melting into the flesh of my hands and I was powerless to stop it, so instead I just watched and screeched, wondering why I didn't feel the pain of this melting into me. Aaron appeared then and whipped it out of my hands. He glared at me and pressed a red button and the house was silent again.

"Thank you," I whispered to him. "Thank you, thank you." I was giggling and crying at the same time. I kept holding up my hands, trying to see where the flesh had melted, but I couldn't find it and found the lack of pain confusing.

ACID WAS DANGEROUS because it took you entirely out of who you were, gave you no sense of your abilities or shortcomings, erased all rational judgment about yourself, about others, about the laws of nature. I'd have jumped off a cliff. I'd have chased a bear. I'd have stolen a police car. Nothing seemed wrong, or dangerous. Marijuana made me tired and hungry. Beer filled me up too much. Cocaine just made me a slightly better, faster version of myself. But acid reordered the world, made me believe I could fly. It was all powerful, in charge, miraculous. It could save you from anything, everything. Something like what God was to my father.

One night I dropped acid with my boyfriend at the time and two others. There was a girl with a car. I don't recall her name now. Just her long brown hair, her pale face in the moonlight, a gap between her front teeth. After the acid we started in on the beer, and then we smoked an eighth of an ounce of weed. My boyfriend and I had cracked up at the hilarity of a piece of paper we found with a phone number on it. He cried for a minute after telling me how much he loved me. We'd been dating about a week. What was love, after all? Did it mean you let a guy have sex with you? Okay, then yeah, sure, I loved him.

By the time we climbed into the girl's car, I was seeing black shadows of spirits careening through the air around us, beautiful demons. Shapes and shadows moved through the atmosphere; I heard crashing, and car alarms that sounded like a symphony. I saw orange, white, red shards light up the view in front of us and it was so beautiful, I marveled at the geom-etries mingling across the windshield. What kind of thing were we seeing? Were these stars fallen to earth for us? Was it a meteor? My body jerked back and forth. Why was my body jerking so much? I laughed and my boyfriend laughed, and I hurt, and the hurting made me laugh. And the sirens were in chorus with one another, and it was wild and wonderful, a strange and beautiful orchestra.

It came to me in slow motion; we had driven through an apartment parking lot, a long row of parked cars, and one after another we slammed into them, crash, crash, crash, crash, crash. The metal bodies crumpling, alarms shooting off, brake and taillights exploding into shards.

We three stumbled out of her car while it was still moving. And the girl kept driving, and I sobbed, because I looked behind me and saw the wreckage of dozens of cars, their severed parts littered across the asphalt, and I understood, even in my acid haze, the treachery. How maybe none of us deserved to be so unscathed as we were.

BY THE TIME I'd run away with Jessica, I was blowing off more school than I attended. What did anything matter? God or the devil? Anger or love? Mothers or fathers? When I blew off school, I went wherever I could, to older kids' houses, or to the houses of kids who had dropped out before us. I went to Tony's house and slept with him because I thought that was the fee for letting us hang out. I went to Cary and Eric's house and smoked bongs in their basement. I went to Billy's house in downtown Naperville, where he had an older sister who would often scream "Suck my dick" if she lost a game of pool. They had a table smack in the middle of their apartment, and they lived above a bar. I went to Chazz's house and dropped acid. Most of these kids had just one parent, usually a single, working mother, and so we were free.

By now, I sat through BAC room at least once a month, and even got out-of-school suspension a couple of times for fighting. My stepmom had been called in to Dean Dollinger's so many times that on Tuesday afternoons I now went to a counselor named Steve Stone. Steve was known among the burnout kids as the go-to guy if you were a troubled teen. He was patient, soft-spoken. I'd talk and talk but wonder what the point was. I expected therapy to work like medicine for a headache and make the problem go away. Sometimes my parents would join me in talking to Steve Stone, but it never got us anywhere. When Steve Stone suggested letting up a little on things like music and television, things that teenagers like me were just naturally drawn to explore and experience, my father was unrelenting. Unwilling to contradict God or my uncle Jim. And Steve's advice contradicted them frequently. "Don't you want to let her live a little?" he said one evening to my father, exasperated. I remember Steve looked like he'd reached some limit himself. I felt vindicated, but to what end?

My father used his soft voice to say that of course he wanted me to live life, so long as that life was in accordance "with her Lord Jesus."

By late spring in my sophomore year, I was hopelessly behind. There were some teachers who tried to reach me, the kinds of teachers you might imagine from a movie. Inspiring, good-hearted. My sophomore math teacher asked me to go to church with him and to have Sunday dinner with his family afterward. I had told my parents I was sleeping over at my friend Laurie's house that Saturday night, but I wound up spending the night at a party, where some guy screwed me under the dining room table in the middle of the night, and I was too wasted to bother moving, so I just slept there afterward. In the morning, I rode to church with the math teacher's family. I sat through church, and then a Sunday roast with his wife and children, and he was so lacking in malice that I felt diseased just sitting there with the stink on me from the night before. I was so ashamed, so utterly disgusted with myself. If my teacher only knew who I really was. If he only saw what I really did. He dropped me off at home later, and I thanked him and could never look him in the eye again.

I'd gotten a job at a Mexican restaurant a mile from my house called El Dorado. I'd been hired as an attendant, which was a fancy way of saying busser, and it turned out that I loved the work. I'd pick up extra shifts here and there, and they'd recently given me a blue linen, off-the-shoulder dress to be a hostess when they were short-staffed. I'd close and get home late on weeknights. I was failing every class. My school absences could no longer be excused, even by Bob Martin, who had advocated for me for two years—with teachers, with my parents, with administrators.

One afternoon, I was summoned to Dean Dollinger's office. He motioned me in from the waiting area and ran his hands across his desk. Dean Dollinger smoked, a lot, and a cigarette burned in his ashtray. Once or twice, he'd even let me smoke a cigarette in there with him. Beside his office was another, identical to his, with another dean meeting another unfortunate student. A calendar tacked up on one wall had large X's across it right up until that day; several picture frames faced him so I could only see their cardboard backing.

The school board had rules, he told me. Rules that went beyond him. He was the head of the school, but there were people above him, people who were in charge of all the schools in Naperville. I could see that, right? He had to answer to those people.

He seemed nervous, going back and forth between not quite meeting my gaze and looking so intently at me that I shuffled in my seat. On my way into his office, I had seen that another student, named Tim, was waiting for his turn in the hot seat; Tim high-fived me as I walked past. It was May 1985. I nodded as Dean Dollinger spoke.

He told me he'd tried to give me a wide berth because he knew I had "a troubled home life." But my number of suspensions and absences was simply too high. He had no choice but to terminate my presence at

Naperville North High School. He said it was never his choice to kick out a student, no matter how poorly they performed, but his hands were tied. I was done here. At this school. It took me a few long minutes to understand that I was being expelled. But once I understood, it felt both shocking and inevitable.

My hand shook as I called my stepmom from Dean Dollinger's phone. My stomach felt weirdly hollow and nauseatingly full simultaneously. Dread and freedom competing for territory. This is what I'd wanted all along, hadn't I? To be the most *in trouble*. To push farthest, fastest. I hated school, hated how far behind I was in so many subjects, hated half the teachers and half the kids.

But also.

Who was I with no one to witness my fistfights, to look at the long line of F's on my report card, to hear me mouthing off to a teacher? Had I done all that for show? To be seen? Would I disappear entirely now, a tiny shell swallowed by the vastness of the sea?

Barb picked it up on the first ring. I told her Dean Dollinger wanted to talk to her, and I quickly handed him the phone. He motioned for me to wait outside. I didn't think, then, about how Barb was herself a high school dropout. She'd gotten pregnant with Holly at sixteen and never went back. I felt myself go cold when I imagined what my father might say. My whole body felt like a snapped wire. But I knew he wouldn't hurt me. He could ground me, but what was the point of that? I wasn't going anywhere anyway. He'd never make me quit my job, because he believed work was good for people, that it made "men out of mice." I'd been working since twelve. Babysitting, Bestline, selling newspaper and magazine subscriptions (mostly the *Chicago Tribune*) door-to-door. My father had always made an exception for work whenever I was grounded. Corn detasseling, working at Cock Robin, and now El Dorado. If there was one place I excelled, it was at work. I worked hard and I was dependable.

I cleaned out my locker, not bothering to take the textbooks, and waited outside until I saw the brown van pull up in front of the school, Barb at the wheel. John-John and baby Joshua were in their car seats in the back. They squealed with excitement when they saw me and I felt my eyes tear up. What would they think when they were older, and knew who I really was?

I climbed into the front seat and shut the door behind me, too ashamed to say anything to Barb. She sat in the driver's seat for a moment and didn't put the van in drive. Then she turned to me, looked hard at my face, and said, "School's not for everyone, Rachel."

There was no anger in her voice. No malice or judgment. I didn't even detect disappointment. It was simply a statement of fact. It would be nearly four decades before I saw the wreckage that had been my high school transcript. I'd had a combined GPA of 0.467.

Seventeen

Summer came, and with it the potential for long hours of boredom. I took on as many shifts as I could at El Dorado, often working in two different parts of the restaurant at different times of the night. Sometimes I'd hostess through the dinner rush, then change my uniform and bus tables. I'd help Charles, the dishwasher, who was sweet with a pimply face and called me Ravishing Rachel, and on weekends, it might be four A.M. before we finished the dishwashing. I no longer had the weight of school, of daily failure, hanging over me. But now I was staring down time itself. I tried not to think about it.

On the nights I worked, it was easy to stay out late. Someone was always up to party. Occasionally, we drove out to Book Road, which was a rural area far southwest of Naperville's downtown where we could light a small bonfire in the woods and toss back cases of beer.

One night, a dozen or so of us stood along the side of Book Road. We had come out from the woods and were on our way home, piling into various cars that were parked along the shoulder of the road on the edge of the woods. There was a shaggy-haired boy in a denim jacket that I noticed because I liked his hair. It curled in loose waves down to his shoulders and shone in the moonlight. He was standing a little out onto the road, a few feet from the shoulder, his back to me.

Suddenly a car came careening down the road. It wasn't a car I recognized. It swerved when it saw the boy—he was young, maybe seventeen or nineteen, maybe twenty or twenty-one—except that it swerved *toward* him and not away. The bumper snagged the side of the boy's body, right around his upper thigh, and he shot up into the sky like a firecracker, his legs and body straight in a plank, and he flipped a few times in the air, and he landed flat—on his chest, his face, his thighs. And he lay still. The car never slowed. No one got the plates, the make, the model; it was too dark to have made out the color. We gathered around him. We covered our mouths, silenced by the morbid and terrifying reality of him, the sudden piercing of our collective illusion that we were wise, that in our rebellion the world's rules somehow did not apply to us. Dark blood trickled from his ear onto the pavement. I heard a slight moan. He was alive. But maybe not for long. Maybe only barely.

This is what I think happened next: someone took off to call the police. And then we all fled.

We left him there, to be saved by someone else.

We were young and we were scared. But still. Some things are unforgivable.

I thought I was getting away with it all. I thought I was smarter than my parents. I'd make all kinds of noise when I got home from a shift at El Dorado, or when I was getting ready for bed, and then I'd sit in my bedroom for an hour or two, or maybe more, and I'd listen for sounds in the house. The cry of a baby brother, the squeak of the floor, the clicking of a door hinge. And if I heard nothing, at some point after midnight I'd be out and off into the night. Then home before dawn.

Except my father knew. He never told me, but he knew. Sometimes, he'd just drive around praying for me, not expecting to find me, but driving familiar streets where he knew I had friends, like he had when Jessica and I had run away. He wouldn't have wanted to say whatever he dreaded aloud for fear it might come to pass. So he stayed quiet all that time, drove around and around in the dark. The power of positive thinking; in some terrifying, silent way it ran his life.

IN SEPTEMBER, AARON and David returned to school, but I did not. Holly was in beauty school, though before long, she would drop out. I worked. And I partied. If I stayed stoned, I never had to grapple with my lack of options.

One Saturday morning, my father and stepmother sat the four of us down in the living room for a family meeting. Family meetings weren't uncommon now since spankings and groundings had proven ineffectual. I was all the evidence they needed to see that all the discipline wasn't working. Although I was unquestionably the least controllable, and certainly the angriest, we all rebelled in our own small ways. Aaron's fury often matched mine. David kept entirely to himself. He worked at the Ponderosa Steakhouse, saved up enough money for a small motorcycle, and more often than not, I'd go days without seeing him. Holly wasn't angry, but she was directionless, floating, and too old now, at age twenty, to really be disciplined for anything she did.

My father passed around a binder to each of us. The binders held a one-page typed list of rules, titled in all caps "TIME FOR A CHANGE." There were eight categories:

1. *Curfew*
2. *TV*
3. *Chores*
4. *Meals*
5. *Church*
6. *Counseling*
7. *Rewards for Excellence*
8. *Un-Christian words, deeds or lifestyles will not be tolerated here!!!*

We had new curfews and wake-up times. Chores to be done by noon on Saturday. No jeans at church. No swearing. Dinner at 5:45 P.M. Snacks "as directed." Counseling was required once per week and we were to make our own appointments; conveniently, there was a phone number. Under "Rewards for Excellence" we were instructed to find a hobby or a sport. "Improved grades, acts of thoughtfulness, going the way you should go" would also earn a reward, though the document did not offer specifics. No secular music, tapes, records, or posters "in house or on property." There was one single line, one allusion to what felt to me like a shattering admission: "No child or parent abuse (verbal or physical). Control your anger and your words."

The author circa 1984.

It was just two sentences buried in the document. But it gave me hope. What it said to me was that my dad bore some responsibility, too. That he had to try, too.

The document ended with an adage from my father: "If you are not self-disciplined, the world's discipline will be painful. You are your own best friend or worst enemy. Go for it and become what you were made for. You can't lose."

Then, my father had written by hand a letter to each of us. This was mine:

> *You are attractive and intelligent. God made you beautiful inside and out. You have a sweet spirit and tender compassionate heart. You are creative and fun to be with. You have an inner strength and resolve to carry through to attain a goal. You have a good sense of humor and infectious smile and laugh. You are a leader and "A" student when disciplined to study and resolve to be the best at whatever you lay your hand to. I am blessed to have you as my daughter and proud of you. —Dad*

Several years ago, I showed this document to my father. He couldn't believe I still had it. It was dated September 14, 1985. As he read it, in my home office, I could see a darkness come over his face, and I had to leave the room to keep him from seeing me tear up, to keep from maybe seeing him tear up.

Because we both knew what happened next.

THAT NIGHT, HOLLY and I went up the street to Gina and Kelly's house. Gina was Holly's friend, and Kelly was mine. They lived with their mom and brother. Kelly was a year older than me with a flaming red afro and freckles and a wild, whole-bodied laugh. Sometime around eleven P.M., Holly and Gina took Holly's green hatchback Citation to the White Hen Pantry for snacks. They should have been back in twenty minutes, but twenty minutes came and went. Then it was 11:30, and 11:45 and 11:55, and I froze, not knowing what to do. Our curfew was midnight. Should I abandon Holly and walk home? Or wait for her? Should I ask Kelly's mom to call my dad? And say what? That Holly had gone out for snacks and wasn't back yet? It felt wrong to just leave Holly on her own—and wouldn't my parents have been angry with me for abandoning her? What if she was hurt? What if the White Hen Pantry had been robbed while Holly and Gina were in there with a bag of Doritos and a liter of Diet Coke?

Sometime after midnight, the phone rang at the Jimmink house and it was Gina saying there'd been a fender bender, and now they were in the emergency room and could Mrs. Jimmink pick them up? Holly's car wasn't drivable.

I called my father. He picked up without saying hello, his voice deep and groggy. "You're late."

"I know," I told him, "but—"

"You're late." He cut me off. His voice had that impatient edge I'd come to recognize.

"No, but—"

"No buts," he said. At other times it was something he'd say to get a laugh. He'd see half a cigarette on the ground and say, "No ifs, ands, or butts!"

"Holly had a car accident," I blurted. I assumed this would change things. He'd soften his voice. He'd see that this time, at least, it wasn't my fault.

"You're late," he said, and he hung up.

*   *   *

ONCE GINA AND Holly returned, Mrs. Jimmink drove us the quarter mile to our house. It was two A.M. now, and the front door was locked. I wasn't surprised, but I'd held out some hope anyway. It was a crisp fall night, the grass dewy as I walked through the front yard, making sure to avoid the black volcanic rocks that had once gashed open John-John's knee. I made my way around the side of the house to my basement bedroom window. The window was locked. This was a surprise. I'd been sneaking in and out of this window for years now, but I assumed my father didn't know. I'd never come home and found it locked.

My breathing got shallow, my hands starting to sweat. *What does this mean? What will happen?* I knew the back door would be locked, too, but I tried it anyway, tiptoeing up the deck stairs so Charley, our dog, wouldn't wake up and bark.

Mrs. Jimmink said we could sleep at her house. It would all be sorted out in the morning. She couldn't understand a parent who didn't ask about his children after a car accident, she said. What was the matter with him? She felt so terribly sorry for us. Maybe my dad had been half asleep and hadn't known what he was saying, Mrs. Jimmink offered. Maybe he hadn't really been paying attention when I said the words "car accident." But even as she presented these rationalizations, I knew the truth: he knew exactly what he was doing. *Time for a change*, his handout had said.

WHEN HOLLY AND I returned to our house the next morning, the front door was unlocked. We let ourselves in and nearly tripped over four empty suitcases lined up in the entryway. My father and stepmother stood at the top of the stairs watching us, their faces stern, final. "Pick one," my dad told us. They were not interested in hearing more, in talking to us at all. Our mirrored wallpaper offered fuzzy outlines of the scene, the shag-carpeted stairs, the railing slats, the four suitcases. I froze there for a long moment, my brain refusing to take in what I was seeing. The suitcases, the stiff line of my father's face. Leave, I finally understood. Leave this house and don't return. I could feel nausea threatening to erupt in my stomach, a chill starting at my fingertips and working its way into my body.

Holly was twenty. Aaron was seventeen. The two of them went to their grandmother's house in Geneva, a suburb a half hour to the west. David stayed with a friend for a month, and then he rented a room at the YMCA in downtown Naperville, where he would finish his last year of high school. But the equation—four kids, four suitcases—was an abyss for me, like staring into a lightless cave. I could not imagine any future life for myself at all.

I picked the most colorful suitcase, a dark blue and maroon soft-bodied Samsonite.

Part IV

AMBUSHED

Eighteen

I stayed at Kelly's for two or three nights, shell-shocked, careening between terror and elation. They'd done it. My parents had finally done it. Just what I'd suspected all along: they couldn't wait to be rid of me, to be rid of all of us. And now they were. No more fights. No more church. No more God. But also, also.

Working at El Dorado, I discovered on my first day gone that if you're going to be unhoused, perhaps the very best place to work is at a restaurant. I never went hungry. If it were up to me, I'd have worked all through the night to avoid the despair that came to me at three A.M., four A.M. Before the day we were kicked out, I might have had options. I could have gone to a SASED-type school somewhere. Though I'd have had to start from the beginning, pass all the classes I'd failed. I'd be in high school until I was twenty. But that option disappeared the minute I packed my Samsonite.

I never deceived myself into thinking that I was innocent. Sneaking out of the house had been a choice. Dissolving a hit of windowpane on my tongue was a choice. Sleeping through classes, skipping school, blowing off homework, all of them had been choices I'd made.

At work, word began to get out that I had been kicked out of my house, and when my shift ended, my coworkers started to ask about my getting home, about where I'd stay, about whether I had eaten. Charles, the dishwasher, told me I could move in with him, which even in my desperate state didn't seem like a good idea. Then an assistant manager named Dawn invited me to her apartment. She could only offer me a couch in the living room, she said, but I'd be welcome.

Dawn had waist-length black hair and came from somewhere in Latin America. She didn't party like the other waiters and waitresses at the restaurant because she had children, and responsibilities. Her apartment was a small one-bed, one-bath. A dark brown couch in the living room sagged in the middle but was still comfortable. Her kids reminded me of John-John and Josh, even though they were older and in elementary school. I wondered if the house felt too quiet for my baby brothers now. If they asked where we'd all suddenly gone. John and Josh were five and three years old—old enough to note the loss of their siblings, even if they couldn't understand why or when we might be back. Their loss was palpable to me, like a piece of my body had been carved away, but I felt I'd forfeited any right to see them. I was so terrible, the worst kid of the worst kids, that I didn't deserve to see them. This, more than any spanking I'd ever gotten, felt like my true punishment. I could conjure their tiny child giggles, the dimples in their hands, the easy way they accepted and returned my love.

I was consumed, equally, with the knowledge that I had to develop some kind of plan for myself immediately. Winter was coming and I needed a way to get around besides my own two feet. In the two or three weeks since I'd left, my father had driven me to work a couple of times when it was raining. So I asked for his help in finding a car. I'd have to use my entire nine-hundred-dollar savings.

Perhaps it's strange to consider that my father kicked me out, but then also helped me once I was out there in the world. Even in those first few weeks, he'd slip a ten- or twenty-dollar bill into my palm when he saw me. He'd ask if I was hungry. He must have been terrified of what might happen to me. I believe my father was as lost as I was. He didn't know how to control me; even I didn't know how to control me. He was prepared for none of what came at him, six children, four of whom were brand-new. What do you do with a child who looks you in the eye and says, simply, "No"? A child who doesn't want your indoctrination, your protection, your control? Or, maybe worse, sees you as the thing from which she needs protection?

* * *

CARS WERE ONE of my dad's great passions. He charted the years of his life by the cars he owned. My mother drove a blue VW Bug and he bought a wood-paneled station wagon when David and I came along. Then she died, and he sold them both and bought that sporty Toyota Celica. He sold that when he married Barb and bought the van, and an Oldsmobile, and on and on. Holly drove the orange Gremlin, then her green Citation, and I lost track of her cars after that. I bought an old car, and Aaron bought an old car, and so there was always a Snyder kid's car up on ramps in my father's garage, or dead in a parking lot somewhere. We all learned basic car maintenance. Months after I left his house, I'd sometimes return on a Sunday afternoon to find my dad on his back on the floor of the garage, planked underneath some sputtering engine. He taught me to change oil, change tires, how pistons and spark plugs worked, and how to grease plugs. I helped him change a clutch in an Oldsmobile once and a water pump in one of his vans. My father never had many close friends, but he always had a loyal mechanic in his life, someone he could call for the jobs he wasn't capable of doing himself, and he'd get the guy's life story before too long.

"Oh, Bob," he'd say, "his wife is due with their second any day now. Good guy, Bob is. Lent me his hydraulic-something-or-other, his multi-function blah, blah, blah." My father would drop the names of workshop gadgets like they were common knowledge.

My father never let a stranger go without talking, finding some connection or point of common interest. He'd chat up cashiers, tell them to have blessed days. One Saturday, when he invited me to lunch after I'd been gone for a few years, we drove up to the local Dominick's grocery store; lunch turned out to be the two of us going from one free sample to the next, talking to each woman giving out the sausages or the chips or the cheese cubes. He knew them all by name. He knew their husbands and kids by name. They greeted him like an old friend.

The car he found for me was a robin's-egg-blue Opel Manta, a tiny two-door with low mileage and a fuchsia defrost button that was pretty much the sole reason I loved it. My dad put me on his insurance and bought me lambswool seat covers for the coming winter. I lugged my suitcase from Dawn's living room to the trunk of the car, and then drove to my dad's house and picked up my albums and the stereo I'd won on Bible Baffle. I had nowhere to plug it in, but having it with me was comforting—the electronic equivalent of a teddy bear.

The car turned out to be a lemon. The engine turned over but wouldn't catch half the time. The battery died; I bought a used one from the junkyard (boneyard, as my father called it) and it, too, died. I could only afford to buy parts from the junkyard, from cars that had been totaled, and often these "new" parts failed immediately: belts, distributor cap, carburetor. I was told by a mechanic that the timing belt likely would need to be changed, but it would cost as much as the car was worth. Every day, when I walked from Dawn's apartment to where it was parked, I'd wonder if it was going to be a good car day or a bad car day. Coworkers started to stay behind after work just to make sure I wouldn't be stranded. I learned to try and start it early, an hour or so before my shift began, so I could still walk to work on time when it failed. Every time I slid into the driver's seat, my heart would pound and I'd whisper, "Please. Please start. Please, just this time." It's not a stretch to say it was as much a storage unit as a means of transportation. I still loved that little fuchsia button, but the rest of the car was a turncoat.

I'D BEEN SLEEPING on Dawn's couch for a month when a manager from the restaurant, Bruce, asked if I'd want to go in on an apartment with him and his girlfriend, Jackie. Jackie waitressed at El Dorado. They'd found the first floor of a two-flat in the old section of Naperville, just a block from Cindy's house, and I could have the second bedroom, which was tiny but had room for a single bed and a small dresser. Bruce and Jackie would share the larger bedroom with their two-year-old. Since I had so much experience with kids, they said they'd give me reduced rent if I could help watch their daughter. At least one of us would always be off work, which would greatly reduce their childcare costs. I'd visited studio apartments in Bolingbrook and Westmont and Aurora—cheaper suburbs than Naperville or Lisle—but the minute anyone learned my age, they said they had no vacancies. How did anyone live if they didn't have parents? I wondered.

I had tried not to be intrusive in Dawn's apartment, but there were five of us all sharing that one space. I came in late, and then the kids would be up early. I was terrified that Dawn would ask me to leave. Not because she hinted at it, or ever seemed annoyed, but because my sense of myself was that I was likely not wanted by anyone. Tolerated, sure, maybe even sympathetic, but certainly nobody would have chosen to live with me. As a result of this unheralded insecurity, I tried to keep my footprint at Dawn's house as small as possible. I kept no food in the kitchen, no clothes in the living room. In the mornings, I'd go to my car, open the trunk, and pull out the day's clothes. If I needed to wash my uniform, I took quarters to a laundromat rather than risk using the machines in Dawn's building. What if she needed them at the exact time I was using them? What if her neighbors needed them and found me there, asked who I was, and learned I wasn't on the lease? What if I got Dawn in trouble? There was no end to the annoyance I could imagine myself to be, every tiny conflict potentially unraveling the webbed life to which I clung.

The new apartment was drafty, with wood floors, a large kitchen that hadn't been updated since the 1940s, and a living room with three tall, single-paned windows. We used space heaters in our bedrooms at night. Jackie was twenty years old, with shiny brown hair cut short and alabaster skin that held just a hint of pink on her cheeks; she was like a doll, fragile, beautiful, perfect. Bruce was older, around twenty-five, balding, and tall with wide shoulders. I'd worked at El Dorado for nearly a year by now; I was a reliable employee who could answer just about any question about any procedure in any position. I wasn't old enough to serve alcohol, which was the only reason I wasn't waitressing and making more money.

One night, as I was driving home from a friend's house, it started to snow. I had had my car for just shy of three months. There were no street-lights; I was on a neighborhood street in a suburb named Darien, leaning far forward in the seat to try and get a better view in the storm. I missed a stop sign, saw it too late, and when I hit the brakes of my Manta, I immediately felt the car go into a skid. I forgot to pump. Forgot where I was supposed to look. I'd been driving slowly because the visibility was so terrible. I had an instant sense of slow-motion spinning, the glimpse of a pine tree, the halo of a streetlight. The little white puffs of snow turning to droplets as they hit the windshield. I spun in my metal cocoon. And then what I imagined a bomb sounded like as I rammed into the driver's side of a Buick Park Avenue, a boat of a car. My car spun once or twice more and came to a standstill on the shoulder of the road. I couldn't breathe. The headlights illuminated the white cottony world outside, the engine cutting off immediately. Was I okay? I could feel my limbs, all four of them. My chin throbbed where I'd crashed it into the steering wheel. My forehead hurt.

Gingerly, I climbed over the gear shift to the passenger side of my car—the driver's door was caved in toward me—and I opened the door, then hobbled toward the other driver. The street was slick and wet. When I got to his passenger window, I knocked loudly, asking if he was okay. He was a middle-aged man, mustachioed, with dark hair and a tan corduroy jacket. He looked groggy, but he nodded. A passing car stopped to help and before long there was a police car and an ambulance. I stood there, out in the snow, as the storm built up. The EMT told me I needed to get on his stretcher. I said I was fine, he should take the other driver first, but he insisted. I lay down on the gurney and he put my neck in a brace. The accident had been my fault. Over and over I said it. It was my fault. I didn't deserve an ambulance. I didn't deserve the kindness of an EMT.

At the hospital, they numbed my forehead, then used long tweezers to pull glass shards from it. I had no memory of breaking through the windshield. I heard tools clanging together, the quiet ping of each glass shard hitting the metal tray. They'd turned off the overhead light so it wouldn't blind me, and they used a spotlight to see my forehead. Curtains kept the other patients hidden from me. When they were finished, I called my father. It must have been nearing midnight. His voice was groggy, deep, impatient. The same voice I'd heard when Holly and Gina had had the car accident. "What is it this time, Rachel?"

I told him what had happened. How I needed him, once again. Could he come get me? His voice never lost that edge of annoyance, but he came and picked me up and dropped me at the apartment I shared with Bruce and Jackie.

In the morning, my body was so stiff it felt as if I'd been ground up and reconstituted. My neck ached. My arms ached from clenching the wheel. My chin and forehead were swollen. After her school day, Cindy came over with some leftover beef stew from her mother, but it hurt my jaw to chew. (She said I called her "Mom," but I don't remember this.) Cindy sat on my couch and watched me eat tentatively for a little while, then my dad showed up to drive me to the junkyard where my car had been towed. I needed to get my things from the car. A spare uniform, a collection of cassette tapes, the lambswool seat covers. We saw a bubble in the windshield where my forehead had hit, a perfect circle protruding out from the glass. I peered closer at the bubble, picked hundreds of my own brown hairs from between the cracks. Small smears of blood were dried on the inside of the glass. I looked at my handful of hair for a moment, then released it into the frigid air. I caught my dad watching, too.

Nineteen

I was continually short on rent, or on money for our utility bills. I used the two-thousand-dollar payout from my totaled Opel to buy an Oldsmobile Omega. The Omega had blue velour seats and a roomy trunk. It was far more reliable than the Opel and I could make it to work for weeks at a time without major car trouble. But Jackie still had to lend me money for my part of the electric bill month after month. "Don't tell Bruce," she'd warn. I'd pay her back in quarters and singles, slowly, as much as I could. If I needed gas, I'd pull up to the pump and put in a dollar. Then I'd get a Little Debbie snack cake for a quarter and that would be my meal. Without my parents, I couldn't sign for a car, rent an apartment, apply for a credit card, put utilities in my name, or open a checking account. All I could really do on my own was work. And so I worked.

One afternoon, I answered a newspaper ad for a receptionist at a place called Crest Lighting in Lisle. It was a nine-to-five job, greeting and directing customers, sending and filing invoices. I'd have to wear professional clothes, skirts and blouses. But I'd inherited my father's knack for talking to anyone about anything, letting people know they'd been seen and acknowledged. I greeted customers at the restaurant like regulars even if I'd never seen them before. "It's so good to see you! Thanks for choosing us tonight!" Some of it was camp, of course, but honestly, it was also just my personality. I liked talking to people.

I was hired on the spot.

I'd get home from El Dorado after midnight and be up six hours later, the salsa smell from El Dorado lingering on me. Then I'd leave the lighting store at five for a five-thirty restaurant shift. I'd pick at untouched leftovers from the tables I cleaned, or I'd cut off the parts where they'd bitten into their burritos, their flautas, their chimichangas. I ate chips from the warming drawer. I got by. But I wouldn't get my first paycheck from Crest for a month, and I was a zombie, walking through my restaurant job at night, half dozing through my day job. Sometimes my body would suddenly jerk awake at the ringing phone and I'd realize I'd fallen asleep at my desk, right there in the middle of the showroom.

When I moved into the apartment with Bruce and Jackie, it was the first time I'd ever had a kitchen. I burned hot dogs because I didn't know to put water in the pot. I made fried bologna sandwiches or macaroni and cheese. I bought squares of ham with tiny flecks of cheese embedded into each slice, figuring that this was two items for the price of one. I'd buy a twenty-five-cent loaf of white bread from the Aldi's in Aurora, a jar of combined peanut butter and grape jelly, and some cans of ravioli. By the end of every month, I'd be limiting myself to one meal a day, or eating half a sleeve of saltines for my lunch, and still barely made rent.

I had fallen in love with a pink lamp on the floor of Crest Lighting. It was rectangular, matte, with one shiny pink stripe going diagonally down the body. With my employee discount, it would cost me forty dollars. I hadn't had savings since I bought my Opel, but now I had a focus. Purchasing a lamp felt so very adult to me, somehow more adult than living in my own apartment with Bruce and Jackie, probably because my name wasn't on the lease. I tried to put away two or three dollars a week, or whatever I could manage, and then one day my manager said she knew I was good for the money and she wanted to let me take it home. I could continue paying her as I was able. I owed her ten dollars total. Her kindness was so unexpected that I threw my arms around her—a gesture not typical in the culture of this place. She was tiny, and hugged me back for a minute, then pushed me off her gently and said she was glad it made me so happy. I took it home that very day, plugging it into my bedroom wall. I had not just fed and clothed myself and paid my rent. I had purchased something for the sheer beauty it brought into my life. It gave me some hope that I could get through all this. The night I took it home, I called Cindy and she came over right away to testify to its beauty. "Oh, wow," she said. She turned it this way and that, looked at the stitching on the shade. Her mother and two brothers all worked at Beidelman Furniture in downtown Naperville, so this was a family who knew home décor. "It's very you." Cindy smiled her wide smile.

"But do you like it?"

She laughed. "I love it. For you."

I FELT THE burgeoning of a routine in my life, some tiny bit of stability, but Bruce and Jackie had a troubled relationship. Often, I'd come in and find him sprawled on the couch in the living room, his eyes glassy, speech slurred. When he wasn't drinking, he was gregarious and funny. But night after night, I'd hear them fighting, their two-year-old daughter crying as her parents screamed at each other. One night, I came home to Jackie sobbing on the couch, the side of her face swelling and red. Another night I found her sitting in the dark at the kitchen table; it wasn't until I turned on the light that I saw her eye was bruising and bloodshot.

I understood that Bruce had inflicted these injuries on her. But it did not occur to me to get help. No one had ever talked about domestic violence at church, at school, or at any job I ever held. I knew my father had spanked me because I smoked. He had slapped me because I swore at him. He had hit me because I broke curfew, or came home wasted, or disobeyed him. *If I didn't do X, he wouldn't do Y.* It was the only kind of equation I understood. It was the one where I shouldered the burden of the blame.

One night I came home near midnight to them arguing in their bedroom. It was late for them. I headed quietly to my bedroom. I shared a wall with them, and I could hear Jackie crying as Bruce slapped her. Their daughter was wailing. I opened my door a crack. Should I at least go in and get the little girl? Would they want me to do that? Should I leave the apartment and go somewhere else? Cindy and her family lived close, but it was too late to call, and what could they do anyway?

Just then, the bedroom door beside me burst open, and Bruce's clumsy frame spilled out. His ruddy face was contorted, his lips in a sneer. His red eyes seemed almost to glow. He was still wearing his uniform from El Dorado, a flaxen shirt with flowered neckline and black trousers.

I quickly shut my door and piled up a few things behind it, as if that might stop him from barging in. A guitar that had once belonged to my mom, heaps of clothes, my stereo. Jackie cried in the bedroom beside mine, her daughter saying, "Mommy, mama."

Bruce didn't try to break into my room. Instead, he lumbered into the kitchen and began to punch the wooden cabinets. Plates and glasses crashed to the ground. Bruce was roaring, howling like a bear. Jackie and I were trapped in our rooms; the only way out of the apartment was through the kitchen to the front door. My father's violence had been mostly predictable, predicated on my having disobeyed him in some way. Bruce seemed like a force unleashed in that moment, his entire body pure danger and destruction. He was enormous and terrifying. Later, in a book I would write on domestic violence, I would describe a scene pulling from this memory: Bruce was like a bear coming toward you and you had one split second to think what you could do. It was his body, his fist careening into cabinet after cabinet that I pictured as I wrote that scene. He had stopped himself before he hurt Jackie too much. Of course he had. He'd left their room. But me? What loyalty did he have to me? What reason did he have to not hurt me?

Eventually, I heard a commotion outside, the voices of several men, and Jackie's door opened. She'd called the police, and now there were two cars in front of our duplex, their red and blue lights throwing purple beams on the green trim of our house. They took Bruce to the front porch. Jackie's face was tear-stained and swollen, her daughter's face buried in her mom's neck. An officer saw me peeking through my bedroom door and motioned me out. I was hesitant, looking left and right, my body behind the door as I stood on piles of clothing. The officer came to where I was standing, pushed at the door gently, and beckoned me out. I slunk to the living room and stood half behind Jackie. I could see Bruce on the porch, shaking his head, trying to make his large body smaller by hunching. He was still in his uniform. I was terrified that they'd learn I was underage and arrest me.

"Do you have somewhere you can go for the night?" the officer asked us.

Jackie and I looked at each other. Did we?

One of the police went to the kitchen and got ice for Bruce's hand. It would turn out that he'd broken it in his rampage. Already his fingers stuck out at odd angles, thick and bloody and blue. Half the cabinet doors dangled by their hinges, the floor covered in broken dishes and glassware.

I didn't think to ask why we were being made to leave. Why Bruce might not even get a charge for this. Destruction of property, maybe. Criminal mischief. He'd give a statement, then bail himself out. We girls needed to be somewhere safe because they couldn't hold a guy even if he had been the one doing wrong. I didn't question any of this.

Jackie and I spent that night at my dad's house. She slept with her daughter on the foldout couch in the den, and I slept in my old room. In the morning, I went to work at Crest Lighting, and Jackie went back to the apartment.

When I drove home after work that night from Crest, I let myself in and saw immediately that they had fled. Everything was gone. The living room was empty. Whatever was salvageable from the kitchen had been packed up, leaving the broken glass and dangling cabinetry behind. Bruce and Jackie's bedroom was empty. In my room, there was my single mattress, and my dresser. My guitar was gone. The stereo I'd won on Bible Baffle was gone. My brand-new pink lamp was gone.

I knew nothing of the dynamics of domestic violence then, that Bruce would likely get worse and worse, that any impetus for change would be on Jackie. She would have to be the one to leave, but then she'd discover how bureaucracies hold victims like her in place. Health insurance and housing deeds and children's school systems all required the signatures of both parties. Wills and life insurance, loans and leases. Everything they'd ever shared as a couple would turn into a negotiation for Jackie, no matter the danger to herself and someday their daughter. The fact that Bruce bailed out just hours after his arrest was all Jackie needed to understand that the systems our society had established—like police, like the judiciary—prioritized Bruce's freedom over her safety.

I drove my Omega to Fox Valley Mall in Aurora late that first night and parked it in a dark spot in the enormous lot. Then I locked the doors, reclined on the velour seats, and tried to sleep. It was chilly and every so often I'd have to turn on the car and get the heat going to warm up. I had a blanket with me, and a trunk full of clothes. I'd left my mattress. I knew I couldn't afford the apartment on my own, and my name wasn't on the lease anyway. I was still illegal.

And now I was back to nothing.

I never saw Bruce and Jackie again.

Twenty

Once again, friends from El Dorado helped with couches and showers. A waitress who had purple streaks in her hair and sang show tunes in the kitchen let me spend a few nights on a couch she had been given by her grandmother. It was green and crunched underneath me when I rolled over. A waiter with a booming laugh and thick brown hair often invited anyone who wanted to come over after work. He'd have parties that started after midnight. I went and stayed, curling up on the floor of his second bedroom one time, and in the living room another. The party went on around me. I wasn't really asleep, but I pretended so they'd leave me alone, leave me there all night. I was underneath my coat, curled in the corner with a vertical blind tapping my face whenever someone breezed across the room.

But many of those nights are lost in my memory. I stopped writing in my journal sometime around age fifteen and didn't pick it up again for several years. The years I lived nowhere. Images dominate my memories from then. Opening my trunk to pull out clothes. Carrying my blue and maroon Samsonite and a series of garbage bags into another temporary room, then out again days or weeks later. Someone's mom would be gone for the weekend and I'd stay there, or someone's roommate would go to visit her family for a week and I'd hunker down for a few nights. I lost track of all the different addresses I used on forms—for my driver's license, for my employer, for my taxes. Clearer in my mind are the few nights I spent at Fox Valley Mall in my car, the wintry afternoons when I'd scour under the driver's seat searching for enough change to put a gallon of gas in my tank, or buy Campbell's mushroom soup that I ate straight from the can with a plastic spoon.

One night, out of desperation, I tried to rent a room at the Green Tree Motel on Ogden Avenue. I had just cashed my paycheck so I had enough money, but I was still only seventeen. The clerk refused. I felt dirty, exhausted, contaminated. I was living out of my trunk, working, but somehow not able to land. I knew it was foolish to spend this much money on a motel anyway, but I wanted that little sliver of a bar of soap. I asked the clerk if I could call my dad. Once again, he came. He signed for my room. As we stood in the dim lobby, I felt such profound shame. I was too terrible a person to be allowed to live with my parents, like a normal teenager. Had I not been expelled, it's likely that Bob Martin would have suggested I get emancipated by the court. That would have allowed me to sign a lease, to get a credit card, to open a checking account. But I didn't know emancipation was something a person could do. I was trying to cobble together life in a world that did not acknowledge me. Tough love, my dad would have called it. I wasn't homeless either. Homeless kids in wealthy suburbs simply did not exist. And my father helped me situationally, wordlessly, though I had been disobedient, ungodly, rebellious. I had *backslid*, I had *turned my back on God*.

An acquaintance who'd once worked at El Dorado and was now at an Italian restaurant called me at Crest Lighting one afternoon because she'd heard I was looking for a place to live. I instantly agreed even though she was practically a stranger. She'd found a small studio apartment in Aurora, but couldn't afford rent on her own. We each put a single mattress in a corner on the floor, and we painted enormous pink stripes on our walls. My lamp would have matched perfectly, and I mourned its loss with a fervor normally reserved for a human, or a pet. We bought a secondhand table and chairs and with that our furnishings were complete.

My roommate, Laura, waitressed in the evenings, and I worked at Crest Lighting during the day, and so we often didn't see one another until late at night. El Dorado eventually fired me after I mouthed off to a manager; I can't remember the substance, only the relief that I wouldn't be so exhausted every minute of every day now. Sometimes my new neighbor across the hall came over and we'd sit on the floor drinking and laughing, plastering green mud masks on our faces. Our neighbor was Black, gay, full of energy, and he laughed at everything I said even if it was a dud of a joke. We didn't talk about his homosexuality or about our lives, or the many forces that had culminated to bring us all together in this shitty building.

If I abided by his rules, my father told me, I would be allowed home, but those rules entailed church three times a week, and daily devotions, and a willingness to, as he put it, "submit to God." And even though I'd only been gone a few months, I couldn't imagine myself living back in my dad's house, waking up for church on Sunday mornings and raising my hands in prayer, singing songs, and sitting through my uncle's sermons. I knew that he meant more than just following rules about curfews and television shows. What he really meant was I'd have to become a Christian—that is, his definition of a Christian, with the super-ficial joy they all projected to one another. I'd have to punctuate my speech like they did, with "Praise the Lord" or "Hallelujah, Lord" or "Jesus doesn't give us more than we can bear." Once, when I was a little older, I asked my dad about retirement and Social Security. He didn't think about those things at all, he said, because his father "owned the cattle on a thousand hills" (a reference to Psalm 50, God will care for his flock in their time of need).

HAD YOU ASKED me at the time, I'd have disavowed my father's religion completely, but that didn't mean I didn't fear it. What if heaven and hell were real? I tried to imagine what it would take to keep me from that burning for eternity and it seemed unlikely that it was a matter of prayers and church. I had so many questions: why did we follow the New Testament, but not the Old? Why did God condemn people from other times and other places to die: the Mayans, the Ashkenazi, the tribes of Peru and Ecuador? It wasn't simply that the Bible seemed unfair to me, it was that God's rules seemed arbitrary. Why this person and not that one? Why AIDS and not malaria? Why the United States and not Gambia? My neighbor: He was kind. He was funny. He liked mud masks and jeans with a crease. He never asked us to take off our shirts, never asked us to give him a blow job, never went where he wasn't invited. Why condemn *him* to burn in an eternal lake of fire?

I QUIT CREST Lighting and took a job at a gas station, working the register. Regulars came in daily for coffee and cigarettes and by the end of the first week, I had begun to recognize them. Like my father, I could talk to anyone. There were truck drivers who'd stop in every few days; they'd been on the road for a long time with very little human interaction, and they'd loiter around the counter and tell me stories. There were professionals in business suits who'd stop in for a donut or coffee and talk for ages, like they were avoiding their own fate. This was a job I loved.

But after a couple of weeks my drawer started to be short. At first it was only every week or so. But then it happened more and more often, until it was nearly every day. I had been trained by a manager named Troy, who was plump with a military haircut, pale skin, and a friendly demeanor. He counted the drawer again and again trying to figure it out. The register calculated change for me automatically, so I wasn't subtracting wrong. Day after day, I'd be twenty or thirty dollars off. As my shift drew to a close, I'd feel the anxiety start to ramp up in my body as the time to balance my drawer ticked closer. I'd walk into the back office and greet Troy, who was always unfailingly nice, but I knew he couldn't go on having a cashier with a drawer off every day. I paid extremely close attention to every single transaction, taking my time, sifting to make sure I wasn't giving out extra ones or quarters. I'd double check the register amount, the cash handed to me by customers, go over it all in my mind multiple times. But without fail, every day I'd still be short.

"I don't understand it," I nearly cried to Troy one afternoon, as we went over the money. The smell of grease and motor oil wafted in from the garage.

"We'll figure it out," Troy said. "Don't worry." We were both smoking Marlboro Reds and the grimy office was hazy with smoke. Troy wore jeans and a blue Izod.

He seemed to have preternatural patience, for which I was grateful and told him so. He nodded and took the cash to lock it in the safe in his office. It must have been my abysmal math abilities. I hadn't studied anything past algebra; what did I expect?

It happened again. And again. I was desperate. The only time I ever left the register was to use the bathroom, or to go and take a half-hour lunch break in Troy's office, and during those times he'd cover for me.

Day after day, I'd say to Troy how I just didn't understand how it could happen. I'd swear to him that I paid attention to every single transaction. And he always nodded, showed endless patience, until finally one day a few months after I'd started, Troy—patient, understanding Troy—told me he was going to have to let me go. I cried, but I didn't fight it. I knew. I'd watched him count my drawer day after day. It would be years before I would understand where Troy's patience had come from, how it must have benefited him to train and retrain naïve, insecure girls. Girls just like me, who'd gotten used to blaming themselves when things went wrong.

IT WAS AT my next job months later, as a file clerk at Aetna Insurance, when my grandmother Erma called to tell me about a "finishing school" she'd learned about. Her voice had an air of desperation in it. I knew, by now, that her best hope for me was marrying me off to a nice Jewish boy, but I also knew she thought I was unrefined and wild—not entirely an inaccurate assessment. Over the years, she'd tried to get me to take tennis lessons, and to return to the piano lessons I'd taken when my mother was alive. If I could just tone myself down a little, learn to serve a nice martini, maybe I'd meet someone. Here, now, was another attempt at turning me into someone more elegant, more like my mother. She'd cover the cost, she said, if I agreed to go. I was sitting at a secondhand kitchen table in an apartment I shared with a girl named Michelle. My stepmother had given me the table, or rather, she had rejected it: it was the yellow wooden kitchen table we'd had in Pittsburgh. She and my dad were clearing out their garage, about to move into a new home, one they'd finally purchased.

As my grandma spoke, I looked down at the Def Leppard T-shirt that I'd slept in, not entirely sure if it was mine or someone else's. Even then, I saw the irony. My rebellious, rock-and-roll, feral midwestern self at some kind of old-fashioned finishing school from which I'd emerge like the kids in *The Sound of Music* saying "Yes, sir" and "No, sir" and sipping quietly from an oversized soup spoon. The school, she said, taught poise, fashion, hostessing, and conversational topics for dinner parties. They also taught modeling and makeup, accessorizing, and how to walk the runway. She called it Barbizon.

Barbizon? I suppressed a laugh. *Barbizon?!* Every teenage girl knew Barbizon from its ads in the back of *Seventeen* magazine: *"Be a model! Or just look like one!"* Was my grandmother really suggesting I attend modeling school? Did she not know what Barbizon was all about? She clearly thought of it as a place where I could finally learn to be the kind of New England Jewish American Princess who might land a decent husband. I thought of it in a very different way: a ticket to the runways of Vidal Sassoon or Christian Dior. It hadn't ever occurred to me to be a model, but sure. Why the hell not?

I agreed to attend what she called "the tryouts." Then I hung up the phone and laughed.

Twenty-One

The "tryouts" turned out to be basically a sign-up sheet. I drove myself down the Eisenhower Expressway into Chicago and up North Michigan Avenue to the plush lobby of the Hancock building, where tables were set up. Hundreds of girls wearing pancake makeup wandered from table to table, picking up sample powders and lipsticks, or checking their faces in the many hand mirrors available. Most of the girls had mothers with them, or they came in small groups of friends. I wore one of my leftover business suits from my time at Crest Lighting in the hope that it would make me appear more serious than the others, even though I felt like I wanted to shrink into the marbled floor. All the girls here had plans, opportunities, chances of something. I was a fraud, looking to fill time and make myself prettier in the process. Barbizon would be my surrogate mom, teaching me the things my own mom hadn't had time enough to teach. How to be better. How to be loved. On the phone with my grandmother this had seemed kooky and fun, but here in person, I felt the weight of my life, the burden of the past few years. Who did I think I was? I was a high school dropout with big hips and big boobs and frosted hair tips. It wasn't that all these girls were perfect, though many were quite stunning. It was a sense that their lives had been, well, poised for it. I felt wild. Loud. Plump. Too many pimples with too much frizz.

"You have perfect bow lips," said a man in powder-blue pants. I looked around, but indeed, he was speaking to me. I gave him a half smile. He motioned me over and handed me a mirror and a lip gloss. "Try it! It's your color!"

I hadn't known I had "a color." But I liked the way my lips shimmered in gold gloss. I was never allowed to wear makeup when I lived at my father's house.

He asked what my name was and pointed me to a sign-in table. I'm not sure what I expected. Some kind of public assessment, perhaps, a silvery diva in a long dress pointing out girls in the crowd, saying, "You! And You! But not you!"

The minimum height for New York models, read a printout, was five foot eight. This was exactly my height. Things were looking up so far as my lips and my height were concerned. I tried to imagine what I might be like as a model in New York City, but the only image that came to mind was me eating a vendor's hot dog in Times Square while my uncle Robert stood by jangling the change in his pocket and probably praying that no one from the Harmonie, Princeton, or Lotus clubs spotted him.

I signed in and was directed to a large conference room with paisley chairs and dozens of attendees waiting for an orientation. The room was arctic, and my toes ached in the blue pumps I wore. The pantyhose constricted my legs. After a few minutes, a slide show began: men, women and children in all manner of advertisements, from the glossy pages of *Vogue* to the circulars in our Sunday newspaper. Modeling, we were told, was everywhere. The opportunities were endless. There were families in matching outfits sitting around a fire smiling. There were women and men on a date in black tie, and children catching bubbles blown by a gorgeous pretend mother. There was a woman draped over what appeared to be a zebra's butt. Barbizon would set us up after graduation with our own photographers, agents, and opportunities. We would learn catalog modeling, we would learn runway modeling, and we would learn etiquette, hostessing, and socializing. We would learn how to engage with people in the highest echelons of society, so even if we didn't find ourselves in those glossy *Vogue* pages—though some of us definitely would!—we'd at least know how to comport ourselves in other universes.

There were hand models and eye models and lip models. There were feet models and leg models. There were stand-ins for movie stars, and emcees for shows, and those game show girls who twirled letters or slid their hands across the hoods of shiny cars on TV. There were endless, endless models. Girls everywhere you looked, being used to sell everything you could ever want. The only limits were our imaginations. Look around, look everywhere, and you'd see models. Models, they said, were the lifeblood of our economy. I did not know what this meant, but it sounded important, like I'd been let in on something the rest of the world didn't know about.

The secrets to this shimmering world could be mine for just a thousand dollars.

I ATTENDED BARBIZON from nine to five on Saturdays, driving myself to the city for a class with a dozen others, all taught by a Snow White beauty named Tamara. At five foot seven, Tamara was an inch too short to be a New York model, but her enthusiasm for modeling was infectious, and her belief that she could make it in this competitive world was absolute. Tamara was thin, with alabaster, poreless skin and inky black hair past her shoulders; she wore bright fuchsia or vampire-red lipstick and she laughed from the waist up, often tossing her arms into the air with joy while she held a mascara tube or lipliner pencil. She got lots of catalog work and shared her portfolio with us on our very first day, pictures of her done up like a mother with a child and dog at her ankles, or like a business professional with her hair in a bun. She had all manner of different looks. Page after page she was reinvented, reimagined, retooled. She never failed to point out our positive attributes. One day she measured the height of every girl in the class and after mine she said, "Whew! Just made it!" as if the stakes of this were ours to share.

Tamara was a decade older than me and had two young daughters who stayed with her grandmother when she was at work. She lived in a small house in northern Indiana and it turned out that she loved heavy metal as much as I did. After a few weeks of classes, I learned that she'd had a fling with Bret Michaels, the lead singer of Poison, a moment of glory which propelled her belief that they were destined to be together. He was diabetic, she informed me, which gave him an air of seriousness about the world.

On Saturdays, we would learn to cross our legs at the ankles in pictures, to lean back, one hand wrapped around a thrust-out hip as we glared into a fake camera. We accented our cheekbones with makeup and covered

The author in her Barbizon days.

our facial deficits—pimples, chicken pox scars—with various concealers. If we had no cheekbones, we drew them in with crème blush. We were taught how to paint liquid eyeliner halfway up our lids, and line our lips before putting on lipstick. When I looked in the mirror at myself, my face buried under a dozen layers of various types of makeup, my lashes thick as twine, my eyes glowing blue orbs popping out from my face, I didn't recognize myself at all. And this was perfect. I didn't want to recognize myself. For the next year, I would wear makeup like this every time I left the house.

One room at Barbizon had a small runway about a foot off the ground, and one Saturday, Tamara took us in there to teach us the proper method of runway sauntering, toe-heel, not heel-toe, which was about as awkward a strut as any I'd ever done. We were to thrust out our hips, walk so that we appeared to be as lithe as sea grass, like our little twig legs could barely hold up the bulk of our tiny torsos. At the end of the runway, we were taught different ways to turn: the Dior method took its cue from ballet. You had a spot, then you turned your body in a kind of twist, starting at the feet, then your shoulders and then your head last, before leaning back with one hand on your hip and your legs bent slightly at the knee. You never smiled on the runway. Ever. Modeling was serious business. On my first turn, a three-inch copper-colored clip-on earring flew from my lobe into the onlookers' seats.

We had a textbook for our lessons, and each week was devoted to a different skill set: runway shows, catalog poses, accessories and jewelry, party talk and tableware. We learned different body types ("Pear," Tamara proclaimed me with a touch of empathy. What New York wanted was the X. Or possibly the Y. But never the pear). We learned exercises for our facial muscles and conversation starters. My grandmother Erma expected me to emerge from Barbizon resembling my real mother. But I was trying to turn myself inside out, into someone else entirely. And maybe secretly become a New York model.

ON SATURDAYS, AFTER Barbizon, I began to follow Tamara out to her house in northern Indiana and spend the night on her couch. Sometimes we'd make dinner with her girls and play, and other times she'd have her grandmother keep the girls overnight so we could go out. At eighteen, I wasn't technically old enough to get into bars yet, but Indiana was far more lenient than Chicago and Tamara was so stunningly beautiful that she was rarely asked for her ID. They accepted me, I suppose, as the age grifter that I was, though Tamara would do my makeup and accessorize me so fully that I looked much older. We'd sit at the bar and drink whiskey sours or fuzzy navels while the bartenders flirted with Tamara. She didn't have a boyfriend, maybe because she was always sort of holding out for Bret Michaels. Or maybe just someone who might make the struggles in her life a bit easier to bear. To me she was aspirational, beautiful, with her own house and her own glamorous career. But she was also a single mother cobbling together a meager living.

One night, we went to a place called Club Dimensions, just across the Illinois border in Indiana. It was a large nightclub, with a big stage and dance floor and two levels of tables, shiny black, with pleather and chrome seats. This night, the stage and main seating area were dark, and most of the patrons gathered around the bar or the high-top tables. Tamara and I sat down and ordered drinks, and the bartender, as usual, did a double take at Tamara. We were dressed as if we had just walked off a television set: miniskirts with tights, high heels. The Barbizon lessons had catapulted me immediately from the tomboy I'd once been into full womanhood.

"It's so quiet tonight," Tamara said. Somehow, no matter what came out of her mouth, it sounded like a compliment, or at the very least, not a complaint.

The bartender nodded and slid our drinks to us. When they had bands play the place wasn't so dead, he told us, but they'd had trouble finding good acts. He asked if we knew any good bands. He was joking, of course, asking us. But Tamara was thoughtful a minute, then she said, "No. But she does!" And suddenly both of them were looking at me and I froze. I wasn't used to having a question directed toward me in a situation with Tamara. "You do!" she reminded me.

And slowly I nodded. "I do," I said. "White Lie."

This was not technically a lie. A friend from high school played drums in White Lie, and sometimes on the weekends I'd hang out in Chris's garage while his band practiced. I had a massive crush on the lead singer, Micky. Chris wore animal print leggings and a torn T-shirt and twirled his drumsticks between his fingers like Tommy Lee. He'd bought a drum cage and he somersaulted around it occasionally.

"White Lion?" the bartender almost yelled and took a step back. White Lion was a fairly popular metal band known for the ballad "Wait." (They've had so many personnel changes over the years that there is an actual colored graph on their Wikipedia page.)

"Lie," I said. "Lie."

He looked surprised. "They any good?"

I took a large sip of my drink. "They're fucking amazing," I told him. First rule of sales: believe in your product.

But White Lie *was* good. They were a metal band, and sure they were derivative in the way that anyone who is young and starting out is derivative, but they were talented and they worked hard. They put in hours of practice, the four of them: Chris, Jimmy, Micky, and Dave. They'd played a few gigs around the western suburbs, for friends' parties or all-ages shows, and every time they played, they drew small crowds—old high school friends, gaggles of screaming, dancing girls, including me and sometimes Cindy.

The bartender waved over a small man in a black button-down shirt and black jeans and introduced him as the manager, then pointed to me and said, "She knows a band."

"You got a promo pack?"

I did not know what a promo pack was, but I nodded anyway. "I can get you one."

I lied about the places they'd played: a lot of Chicago clubs, I said, and a popular place in Naperville called Potter's, which was a bar that I just happened to know the name of. I was banking on his ignorance, and filling the space with talk. They were a four-piece metal band, I told him. And girls? They had groupies galore.

This wasn't all that much of a stretch for me, really. I'd been pretending something or other for years by now. I'd been pretending to be tough, pretending to know more than I did, pretending not to be scared.

The manager talked to me about percentages of the door versus flat rates—I didn't have any idea which was preferable. Then he offered to take me on a tour. We could see the darkened club more or less entirely from where we sat, but I jumped down from the bar stool anyway, assuming this was what a serious businessperson would do, get a look at what was being offered. Tamara stayed at the bar and we zigzagged among empty tables and toward the stage, which stood about waist-high off the ground and was fairly expansive. To the side of the stage was a small dressing room.

He walked me to the far end of the dance floor and told me he had a "twenty-four-track mixing board" and had recently upgraded his light-board. He motioned for me to try it out. I pressed a white button and a set of lights rained down onto the stage. I pressed a few more. Blues, reds, yellows. I flooded the stage with lights, played the board buttons like a keyboard. I tried to look nonchalant, nodding sagely as if to say, "This'll do." I didn't touch the mixing board. It was too complicated, too many levers and buttons and lines and numbers. But I memorized the information anyway, assuming it would be of use to the band:

twenty-four-track mixing board, upgraded light board, percentage of the door versus flat rate.

The manager gave me his business card, and I promised him I'd have him a promo pack within a week—lightning speed for the 1980s. I made up some excuse about being out of my own cards, but I shook his hand. Handshaking was always part of my father's business deals. If you shook on something, it meant you were serious and trustworthy.

Tamara and I clicked our high-heeled way out of there, got in the car, and roared with laughter all the way back to her house.

Twenty-Two

I wore my backstage pass on a lanyard, making sure to keep it outside my shirt where everyone could see it. A couple of roadies, my roommate, Michelle—who was also the bass player's girlfriend—and I were huddled in the tiny dressing room; we had become de facto makeup artists and hair stylists. We ratted and sprayed Chris's brown curly hair. I put eyeliner on everyone. I wore a black and white snakeskin jacket with pleather collar. The lead singer, Micky, had a T-shirt ripped down the sides all the way to his waist and bandannas tied around one thigh. Chris wore his tiger spandex.

The place was packed. I was surprised at the turnout. Tamara and I had put up colored fliers on telephone poles all over Hammond, Indiana, and Michelle and I had passed them out at the Riverwalk in Naperville. The stage was dark. We were all jumpy. Chris twirled a drumstick nervously. Someone turned on a fog machine, and the four of them whooshed past us from the dressing room. Then there they were, on the stage that I'd put them on. There was a part of me, as I watched the first moments from the dressing room, that couldn't get over how this had all happened, what a wild left turn it was. Just weeks earlier, Tamara and I had sat in this very place lying our way toward this moment.

Girls were immediately up and on the dance floor and Michelle and I went out to join them. The band played a mixture of originals and covers. Aerosmith's "Sweet Emotion," Kiss's "Rock and Roll All Nite," the Kinks' "You Really Got Me." People screamed. Micky held out the mic and the audience sang along. With the fog machine, and the constant smoking in those days, the air was hazy and warm, which added a kind of romance to the show. White Lie played two or three sets that night, and by the end of the show, we were all buzzing, collectively in love with each other and with whatever had just happened. I felt part of something then, the instigator of *something good*. I had brought us all here. The very thing that my father had denounced over and over through the years—the devil's music—had given me something I hadn't felt in years: hope.

THERE WAS ANOTHER club, Tamara told me. Not as nice as Club Dimensions, but they might be interested. And then I went to the entire Chicagoland yellow pages: who else needed bands to play? What other possibilities existed? We got a cassette tape of White Lie's best songs, recorded by Jimmy, the guitarist, on his four-track. The band hired a photographer, and I wrote up a bio for them with my contact information. I called myself "Midwest Artist Management" and I went by Rachel Lee because it was my mother's maiden name, and because I thought it sounded cool, like Tommy Lee of Mötley Crüe.

By day, I filed documents at Aetna Insurance, and then I'd scour the yellow pages for clubs. The gatekeeper was a club called the Thirsty Whale, booked by a guy who went by Tony Shark (his real name was Tony LaBarbera). Tony was the king of the Chicago heavy metal scene in the 1980s. You didn't play anywhere without Tony knowing about you. He had started a fanzine called the *Chicago Rocker*. The Thirsty Whale came up time and again when I'd talk to people about booking White Lie. You can't do anything without getting Tony involved, I was told. You gotta call Tony. Talk to Tony. Tony was like Oz, a powerful figure operating from behind the curtain. I didn't want to seem like I was moving in on Tony's territory, but I knew playing the Thirsty Whale would be a huge endorsement for White Lie.

White Lie appreciated my booking them. We had no contract, of course. I didn't know to offer them one. I took no proceeds, at least in the beginning. The sum total of our partnership was a conversation that went something like this:

Me: "Can I book you some more shows?"

Them: "Sure!"

I began to learn about the business of small-time booking. I made dozens of promo packs and mailed them out to clubs across Illinois and Indiana. I followed up with phone calls. I was relentless, and somehow the swagger of it all appealed to me. No one ever asked me how old I was; Tamara's makeup lessons came in handy. I'd been living on my own for more than two years at this point, and I acted like it.

The band had instituted something they called the Girlfriend Rule. The Girlfriend Rule dictated that no one in or around the band would ever publicly admit that any of the four guys had a girlfriend. If a girlfriend attended a concert, she had to agree to hide her status while said member of White Lie consorted with the groupies and fans. It speaks to how insecure we all were, not just us girls, but the bandmembers, too, who didn't yet have enough faith in their own talent.

Michelle would hang around with me in the dressing room, or somewhere backstage, and if asked by another girl about whether or not any of the guys had a girlfriend, Michelle would have to say, "No! Crazy, right?" Or maybe, "Sure, he'd love for you to buy him a drink," speaking of her own boyfriend. She'd watch as girls with big hair and miniskirts hit on Dave, the bass player, all night. For me, it was easier. I hid behind a title. I'd say "booking agent" or "manager" and feel like a groupie who'd figured out how to game the system.

Boys on stage; girls on the sidelines screaming for them. We were cheerleaders, hollering at the star players. We existed because they existed. We knew girls played music. Joan Jett had proven that girls could rock. Pat Benatar, Heart, Lita Ford, Fleetwood Mac. Sure, we could name hard-rock bands with girls in them (though not heavy metal, not really). We'd go to showcases with half a dozen other bands. But I never saw a girl on stage.

IT TOOK ME months to work up the nerve to call the Thirsty Whale and leave a message for Tony. He got back to me the same day, inviting me to meet with him. I knew better than to wait for a bouncer to talk first. "Rachel Lee," I told the guy at the door. "I have a meeting with Tony."

I'm not sure what I had imagined Tony would look like; most definitely not like the person who stood in front of me. He was tall, with thick, nerdy glasses and short hair. Short hair! Tony was friendly. He shook my hand. He did not ask me what I thought I was doing horning in on his territory. He took my White Lie promo pack and talked to me about setting up a show for them. He was exuberant. The guy really, truly just loved music. He understood the business of it and he loved to be surrounded by it. Perhaps he was nice to me because he understood I was small-time, no threat to him. Perhaps he was nice to me because I was the only girl around doing what I was doing. But whatever it was, Tony said if he could ever help me, I should let him know. He told me I could come to any show at the Thirsty Whale that I wanted to, anytime, just let him know. He told me he'd listen to the White Lie demo tape and get back to me.

Which he did. With a date for a show.

Sometimes, the clubs we played had female managers, and they always struck me as intimidating and tough. Was I like them? I knew I came from a long line of women doing things on their own in a world of men. My great-grandmother, Florence Carp, had had her design business. Or maybe I was more like my grandma Erma, going off to dance in New York alone when she was sixteen. Music had given me the language for my feelings; I could chart that language all the way back to those afternoons in Pittsburgh dancing around to Styx with my babysitter Cherry the year after my mom died. The world of music was so often a world of pain and heartbreak and yearning and despair, all things I'd felt for years. Now it gave me some control. The more shows I booked for White Lie, the more I thought I *could* book. I had nothing else in my life to really strive for, no one expecting or believing much of me.

AS TIME WENT on, Micky and I started to see each other, getting together after practices or shows. Sometimes we'd get in my car in the parking lot of a club. Other times, we'd drive to the end of a dark street. I drove my Oldsmobile Omega, or if it was warm, we'd sometimes sit on the hood together. I began to yearn for those times with him, times when he would barely talk above a whisper. He'd told me some things about his life. He'd gotten in some kind of trouble when he was younger. He had been adopted and knew nothing of his real parents, which sounded hopelessly romantic. He'd been raised an only child. I'd watch his mouth move as he talked, and I'd listen until there was a break in the conversation, and I'd kiss him and think somehow that I could kiss the pain out of his stories. Because when you're eighteen you think you have the power to do this.

I would have stayed all night in my car with Micky if he'd asked, but he always had to get up for work, or something in the city, and he could never stay. He never came back to the apartment I shared with Michelle, but then I'm not sure I ever suggested it, and Dave was often there anyway. It didn't occur to me to wonder why the only thing we ever did was screw in the back of my car. We never went on a date. We never saw each other during the day. He never called me, but then I worked during the day at Aetna, and White Lie played more or less every weekend and practiced a couple of times during the week and so it seemed like I saw him all the time anyway. I told myself I was unconventional. I hadn't lived a normal life, so I wasn't going to be a normal girlfriend. I didn't know to ask for more, what "more" even really meant. How did a girl go from being kissed to being loved? From being a date to being a girlfriend? It seemed like one more mystery that surely would have been solved had my mother only been around to give me the instructions.

IT DIDN'T TAKE long for the other guys to find out about Micky and me. One night Chris suggested in the most passive way possible that maybe it wasn't such a good idea. We were sitting in his living room where we'd once made prank calls to bowling alleys when we were freshmen in high school ("Do you have ten-pound balls?" we'd ask. "Yes," the person would answer. "Then how do you walk?" We'd howl with laughter, owing to our being the most hilarious teenagers alive).

Chris wouldn't look directly at me when he said, "I don't know, Rachel. Maybe you guys just shouldn't."

"But why?" I asked. I was sitting on his couch, my feet resting on the coffee table.

Chris got a pained look on his face, fidgeted on the seat beside me.

"No one ever says anything about Dave and Michelle."

Chris nodded. "I know." I ignored how obviously uncomfortable he was as he rubbed his hands together and looked around the room. I thought maybe I hadn't explained it well enough, that Micky and I talked, that he told me stuff about his life. (Sometimes a story isn't a window into vulnerability. Sometimes it's just a story. But I didn't know that then.)

"I mean, I think we love each other."

Dave was the one who finally told me. He had a habit of shaking his bangs out of his eyes when he was uncomfortable. He leaned toward me and put his elbows on his knees; I could see every freckle on his face. "Dude," he finally said. "Micky's married." And he had a child with his wife, Peggy.

I bawled for days. I thought I felt for Micky exactly what you were supposed to feel about someone when you loved them. But of course, it's equally true that I didn't quite know what I was feeling. When you're as lonely as I felt all the time, as weightless and disconnected from your people, you cling to anything, anyone. I had screwed a fair number of guys by then, but none of them that I knew of had lied to me. They'd used me, sure. And sometimes I used them. But I didn't love any of them. Many of them I didn't even like. Micky was different. Micky took my breath away. I wanted to sleep for a year and wake up forgetting he'd ever even existed.

I told myself a lie about him. That he had been trapped by this woman, Peggy, when she knew he had no other place to live, and then she had had a child with him, trapping him further, but I, who never forced him to do anything—even acknowledge our relationship publicly—I was who he really loved. I couldn't even envision the kind of home life Micky and Peggy and their son had. Or conceive that this family might be more important, more real to him than the band.

How could it be? He was so vital and losing him could mean the end of the band. His charisma as a front man was undeniable. One time, White Lie played a summer festival and girls stormed the stage, tearing his shirt in pieces right off him. It was that ebony hair, those intense green eyes. It was the sexiness with which he simply moved through the world. Even months into my relationship with him, I could barely stand next to him without feeling his presence zing through me. I mistook this zinging for love. I understand now that part of what loving someone means is that you let them choose the life they want for themselves.

One day, I drove out to the house Peggy shared with Micky while Micky was at work. Had she invited me? Had I just shown up? I no longer remember. Their son was asleep in his room. Peggy had curly brown hair and smelled like fresh shampoo. I wanted to hate her. I also wanted her to hate me. Maybe she'd hit me, so I could have an excuse to hate her. Maybe she'd swear at me and push me down the stairs and Micky would come and see what a ghastly thing she'd done, and he'd sweep me up in his arms.

She was older, maybe twenty-nine or thirty. I was eighteen. I didn't understand that she would see me for exactly who I was: a distraction, a shadow in her husband's life that would soon pass. She didn't scream or punch or tear at my clothes. Instead, she brought out a photo album and began to turn each page, slowly, so that I could take in the photos, one by one. Their life together. What they shared. Micky and Peggy laughing, holding each other, kissing their baby. I thought of my love for John-John and Joshua, the purity of it. How I'd fly in front of a Mack truck to save those little boys, and how Micky and Peggy must have felt the same way about their child. The photos were of a couple, away from crowds, stages, groupies. I had misunderstood. I thought the band was Micky's life. His real life was here, with this woman and this child, in this house in Berwyn. To me, family had been something you escaped, not something you formed.

I'd had it backwards. The band was a hobby for Micky. And so was I. Peggy's life, as a young mother, was far more serious than I understood. I had a serious life, too, in its own way, but I wasn't yet a woman with any sense of her own power. And Peggy was, despite how we'd both been played.

Micky quit the band.

Twenty-Three

One Sunday afternoon, I rang the doorbell at the house of a man named Frank Pappalardo. Frank was a recording engineer at a new state-of-the-art studio in the city called River North. White Lie had started recording an album with him, their first time in a real studio, the kind that was so soundproof it was like sitting inside snowfall. I'd gone down one Sunday night to listen to a session, and Frank had invited me over to learn about contracts and booking and band management. Frank would go on to mix sound for hundreds of bands—live shows, studio recordings, television mixes. Groups like Fleetwood Mac, Foreigner, Chicago, Fall Out Boy, and too many others to name (Stevie Nicks once gifted him a signed guitar). He'd played for years with a regionally successful band named Rampage. And he offered to teach me everything he knew about booking.

For as connected and cool as he seemed, Frank's neighborhood was suburban and conventional. He was surrounded by young families in 1970s-era two-story brick homes. He had a goofy, lopsided smile and short brown hair. He was constantly cracking jokes: about groupies, about the sometimes ridiculous culture of rock and roll, about the stage clothes—in the '80s the spandex stage clothes could write their own jokes. He cracked up at lead singers who played garage-sized clubs, but screamed into microphones at stadium volume. "Do they think no one can hear them?" he'd say.

He said things aloud that the rest of us might only think, about the amount of hair spray necessary to play rock and roll, or why no one but him seemed to notice the unforgiving nature of stage wear. Frank could hear things through his headphones that even with instructions and maxed-out volume would elude me. I loved watching him communicate with the band, ask for a little less reverb, instruct one of the guys to hit *that* note harder, softer, longer. It was thrilling to hear what took shape—how an idea became a chorus, and a chorus became a song, and then a song got filled in with lyrics, and other instruments, a melody and a rhythm playing off each other, complementing each other.

I had been booking White Lie for close to a year when I met Frank. I had long since dropped out of Barbizon and almost immediately lost touch with Tamara. Apart from my day job, I had devoted my life to cold-calling clubs all over Illinois and northern Indiana, so long as they were in my area code. I couldn't afford long-distance fees.

Frank offered me a drink, maybe a rum and Coke, which I accepted, and then we sat at his dining room table—he had both a dining room table *and* a kitchen table. It had been several months since Micky quit White Lie and Michelle's older brother, Stacy, was the lead singer now. I couldn't get over how adult Frank's life seemed. He'd bought his house when he was twenty-five years old; I could barely imagine even being alive at twenty-five, let alone having enough direction to buy your own real estate. With Micky gone, now all four of the band members lived with their parents.

An enormous box sat on the floor beside the table, and Frank began to pull out contracts, posters, fliers, photos, cassette tapes, and old show tickets. When he played in Rampage, the band used to sell themselves to high schools as an education in the history of rock and roll for the students. They'd play at an assembly, songs from the '50s, '60s, '70s, and talk a little about how music affected politics. Then they'd sell tickets to a show in town that night and thousands of kids from the area high schools would come.

Frank explained to me what a rider was, and the essentials of a contract. How many sets and how long would the band play? How big was the space itself? Would the band load in and out themselves, or did the club have people to help? How long would their breaks be? Would they have access to a dressing room and a place to rest between sets? If the gig was out of town, what were the sleeping arrangements and who paid? How many rooms did the band require? Who was in charge of promotional material and was there an opening act? I sipped at my drink and took copious notes on a legal pad. We looked through the old black-and-white photos of Rampage at their live shows, Frank onstage with a guitar and long hair. He pulled out their records and tapes, talked about how he loved music but knew he wasn't good enough to be a player himself. But he had these incredible ears, this auditory gift. It was a lesson for me in how he had taken the thing he loved most in the world and bent it to his will, found a place to fit himself.

Frank wasn't impatient with me. He didn't ridicule my obvious lack of knowledge. He told me later that he had seen right away that I was smart. We spent the entire afternoon poring over papers. He told me I needed to negotiate everything from food service to the guest list to whether or not the entourage got free drinks and, if so, how many. And as the band's booking agent, I needed a contract with them, too. Was I taking 15 percent of the gross? That was standard (I was not, though I started that day). After all, I might have just fallen into this, but the band was farther along than they'd been a year ago and that was, at least in some small measure, due to my hard work.

"You have to know what kind of security these clubs provide," Frank told me. "You get people and alcohol. Shit happens." I remembered the festival where Micky's shirt had been torn off him, how we had picked up tiny pieces of it scattered all over the lawn later. We'd laughed about it at the time, but it was also a little terrifying.

"Clubs need security," Frank advised, "in the contract." Recording had to be explicitly disallowed.

I put aside sample contracts that Frank said he'd let me borrow. We were drinking, laughing, sharing stories. I recounted how I'd convinced the guys to switch instruments once by having Chris go up onstage at the start of the show and tell the crowd there'd been an accident. The band was okay, but they needed volunteers from the audience to play. Jimmy, Dave, and Stacy volunteered, each of them going to a different instrument. They played a few off-key bars, the crowd increasingly confused, before switching to their own instruments; they launched into the show, the crowd wild with laughter and applause. Another time, Stacy had wanted to make a grand entrance from the dressing room as the first chords were played. He ran out, crashed headfirst into a beam, and knocked himself out cold. Chris, Jimmy, and Dave played that opening chord over and over, looking toward where Stacy was supposed to emerge. Seconds went by. A minute. Then Stacy, dizzy and stumbling, made his way to the stage and sang the rest of the show in a concussive haze.

The afternoon waned, and night fell. Frank asked if I wanted to stay and watch a movie. He'd make popcorn. Several steps down from the kitchen was a den in deep shades of brown with a giant wraparound couch and a home theater. Every room in the house had a different color carpet.

Truth is, I never wanted to leave. The carpet swallowed our steps, and his house was deeply quiet. More than all I was learning, it was Frank taking me seriously that mattered. I had never stopped feeling like a fraud in any of the clubs I booked. With Frank, I didn't feel ashamed of what I didn't know.

During the movie, Frank put his arm around me. He couldn't possibly like me, I thought. I was just this kid who knew nothing and was walking around broken-hearted and lost. But I didn't move away.

Frank became the sound guy for White Lie. He encouraged me to branch out to other parts of the Midwest, especially college towns, where the pay was decent and attendance was always high. We began to play in Champaign-Urbana, Effingham, Milwaukee, Muncie, Indianapolis, Carbondale.

Meanwhile, Frank and I were spending more and more time at his house. One night he told me he'd forgotten to mention a waiver for Chris. Chris was underage, too young to be in the clubs we played, and the owners needed indemnity. I'd never heard of this. Mostly, since Chris and Michelle and I were the only ones under twenty-one, we just didn't drink. Or we drank secretly. It hadn't occurred to me that Chris's age was something to address with clubs. Frank said he'd been meaning to mention it to me for weeks. We were sitting in his TV room downstairs, on the couch with the lights dimmed.

"Me, too, though," I told him.

"You, too, what?"

"I mean, I'd have to say how old I was too, then."

"Wait." Frank shifted on the couch. "How old *are* you?"

"Eighteen."

He covered his eyes with one hand. "Eighteen? Eighteen fucking years old?" He seemed equally incredulous and amused. I hadn't lied to him intentionally. I'd gone to high school (briefly) with Chris, so the rest of the guys all knew my age. It had simply not come up with Frank.

He didn't seem angry, just floored. He'd thought I was in my mid-twenties.

I shrugged. "No one ever asks."

He ran his hands through his brown hair and it stuck up at all angles. He said, with a half-laugh, "Yeah, and don't tell anyone."

I told him I wouldn't.

Then he asked me how I'd wound up here, eighteen, on my own, booking a rock band, filing insurance papers.

So I told him about my life. And after that, I suppose it's truthful to say that Frank and I dated. Except that we never went out to dinner, or to the movies, or anywhere public. We stayed at his house, watched movies, had a lot of sex, went to White Lie shows. My body didn't zing around him like it had with Micky, but he made me laugh so hard I'd double over. And he never hid the fact of our relationship in front of anyone. He helped me with professionalizing my business, had someone help me design new business cards and promo packs for Midwest Artist Management by Rachel Lee. He said if I really wanted to make it as a booking agent, I had to represent multiple bands, playing on multiple nights, not just one group playing once or twice a week. I couldn't be both fan and agent, friend and manager. I auditioned one band, but my heart wasn't in it. I loved White Lie because they were my friends and I loved their music. I couldn't picture myself being loyal to some other group in the same way. This was the difference, I supposed, between me and a real booking agent. Me and someone like Tony LaBarbera.

One night, Frank cooked me dinner. Bow-tie pasta with Parmesan cheese, butter, and dried parsley. I'd been up showering when he called me down. He hadn't made a big thing of it, just said, "Dinner's ready." No man had ever cooked for me before. I couldn't even recall ever seeing a man cook unless it was behind a commercial grill at a restaurant. Certainly, my father never cooked, and my friends' fathers never cooked, and none of the guys I knew from the band or anywhere else ever cooked. I sat down at the kitchen table as if I were being hosted by the queen of England. I could feel tears welling up in my eyes, and I told myself not to be stupid, not to ruin this moment. Frank dug in and was probably a third of the way through his pasta when he looked up at me and said, "What?"

I didn't know what to say, so I smiled and took a bite. It was so extraordinarily delicious. Though I'd lived on my own for two years, I couldn't cook at all. My stepmother was at best an embittered home assembler, called in to action entirely against her will. The only person who'd given me even the haziest of lessons was Cindy's mom, and my largest lesson from her had been to tell me to cook hot dogs in water.

I asked Frank to show me how to do it.

"It's just pasta, butter, and Parmesan," he said. "A little dried parsley if you have it."

"But how," I wanted to know, "could it taste *so* good? Like this?"

Frank stared at me for a moment. "It's just pasta." He seemed genuinely confused.

I didn't want to tell him that I ate those square slices of ham with bits of American cheese embedded into them. I ate cereal. And I ate toast. Sometimes peanut butter and jelly, or Chef Boyardee ravioli. "Sure," I said. "Never mind."

Twenty-Four

I had to move again. Michelle was going to move in with Dave, and I needed to find my own place. Finally, I was old enough to sign a lease. I'd had my job at Aetna for a year, and even though I was convinced a job couldn't possibly offer a more boring way to spend eight hours every day than extracting and returning the same files over and over again, the job had at least given me some sense of stability.

This time, my stepmother called me and told me she'd found the perfect studio apartment for me. It was in Aurora, Illinois, in a small building, but the apartment was beside the manager, so if I needed anything, he'd be right there. His name was Vic, and he wore green janitor's pants and was always shirtless. The apartment was one large room, with an alcove for my twin bed, and a tiny kitchen around the corner. The clothes closet was in the bathroom beside the toilet. The linoleum flooring curled up in spots, but my stepmom said I could buy some kind of rug and cover it so I wasn't slicing my feet all the time. And the price, at two hundred dollars a month, was as much as I could afford anyway. I signed a lease at Vic's kitchen table. That following weekend, just before I moved in, someone was murdered in the adjacent parking lot. But a lease was a lease and I'd paid my deposit. There was a liquor store around the corner with bars over the window where I would sometimes buy a bottle of Mad Dog 20/20. Vic told me to watch myself at night, to park in my assigned space, and go straight up to my apartment, not linger outside.

One night, coming home late from a show, I saw the headlights of a car that seemed to be following me. I exited I-5 and so did the car. I made a left off the ramp and the car turned left. I started to feel a tingling in my belly. It was four A.M. What should I do? Why would someone follow me? He didn't have the headlights of a cop car.

I turned once, then twice. The car followed. My heart started thumping. In the parking lot of my apartment, the car turned, too. A red sports car. Frank had followed me home.

"I wanted to make sure you got home okay," he said. He could have told me to call him when I got home if he wanted to look out for me. I was so insecure in those days, and so unsure of my standing with Frank, that it never occurred to me to ask if I was his girlfriend, or if he was my boyfriend. I didn't think he was seeing anyone else, but I didn't really know. I'd never had a guy come to one of my apartments before. Was this what it was like to have a boyfriend? Someone who showed up unannounced to make sure you were okay? I felt a kind of joy wash over me. Someone in the world had sought out my safety. And my company.

Because I never initiated anything, never asked anything of him, I had become, in fact, what the evangelicalism of my father told me to be: a subservient girl, never speaking of my own needs or desires, never even acknowledging them to myself. This wasn't something Frank, or any other man, demanded of me, but we all operated within the same cultural and gender norms. Women pleased men and rarely if ever considered their own desires. I was twenty-six before I would have my first orgasm and it would only be then that I started to understand how much was kept from women in this culture. Evangelicalism didn't invent this imbalance, but it certainly perfected it.

I was available when Frank wanted to see me and gone when he didn't. Just as I'd been with Micky. Just as I'd been with Jackson: never sure of my status. It was connected to what I had always felt about girlhood: that the loss of my mother left me no blueprint for how to be a woman. It seemed to me that other girls had clarity when it came to dating; they had been gifted knowledge that I lacked about how to be a girlfriend. Mothers, I was sure, had given them such wisdom. Even back in high school, I would watch couples and wonder how they'd arrived at being couples. Cindy had met her boyfriend in her sophomore year, and they were still together, five years later. (They would, in fact, still be together in thirty years.) It wasn't that I equated Frank and Micky and Jackson with one another, not by a long shot. But questions I could not articulate about my own acquiescence remained. If I wanted to be Frank's girlfriend, why wasn't I? I didn't even know myself enough to consider this question. I was just a lost soul; I was who my parents had warned me about. Someone who was always lonely. Someone who would always feel like an outcast. But then Frank came into my life offering some measure of protection and care.

Frank spent the night in my twin bed with me, which was sweaty and ridiculous, and in the morning, he said, "This apartment sucks." Which was true, it did, especially compared to his large and nicely furnished house. We laughed. Secretly, I loved that apartment. Even if the next-door neighbors were always tossing each other into walls and Vic walked around the hallways with his hairy belly on full view. Even if the floor curled up and the doorless closet sat directly beside the toilet. It was entirely my own.

ONE MORNING, ON my way to work at Aetna, I crashed into the back of a truck during rush hour traffic. It wasn't a huge crash, not like breaking the windshield of my Opel when I was sixteen. But the car was totaled and had to be towed away. I didn't know who else to call, so I called Frank. He came and got me, and I took the day off work. I was dazed, but not really hurt. By now, I'd grown used to my nine-to-five schedule in the filing banks, and to have a whole weekday stretch out before me felt strange and wonderful. Frank took me to his house, and we had sex. I was sore, and shaken up, but it didn't occur to me to communicate this with him in any way. Afterward, he went downstairs and made me a sandwich and brought it to me in bed, and it seemed like the most caring thing a man could ever do for a woman.

Frank and I sat on his king-sized bed across from each other as I ate my sandwich. I had just turned nineteen. My friend from Aetna was working to be promoted to an underwriting position. This seemed like something possible for me, except I was terrible at math, and most of the underwriters had had college courses or were at least comfortable with equations, which I was most definitely not.

Frank asked me what I planned to do. I couldn't ever remember even seeing him in the daytime. "With your life," he clarified. "I mean what do you plan to do with your life?"

No one had ever directly asked me this, though it was the primary occupation of my mind. I'd worked more than a dozen different jobs, all of them minimum wage, and at all of them I'd still struggled to pay my bills and always, every month, ended in the red. How did people live? How did they survive working these jobs? I didn't have the contours of these questions quite yet, but they had begun to form in me, shapeless as raw clay. I'd gotten my first grocery store membership rewards card from the local Jewel several months earlier, and the day I got it, I ran straight to the store. I had no food in my house and had no money to buy any. My biweekly check was still several days away. I went up and down the grocery aisles filling my cart, and when I got to the cashier, I handed her my Jewel card. She looked confused for a minute, then said, "No, sweetheart. This is just a membership card. It's not a credit card."

I fled the store in shame, leaving my groceries behind.

I told Frank I liked booking White Lie, that maybe I could take on more bands, do that professionally someday. It sounded hollow even to me.

Frank had a way of talking that made everything seem not merely possible, but inevitable, a wry sense of humor that made the unspeakable terror of my whole life seem less terrifying if I only did what was crushingly obvious to him. "It's a business," he reminded me, as he had a thousand times, "just like any other business. You have to learn the business."

I told him he was teaching me everything I needed to know.

"No." He shook his head. "Not contracts. I mean a real education. You have to go to college." Out of our entire entourage, Frank was the only one who had gone to college and graduated with a bachelor's degree. I'd never thought about this in any meaningful way.

I reminded him that I had been expelled. I was not exactly the kind of student colleges were courting.

He looked at me with a seriousness that was rare for him. He was sitting cross-legged on top of his bed. I was wrapped up to my neck in the covers. "So, what," he said, "you want to be a loser for the rest of your life?"

It was a blade right through my abdomen. I had to catch my breath. He had articulated instantly the simmering terror that swirled around me every minute of every day, that my immediate past would be my forever future if something didn't intervene. I knew that he had not meant it to be cruel. That he was trying to make me think beyond the struggle of day-to-day. The word *loser*—*loser* as in the rest of the life I was staring down—felt nauseatingly true. But college? It sounded so far-fetched, like those stories of people who get knocked on the head and wake up fluent in some language they never knew they knew. College was beyond my capabilities. The two years I'd spent in high school I'd been absent, stoned, depressed, or otherwise disengaged.

"So get your GED," Frank said.

"I can't."

"Why?"

I had no answer for this, except a sharpening anxiety that everyone would be smarter than me, that my ignorance would thereafter be quantifiable. "I can't pass," I said.

"Of course you can." He brushed off this insecurity as if I were ridiculous for suggesting it.

I shook my head. I couldn't dissect the worm in biology, let alone a fetal pig. I didn't understand basic math. The books I loved were Harlequin romances or things you'd buy at a gas station, like Michael Korda's *Queenie*. I knew they weren't teaching Michael Korda in college classes. My brother was the brilliant one, I told Frank. David would eventually earn a PhD.

"Look," Frank stopped me, "college is so much easier than high school. You have a few required classes, but you basically study what you want. No one's going to force you to major in math." He laughed. "And you don't take classes all day. You take a couple, then you have a break. You study, you work. Whatever." I was skeptical of this. How could college be a higher education level than high school, but not require you to be there all day? Frank had gone to North Central College, a tiny private school smack in the middle of Naperville that I'd driven past a thousand times but never really noted. At the time, North Central's classes were held on Mondays, Tuesdays, Thursdays, and Fridays, and everyone had Wednesday off. He told me I'd take maybe three classes a quarter at most.

I'd have a break from Thanksgiving until January, and then be done for summer in the middle of May.

"Just meet with someone," he said. "It won't hurt to have a conversation."

I BOUGHT A GED study guide from Barnes & Noble Booksellers, and at work, my boss, Mary, let me study during down times in the filing stacks. Mary was a joyful person, always smiling, always patient. She wore silky, flowered blouses, and she knew that filing was sheer drudgery. She fully supported my coworker's ambitions to try for an underwriting position. She sometimes quizzed me using my GED book.

Frank made good on his promise to find me someone to talk with at North Central College. In fact, he'd found the head of admissions: Rick Spencer. Rick told him to have me come in after I had my GED in hand, and we'd talk. I dared not hope. But I studied.

I took the GED test that winter on a Saturday morning at the College of DuPage, a local community college in Glen Ellyn where Cindy had begun taking classes, while working full time as a bank teller. I was the youngest person in the room by far. There were a handful of men, probably in their forties, and two or three women. Maybe half a dozen of us. We were told to put our bags under our desks, that we would get one break, that we could have nothing else but the test, some number-two pencils, and scratch paper in front of us. We'd be required to turn in the scratch paper when we finished. My hands shook a little, my stomach in knots. I had done okay on the practice tests in my GED book, except when it came to the math. I tried to do the word problems, but even those were hard for me. (If a train is traveling at seventy miles an hour and a second train leaves the station one hour later traveling at eighty, when can the two expect to meet?) It had been maybe three months since that afternoon at Frank's house. I hadn't dared to think too much about college, but when I'd mentioned it to my father he'd nodded his approval and said, "Amen. Get that sheepskin, Rachel."

He was also moving on in his way, from Shaklee and Herbalife to Amway, and eventually to round houses and no-run pantyhose and specu- lative land in California. He and my stepmom had bought a house in the same neighborhood where Chris lived with his mom. It was a four-bedroom ranch with a renovated upstairs attic that my dad used as his office. My real mother's furniture still sat in the dining and living rooms, except now my stepmother had begun collecting stuffed animal lambs and they were spread out across the settee. An embroidered wedding gift hung on the kitchen wall with my dad's and Barbara's names, as well as all four kids' names, stitched on it, along with a Bible verse: "What God hath wrought together, let no man tear asunder." Beside it hung my stepmother's plasticene McDonald's collectible dinnerware: the Hamburglar, Mayor McCheese, et cetera.

I don't remember how long I sat there, with my clutch of number-two pencils and my scratch paper, but I remember exactly the thought I had when I turned in my test and made my way to my car in the parking lot, and it was this: if everyone knew how easy the GED was, no one would ever finish high school.

Several weeks later, my GED came in the mail with a letter of congratulations. It felt like a door creaking open.

I WAS A heavy-metal girl. I wore jeans and miniskirts, leather jackets in an array of colors, torn fishnets and black strappy tops. At Aetna, I had to dress professionally, but I got away with as much rock and roll as Mary would allow, which usually meant black pants of some sort and a button-down shirt. The day of my meeting with Rick Spencer I bought a new skirt and matching long-sleeved jersey in soft peach cotton.

I parked my car and climbed a flight of stairs to his office. I hadn't been able to eat at all that day. I didn't know what terrified me more: that he wouldn't accept me, or that he would. The stairs had old linoleum on them and carried the wonderful musty smell of a library. There were two thousand students total at the school—fewer than at Naperville North High School—and the campus took up a couple of blocks just east of downtown in the tree-lined historic section of Naperville, where the Victorian houses were extravagantly painted in plums, turquoises, yellows. It was a charming campus, with flowers and squirrels and old, stately buildings set between walkways. I tried to picture myself walking along the sidewalk with a stack of books, nodding with confidence as I passed fellow students.

Rick Spencer shook my hand and motioned for me to come into his office. I'd pictured a gray-haired elderly man, but he seemed young. He was dressed casually, in slacks and button-down shirt, a maroon V-neck sweater over top, and his smile put me instantly at ease. We sat on either end of a couch. I'd been prepared to talk about how David and I had once been accepted into Sewickley Academy in Pennsylvania, but then had moved to Illinois, and how I'd worked ahead in several subjects at FCCA.

But Rick didn't ask me about any of that. In fact, he didn't seem particularly interested in my educational background at all. Instead, he asked me why I hadn't finished high school. I started to tell Rick about my life, my dead mother and my stepmother and the Christianity and running away and being kicked out. I talked for more than an hour. I told him at the end that I did not want to spend the next thirty years of my life living as I had for the past three. And that I didn't exactly know my way out, but I knew I was the only one who could change the trajectory.

AT THE END of that meeting, Rick Spencer and I stood. He reached out his hand and said, "I'm going to take a chance on you, Rachel Snyder." My blood pressure dropped and I went light-headed, but I managed to shake his hand.

Twenty-Five

Shortly after my meeting with Rick Spencer, my father invited me to lunch. This was out of character for him. He never called me. He rarely even returned my calls now that I had found some level of stability.

We met over cheese fondue at a restaurant called J.B. Winberie's. My dad was wearing a tie. I knew there was a reason for this meal, for this meeting, but I couldn't imagine what that might be. Would he invite me to live in his house now that I was in college? Would he offer some profound parental wisdom I'd never heard before?

My father and I finished lunch and walked to our cars. I was driving a Volkswagen Rabbit, he an Audi. Outside was bitter cold and my father's overcoat flapped around him as we stood. The air was tinged gray, the clouds low and thin. It was the kind of ugly midwestern winter day that makes retirees move to Florida.

My father rubbed at his eyes. I'd inherited the same dark circles, the same bags. He looked up toward the sky. "Your mother left you some money," he said. "A college fund for you and David." So this was why he'd invited me to lunch.

MY FATHER SAID he'd invested our money in gold and silver, trying to "grow it," as he put it. But the market for metals had tanked. He'd lost it all. Every penny. My mother had understood something that only came to me in that moment: I couldn't trust him to provide for me in her absence. "I was trying to help," he said. "I wanted to take care of you."

He was tearing up, holding his mouth in a thin line. It tore me in half. Both his own sorrow and his abject failure. Both her foresight and her absence.

"It's okay, Dad," I told him. "It's okay." Although it was very much not okay. I wanted to scratch his eyes out, punch him in the face as hard as I could, shake him till he passed out. But as much as I wanted to rage at him, I also couldn't, not when he was showing such clear vulnerability. Sympathy and anger tangled inside me.

In the space of two minutes I'd gained and lost a college fund.

I now see the church as the first in a long line of my father's "opportunities," his shaky investments and get-rich schemes. Bestline, Amway, Shaklee, Herbalife, no-run pantyhose, land in California, water purifiers, round houses, and some kind of magnets that were supposed to make hard water soft. He got a financial broker's license and tried to give free seminars at libraries, but no one ever came. He'd up the ante into currency trading, into some investment scheme so secretive that he once took me out to his car to talk about it for fear that his house was bugged. A land lease in Texas for oil. Later, a portion of a bitcoin.

But this time it had been my money, my future, a promise made by a dying mother to her children. A mother who *knew* her husband, her widower, couldn't be counted on to care for us.

People would say of my father that he was the most generous person they knew. And it's true that he'd give away his last dollar. He knew the life story of his mechanics and his grocery cashiers. He knew his bank tellers and he took in every stray dog that ever wandered past him. But he also took things he was not entitled to take. This is the part of my dad that is so difficult to reconcile. The part that is arrogant and foolish, the part that believes he deserves more than others because his God supposedly told him so.

"Do you forgive me?" he asked.

What could I say?

I told him I forgave him. Then I drove ninety miles an hour home and raged in my apartment, playing music so loud Vic pounded on my door to shut the hell up.

* * *

MY TUITION WAS twelve thousand dollars a year. I had a Pell Grant.
I took out loans. I got a work-study job on campus. My grandma Erma
gave me a thousand dollars on the condition that I live in the dorms; she
insisted that I would miss some important element of the college experience if I didn't.

I moved into a triple in a brand-new building, much to the envy of
the girls stuck in doubles. We had two rooms with cinder-block walls
painted cream, a set of twin beds in one room, and one twin alone in the
other, which I took. I felt dread as I unpacked my clothes into a closet
just larger than a footlocker. I could hear the chatter among the other
girls as they moved in, and they all seemed to know each other, or to
know what to do. My roommates had pretty little plastic buckets to carry
their toiletries back and forth to the showers. They had pictures of their
families that they taped above their desks. Planners with to-do lists,
sweatpants with the college letters across their butts. They had different
color folders for each subject, and an array of pens and pencils.

But I had Cindy. She'd decided to transfer from the community college
to North Central and we'd be schoolmates once again. I wanted to jump
up and wrap my body around her like a monkey, I was so elated. She'd
decided to major in accounting, so we wouldn't have many classes together,
but at least she'd be there. My oldest, dearest friend, in the background
everywhere I went on that campus. When I'd been too broke to buy food,
she'd given me baggies of leftovers from her mother's kitchen, invited me
over for dinner. When I needed help with math, she'd tried her best. We
went to concerts together, and watched movies, and occasionally I was
invited to tag along with her family to their cabin near the Wisconsin
Dells, where we went tubing and drank beer around a fire.

I was only a year older than the other freshmen around me, but I felt
ancient. I imagined none of them had struggled to pay their electric bill.
I imagined none of them had left a conveyor belt of food at a grocery
store, or picked through their belongings in the trunk of their car,
searching for a clean work uniform. They all seemed to know instinctively
how to navigate college: that the registrar's office was where you changed
classes, that the bursar's office was where you worked out financial questions, that you needed a meal card in order to get food from the cafeteria. That a syllabus was what told you which books to buy. I was

surprised to learn there was a health center on campus where students could just go and see a nurse if they needed to. I couldn't remember the last time I'd been in a doctor's office. The students spoke about subjects I'd never heard of: sociology, anthropology, public health.

In my first quarter at North Central, I immediately dropped two classes because they sounded difficult: political science and psychology. Rick Spencer had told me I'd be on academic probation for my entire freshman year, even if I got straight As my first quarter. This meant I had to maintain a B average, and given my wild insecurity around academics, I didn't want to take on any classes that could threaten my standing. I stuck to subjects I knew I'd be good at: literature, creative writing, history. I'd quit my job at Aetna, and I spent nearly every weekend traveling with White Lie. None of us were making much money, but I brought in enough to pay for most of my books and my meal card.

My professors didn't know I'd been expelled from high school after years of subpar schooling. They didn't know I was gone every weekend with a band. I was shocked to learn that a student could just go to a professor's office to talk about coursework. For months I never uttered a word in class. I took furious notes. I tried not to make eye contact with the professors lest they call on me. But soon, I found that I was able to follow what I was learning, whether it was the history of World War I or the diagramming of sentences. I began to go to the library just for the orderly calm of the building. And very often, Cindy and I would hunker down in her parents' basement amid piles of laundry and Christmas ornaments and we'd study, then snack, then study, then watch David Letterman, then study. We had more all-nighters than I can count, and certainly more than were necessary.

One of my mentors was a history professor named Clark Halker, who went by Bucky. Tall and thin with piercing blue eyes and long, shaggy gray hair, he'd slink into class long-legged and fill the board with notes, top to bottom and left to right. Then, he'd lean on his lectern and spend the next hour just talking off the cuff. He said most students thought history was a series of dates and places and this was bullshit. History was a series of systems and forces, human wrought, that connected us. In order to understand history, he said, we had to understand these larger forces. Fuck the dates. We could memorize dates on our own time. He told us there was "a war going on somewhere in the world every second of every day." I walked back to my dorm in shock. To think that while I was sitting in my air-conditioned class in suburban Illinois, some family across the planet was fleeing bombs and guns. While I was living out of my trunk or sleeping in a parking lot, some teenagers in Ethiopia or Guatemala were foraging for food.

I began to visit Professor Halker during his office hours. He was brilliant, sardonic, unafraid to remind us of how little we knew. He wasn't there to be our friend. He was there to wake us up to the world and our part in it. He was also in a zydeco rock band called the Remainders that was hugely popular around Chicago. He was the first person I told about my weekend life, about booking White Lie. We recognized the misfit in each other. One afternoon, when our conversation turned to politics, I told him that I would have voted for Ronald Reagan for president if I'd been old enough and he laughed out loud. "There is no part of you that's Republican," he said.

I told him my father was a Republican. I had assumed it was a kind of requirement to register as the political party of your family.

He shook his head. His desk was covered in books and papers, and he leaned way back in his chair across from me. Then he talked to me about Republicans and Democrats, the New Deal and Franklin Roosevelt. He told me about Reaganomics, how Reagan attacked unions, how his conservative stance on government reeled in religious voters. My family had been on food stamps, my father on unemployment multiple times, yet still my dad railed about "welfare cheats" as if they were the true culprits of government waste.

I was sure my father didn't want anyone dying because they couldn't pay their medical bills, yet he had voted for a man who slashed the budget for mental health care such that decades later, the country would still be reeling from a lack of mental health resources. I was sure he didn't want wars around the world, yet he had voted for massive increases in military spending. Dr. Halker explained to me the idea of cognitive dissonance, how you could profess to be one thing while every action you took suggested something else. By the next presidential election that came around, in 1992, I was a proud Democrat.

Another day, Dr. Halker walked into our class and, instead of writing notes on the board, pointed to one student and then another and asked who our local government representatives were. Who were our state representatives? Who were our aldermen, or council members? Who were our state senators, our attorneys general, our mayors? Who were the senators and members of the general assembly for our district down in Springfield, the capital of Illinois? I didn't know. Had any of us ever been to a meeting of our local government? Had any of us attended, say, a zoning board meeting? A budget meeting? An economic development meeting? "Local government," Dr. Halker said, incredulous at our ignorance, "has more effect on your lives than any president ever will." He dismissed class and told us we would not be welcome again until we knew the names of our local elected officials.

One afternoon, he called me into his office after class. With Dr. Halker, you never knew if you were in his favor or not. He was so smart that I always had a terror of being asked not so much a question that I couldn't answer—that happened often—but a question that I didn't even understand. Over the months, I had shared small parts of my life with Dr. Halker, how I booked a rock band and traveled with them on the weekends. How I'd been living on my own for years.

He reached into his beat-up leather briefcase and handed me a thick spiral-ringed book. It was five different colors, and each color corresponded to a different midwestern state—Illinois, Indiana, Wisconsin, Iowa, and Michigan. It was a state-by-state list of every live music venue and every music festival, with the contact information of the primary booker. I hadn't known such a thing even existed. I'd spent countless dollars calling the operator for phone numbers for years by then. Dr. Halker gestured toward the binder. "Thought you could use it," he said. I hugged the book to my chest all the way back to my dorm room. And I signed up to minor in history.

Twenty-Six

Toward the end of my first year in college, White Lie and I parted ways. I was growing more consumed with my education, and the guys were starting to think of different paths for their own lives. Frank had started dating a woman he would go on to marry, so I didn't see him much. I was also exhausted all the time, between my two other part-time jobs and my schoolwork, the world of rock and roll began to seem less and less relevant to where my life was headed.

And writing was taking up more of my free time. My papa Chuck was sending me little encouraging notes ("Not all poetry has to rhyme!") and authors he thought I should read (Philip Roth! Ernest Hemingway! Anton Chekhov!). Sometimes we held classes outside on the lawn if the weather permitted. My imagined characters were romantic, solitary, and deeply unhappy. I wrote often about a character named Andi who lived in a cabin and spent her days painting. In some ways, I was rewriting those Harlequin romances that I'd snuck off my neighbor's mother's shelves so many years earlier. But what I developed was discipline.

I wrote a story in which I created multiple versions of a scenario: driving with two characters as they are breaking up. They're in a snowstorm in one. In the mountains in another. In city traffic in another, and so on. The descriptions suggested the pain of the breakup. It was the world as we all saw it and also a shadow world operating behind the characters that only the reader saw. Another class exercise: create a scene in which one character knows something the other character does not, and let the reader in on it. Years later, I would find myself using the same technique in nonfiction to show how the signs of intimate partner abuse become visible in victims—in their choices and movements, their speech and silence, their interactions with police, lawyers, judges—once we know (often too late) that they feared for their lives.

Slowly, I began to understand that writing, at least for me, was an empathic exercise in which to examine the complexities and seeming contradictions of people. My fictional creations, but also people like my father, who was authoritarian *and* loving, inflexible *and* hilarious. Or my stepmother, who could be every bit as strict as my father, but was also someone you could trust with your secrets. Far from being paradoxical, I eventually understood that we all embody these extremes. I hold in equal measure both cynicism and idealism as an adult now, in much the same way that as a child, I was filled with both violence and grief.

I'd been taking history classes every quarter, learning about past and current wars, refugees, political geography. I had always been taught the secular world was something to fear, to turn away from, that it held nothing but emptiness and destruction. But Christians like my parents belonged to that world as much as the rest of us. You could no more absent yourself from history than you could escape your own body. My father may have believed he was separate from those who declared war on non-Christians, or those who drew blood in the name of God, but I was beginning to believe there was a kind of collusion in this willful ignorance. You could admit you lived in these same systems and try to change what was wrong from the inside, or you could stay forever uninformed about them and claim liberation through determined obliviousness.

I took a class my sophomore year in Harlem Renaissance and Black literature. I was introduced to Zora Neale Hurston, Langston Hughes, Richard Wright, James Baldwin, Claude McKay, James Weldon Johnson, Jean Toomer, Toni Morrison, and others. They wrote of a pain that went so deep it was neurological, generational. One night, lying on my bed, I read a line from James Baldwin. "The most dangerous creation of any society is the man who has nothing to lose." I felt my brain buzz. I bolted upright in my bed and read it again. Then again and again. *The most dangerous creation of any society is the man who has nothing to lose.*

I imagine I am far from what Baldwin had in mind when he wrote that line. But sitting up in my bed with *The Fire Next Time*, it was as if someone had held a mirror to the child I'd been at thirteen, fourteen years old. Grief-stricken and angry. I had, even then, so many built-in advantages. But I understood the danger of desperate rage. I remember feeling astonished at the power of Baldwin's language, enlivened by the raw truth of his words.

BY THE END of my sophomore year, I was feeling more and more like I belonged in school. My grades were generally As and Bs. I was majoring in English with minors in history and art.

I made some friends on campus. A few guys who all hailed from Alpena, Michigan. The captain of the soccer team and a student so good-looking that the women on campus secretly referred to him as "Jesus." And his friend, a poet and intellectual who became my best friend for a while. The guys all had nicknames that they'd given one another years earlier—there was Doc and Pine Needle, and the Prophet, and Birdman. They gave me an honorary nickname: Womanchild.

One night toward the end of my sophomore year in college, a single line of exposition came to me: *so you want to know what it's like when your mother dies.* I felt the line in my whole body, calling me with an urgency I don't recall ever having felt.

I had always kept a journal. I took seriously my papa Chuck's advice to always carry a pen and paper. And I had taken creative writing nearly every semester since I began at North Central, but it wasn't until this night, this moment, that writing became a gravitational pull. I sat down at my black Ikea desk, the sides of which were slowly collapsing outward because I'd done something wrong when I put it together. I wrote in colored pen on lined paper.

> *So you want to know what it's like when your mother dies? You want to know about the years of desperate pain? You want to know what it's like to make your father Mother's Day gifts, to have your classmates laugh at your loss, to have a gravesite to visit on Christmas, rather than a glittering tree?*

It was sentimental and maudlin, but it spoke to my deepest loss, the absence that had built a darkness in me over the decades. I'd never articulated this aloud, not in detail, not in a nuanced or even detailed way. Now, I wrote about getting my period. I wrote about Jackson. I wrote about Judaism. I wrote about kissing and dating. I wrote about Christmases and birthdays missed. I wrote about all the things I imagined I'd know now if she had lived. I felt the piece as I was writing it, a current that ran all the way down to my fingers as I sat gingerly at that black particleboard desk. And as I wrote, I wept.

I had to share it. I had to know if it was as powerful to someone else as it felt to me. And there was only one person I could trust to be honest. I grabbed the paper, ran down the stairs of my apartment, and drove to Cindy's house. It was eleven o'clock. Her parents had long since grown accustomed to our late nights, our basement study sessions. To my showing up at odd hours.

I knocked on the back door and when Cindy answered, I motioned for her to come outside, shaking with adrenaline. We sat on the sidewalk next to her house, under a streetlight. Cindy had grown into a beautiful woman. Her sandy blond hair was long, halfway down her back, her brown eyes dark and glinty. She no longer dressed in moccasins and concert T-shirts, but wore long, loose skirts and ironed shirts.

"Tell me what you think," I said. "But be honest."

I may have been wearing pajamas. I can only remember the rush to share.

And I read it aloud, there under the streetlamp on that spring night. The memory of this moment is as palpable to me as my mother's funeral, one of those experiences in which every detail stays. The piece was three pages. A short, sharp, deeply personal essay, told in the second person, but felt in the first.

I didn't look up until I was finished. Cindy held her hand over her mouth. I knew something in me had changed.

Twenty-Seven

One afternoon, in the spring of my junior year, a large envelope from my uncle Robert came in the mail. Inside, a brochure with what looked like a cruise ship on the cover announced a program for college students called Semester at Sea. I don't know how my uncle happened upon it, but he had always been a consummate traveler. After World War II, his business as a jewelry broker took him all over the world, to Western Europe and Russia, China, and Central Asia. He figured he'd been to Paris more than two dozen times. He talked often about a life-changing trip he took up the Volga River in Russia. He was among the first group of Americans allowed in Vietnam after the war.

In the brochure, he had included a note that said he would pay half the twelve-thousand-dollar tuition if I could find a way to cover the other half. I turned the cover and found pictures of Masai tribespeople posing with college students on ochre-colored earth, and a group of Chinese students in front of a Peking University sign holding up a peace sign and smiling. There were pictures of the Great Wall and Hiroshima and Buckingham Palace. There were zebras running across the plains of Kenya and women carrying enormous baskets of fabric on their heads. There were fishermen with sun-aged faces and smiling women exposing teeth stained red by betel-nut juice. It was a program to study aboard a ship for a semester, visiting nine or ten countries and sailing, literally, twenty-six thousand miles around the whole of the world.

What I felt, looking through these images, was deep-boned dread. I knew, instantly, that this was the kind of opportunity one could not reasonably turn down, but I'd never left the country. Never even imagined leaving the country. I pictured getting lost in the desert, or being left behind in some village that had no electricity and from which I'd have no way to contact anyone, no way to ever leave. (That someone would come looking for me did not occur to me.) I still carried the residue of evangelicalism—the world was full of evil and corrupt people who would do whatever they could to take what I had. But was it, *really*? Could it be that the danger lay more with all that I imagined, but didn't really know? Could the danger exist merely in the abstraction of it?

I had no idea.

I showed the brochure to a friend from school. She was married, in her late twenties, another "nontraditional" undergrad. She thumbed through page after page, sucking in her breath at a beautiful sunset on the ship over endless ocean, or covering her mouth in awe at the Masai beadwork. "It's incredible," she said. "Just incredible."

"I'm not sure," I told her. I had a good job working in the field office of a textbook publisher based in Iowa and thought maybe I could turn that into a career.

She put the brochure down and looked at me. "You can't *not* do this, Rachel.

How to share my fear with her? Lions! Poverty! Malaria!

"I'd kill to go on this," she said.

"I know." I took the brochure back from her, opened it randomly to a page from India.

Mahabalipuram and Kanchipuram in a state called Tamil Nadu. India had states, just like the United States? There were sand-colored stone carvings of gods and goddesses in temples that dated back to the seventh century. I tried to calculate the years.

"What are you afraid of?"

I told her I didn't know. Maybe dying? Apart from my uncle, who stayed at fancy hotels and was, in any case, a single man not likely to be marked as vulnerable by international hoodlums, I knew no one who'd left America, apart from my dad and Barb visiting the Holy Land for their honeymoon. My family counted Orlando and Denver as exotic locales, the highly orchestrated voyages of those cruise ships, where I had adults protecting me from—I don't know—the tin drum players along the docks?

She said if I didn't go I'd regret it forever. It might become the biggest regret of my life.

"Jobs will be here when you get back. We'll all be here," she said. "You *have* to do this. I won't let you pass it up."

I worked as many hours as I could in the field office. I tutored in the English lab at school, taking on extra shifts. When summer came, I once again answered want ads and put up fliers to clean apartments. I took a bonkers job installing cable channels in motel chains in Ohio over two months of the summer. I was the only girl and got to wear a tool belt.

Come August, I was still $1,500 short. Just weeks before I was due to fly to Vancouver to join the ship, the SS *Universe*, the financial aid office at North Central called to tell me that my loan amount had increased, miraculously, by three thousand dollars.

I got my first passport. I got vaccinations or boosters for yellow fever; typhoid; Japanese encephalitis; hepatitis A and B; measles, mumps, and rubella; tetanus; and meningitis. And then I was off, no less scared, but resigned to an adventure that I feared might possibly kill me.

ON BOARD THE ship, I felt once again neither adult nor child, neither student nor teacher, but something in between. Only slightly older than my fellow students, but not old enough to fit in with the professors, who came from all over the world. I carved out friendships among the resident advisors, most of whom were graduate students on leave from their home universities. For the first time in my life, I met people who had lived and traveled around the world. My fellow students talked about visiting Paris and London with their families. I had nothing to contribute, so I listened to how they'd talk about these sights with a banal world-weariness, while I struggled to even conjure images of the Tower of London or the Arc de Triomphe. I had never heard of a job in international development or the State Department, which a number of parents apparently had. Professors who'd done research around the world or been Fulbright and Rhodes scholars. Other study-abroad programs had students go to one place for an entire semester, Barcelona, say, or Oxford. Semester at Sea was something else. We were travelers, and the trip was about connecting, across language and culture, the emphasis on meeting students like us at universities in Beijing, Delhi, Cape Town.

At the very beginning of our journey, a typhoon took us off schedule and we docked two days late in Kobe, then splintered off into groups, some of us taking a train to Kyoto. The narrow passages and dark woods of entryways, the colorful blushes of fruit markets, the white-gloved cab drivers filled me with something like joy. I smelled incense everywhere as I wandered around; stood watching outside cacophonous Pachinko parlors, the game an utter mystery; breathed in the quiet formality of the Shinto shrines. I loved immediately the feeling that no one at home knew where I was. I had to laugh at the images I'd once conjured of the secular world, empty-eyed zombies in search of Jesus. Instead, there were glossy-haired women in salmon, mint, lavender kimonos. There were giggling schoolkids in dark blue uniforms and crisp white shirts. There was that patient woman who smilingly led me next door after I walked into her house, thinking it was a restaurant. I watched kabuki theater and downed a cup of green tea, declaring it just slightly less delicious than grass. I was a giant, loud American. I was a tourist brochure. I didn't care. I loved it all.

That same storm system that forced us off course stranded us one night in Kyoto. We were to take the last train back to Kobe and spend the night on the ship, but Kyoto had stopped all their trains. It was nearing midnight, in this strange city that smelled of fish and rice, and I felt an all too familiar panic begin to rise in me. Where would we sleep? How would we stay safe? I was with two other friends, but this gave me no reassurance. Could we find a guesthouse this late at night? I didn't yet know about youth hostels. We didn't have credit cards. Our extra traveler's checks were locked away in the ship's bursar's office.

The station floors gleamed. There was no litter anywhere, and we sat on the ground against the wall. My two friends talked and told stories and I sat beside them, silent, wondering how they seemed so unfazed. One of them had lived for some months in Tokyo and earlier that day he had taken me to a food market and introduced me to nashi fruit that tasted like a blend of a pear and an apple; takoyaki, which he told me only later was fried octopus; and inari, an envelope of sweet tofu filled with rice.

Everything in the station was mechanized. Clean and quiet. A row of vending machines sold sake, beer, soda, ramen, yogurt, hot dogs, T-shirts, toys, cigarettes, and whole rows of packaged goods I could not identify. As my friends chattered, one of them moved to lie down, using his backpack as a pillow. Finally, my attempt at bravery unraveled, and I blurted, "What are we doing? Where should we go?" I didn't want to tell them I was scared, how the idea of sleeping in a public train station brought me right back to Fox Valley Mall, freezing in the middle of the night inside my car.

My friend understood immediately what I didn't admit. "This is the safest country in the world," he said. People trusted each other here, he said. I could surround my body with scattered yen and the worst thing that would happen is the wind might take it. "You can go where you want, but I'm staying."

And that became our mantra. Be open. Be flexible. Move like the sea grass with whatever comes at you. There are no plans, only ideas.

In South Africa, I went to a meeting for the Congress of South Africa Writers. I met poets who'd been imprisoned for their writing, playwrights and novelists who'd written under threat of death. They'd invented love stories between Blacks and whites that were considered by the government to be subversive, treasonous. Yet they had never stopped writing.

A poet named Dennis Brutus had arranged our visit with the South African writers. Professor Brutus had tried to get South Africa banned from the 1964 Olympics on the basis of the country's apartheid laws. He was shot trying to flee to Zimbabwe and was imprisoned in the cell next to Nelson Mandela at Robben Island. After his release in 1965, he left South Africa on what was then called a permanent exit visa, forever in exile from his homeland. It wasn't until 1990, after apartheid was banned, that he was finally able to return. And that is how, in the fall of 1991, he came to arrive with us at the port in Cape Town, tears streaming down his face. Archbishop Desmond Tutu met our ship, and I watched the two of them embrace for a long time.

BETWEEN PORTS, WE sailed for days. It allowed for considerable reflection on whatever experiences we'd just had, the interactions with people we'd never have been able to otherwise meet. On the ship, the constant view was ocean and sky. Sometimes schools of dolphins would swim beside us, breaching the water like ribbons. The outside world felt a universe away. The ship was a country unto itself.

I found a spot on a high deck, where I could dangle my feet over the edge and watch the ship slice through the water. The engine was loud, the wind billowing my hair, the waves frothing, and I began to spend hour after hour just watching the water, writing in my journal. Sometimes I sang and it was so loud my own voice was lost in the wind. I felt like everything in my life had prepared me for those hours of chosen solitude in that crevice, where something like a future began to palpate inside me. I called it a *wild whatever.* Possibility. It was delicate. I thought often of Baldwin: "The most dangerous creation of any society is the man who has nothing to lose." I sensed the ship was a way to forge that future. To create a life in which I had something to lose.

DURING THOSE FOUR months of travel, it is the sea I remember most vividly, the long afternoons when I'd be done with my classes for the day and I could just watch the sun flash off the crest of the waves, the rippling foam of the wake as we sluiced through the water. The ship had been built for the Korean War, which meant all the fuel tanks were on one side and we had a perpetual list from the weight. My cabin was several stories below deck, windowless with metal bunk beds. We had some exercise equipment, a saltwater pool, and a projector for screening movies. Sometimes, late at night, I'd spot a rat lumbering across the deck; if vermin found their way onto the ship in any given port, we had to dump them at sea, or keep them aboard so diseases wouldn't be spread between countries. Some of the kids on board were wealthy, but many were not. We had professors from all over the world who introduced us to everyday people that tourists were unlikely to meet.

We sailed across the Pacific for two solid weeks, then through the Indian Ocean, down around the Cape of Good Hope, and up to the Atlantic. The entirety of the world via water. So many of the places I went exist in my mind like a brochure when I try to recall them. Elephants in Tsavo East National Park, an elevator packed with people riding from

Salvador's upper to lower city. The rippling heat of Delhi and the bright turquoises, saffrons, and fuchsias of women's saris. I learned about silk and sashimi, about wild animals and barren deserts. I also learned about intractable poverty, caste systems, indigenous tribes—things I might have learned about America if I'd been paying closer attention. But this is perhaps the most profound lesson of travel, that you don't really know the place and culture you've come from until you've left it.

Today, I think that even if I had someday left the States, without that voyage, I'd have trod the familiar: London, Paris, Amsterdam, Montreal. Instead, Semester at Sea gave me the courage to imagine a different kind of travel, and a blueprint for how to do it. To see the sights, certainly, but to understand that it was meeting people that really mattered. In this, I also count a legacy from my father, the salesman who could talk to anyone about anything.

There was a curious fact about my fellow students that I began more and more to note as the days at sea wore on and we slowly formed friendships. Many of us had lost a parent. I talked to students who'd had fathers die from heart attacks or cancer, mothers die from car accidents or leukemia. I began to write about them in my journal, how every day I met another student with only one living parent, or in some instances none, people like myself for whom residual grief had forged entirely new patterns in their lives. We were land masses reordered after disaster.

What was it about all of us that drew us here to this *wild whatever*? Why did we choose India and Kenya over Ireland and Spain? I pondered this constantly from my little perch above the ocean. So many parents gone, their children alive and pushing themselves toward places many, perhaps most, Americans would never visit.

I befriended a dean and his family. They'd traveled all over the world, lived in foreign countries. All four of them spoke multiple languages, understood things about the world that I was only beginning to learn. One afternoon, the dean and I were on deck near a small group of stationary bikes. If I had to estimate, I told him, I'd bet something like 20 percent, maybe even 25 percent, of us had lost a parent. "This can't be just a coincidence," I said.

He shook his head. He had a thick beard with graying hair and an air of both intellect and mischievousness. When we'd crossed the equator, he'd dressed up as Poseidon, with seaweed in his hair. "I wouldn't think so."

I asked him what it meant, that so many of us had ended up here. The salty air whipped the hair around my face and I tried to hold it back with one hand.

Maybe knowing death at such an early age, he said, made us understand what it meant to live.

It knocked me sideways, the hard truth of it. That my mom's early death had been a warning shot, a directive about life itself. I had never considered it as a source of anything positive. I think he was telling me that it wasn't a betrayal to her memory to seek a life in which joy was deliberate. And nothing in my life had brought me the kind of joy I experienced as I watched the ocean move under me day after day.

I WAS PART of the ship's theater troupe that performed in orphanages in the ports where we docked. Our professor was from South Africa and had directed the opera at the Nico Malan Theatre Centre in Cape Town. He taught us that we could not rely on English for our performances. So we researched folktales in the countries we were due to visit, and then created performances around them, using props, hand gestures, facial expressions, sometimes dance and song. I choreographed a dance with another student about the beginning of humanity, when man and woman first meet, because every culture has an origin story. We twirled and moved around one another at first hesitantly, with both suspicion and curiosity, and then closer and closer. The children clamored around us afterward, tugging on our arms, giggling. We passed out Life Savers and Pringles. I began to understand how the language barrier didn't have to be a barrier to connection. It didn't have to be a barrier at all. We performed stories of love and punishment, of raging seas and heroic animals. The children screamed with laughter and recognition.

One afternoon, after a performance at an orphanage full of girls in Beijing, we were taken to spend the night at the People's University. I took a freezing cold shower. I'd never been anywhere that had no running hot water. We were due to be taken by a tour guide to the Forbidden City and then Tiananmen Square. In 1991, many people in China were still wearing Mao suits. The Cultural Revolution had ended only fifteen years earlier. Our guide was a young Chinese woman in a dark blue skirted business suit and a light blue button-down shirt. She was very serious and her English was impeccable.

As we wandered through Tiananmen Square, I sidled up to her. From which direction, I asked her, had the tanks entered? I'd remembered the images on television just two years earlier during my sophomore year. Thousands of students protesting in cities across the whole country. The tanks, one after another, all lined up.

"Oh no," she said, smiling. "There were no tanks here."

I thought maybe she had misheard me. I told her that I'd seen the tanks myself, all lined up. Dozens of them, maybe more. I couldn't remember now.

"That is western propaganda," she said. "It was a very peaceful march."

"But so many people died!" I said. On the ship we'd been given a rudimentary lesson on the concept of *face*, how important it was to Chinese cultural identity. I thought maybe there was something in my asking that was insulting.

"That is not correct," she told me. "Only six people were injured. But no one died."

Did she really believe that, or had she been trained to lie? I understood only in time that the protesters in Tiananmen Square and in cities all across China in the spring of 1989 were fighting, in part, for the freedom of speech that she could not practice.

Beyond all of the travel itself, language was taking on a deadly seriousness I had never considered. The privilege it could afford someone. How it threatened, rescued, connected. Whether you were banned from speaking your language, or killed for the way you used it; whether it betrayed you, propagated an unknown lie, or liberated you—its stakes had never been palpable to me in this way. It has been three decades now since I took this voyage, and still what remains in my mind is this mutability of language, its power to silence, or to resurrect. I can scarcely recall what I ate in each country, yet these moments when language transcended information, took shape as a tool of power, stay with me.

In the waning days of the voyage, a group of us got pillows and blankets and took them to the top deck to sleep under the stars. We wanted to watch dawn emerge from the shadow of space, the broiling black ocean turn turquoise and sparkle. Instead, we saw the sky split in half, the vertical vein separating night from day, that trick of nature. We lay there silenced by the miracle that unfolded above us.

Later, we would wonder, was it real, what we'd seen?

Part V

CAN ONE KNOW LIGHT

Twenty-Eight

My first apartment in Phnom Penh, Cambodia, had an enormous terrace that my boyfriend and I filled with lush tropical plants. A crane hoisted up a frangipani tree and a traveler's palm. We had a trellis built for shade and braided passion fruit through it. We planted red and orange lantana, pink desert roses, white jasmine, and column cacti with melon-colored flowers. At night, the rich aroma snaked into our living room. We slung a hammock between palm trees and at dusk we'd see the shadows of swift-flying bats as they dive-bombed the air around us. The neighborhood was built up with apartments and single-family homes behind large metal gates painted in dark blues, ambers, creams. An open sewer colloquially referred to as Shit River ran two blocks down. Around the corner was a cobbler who'd try his best to make imitations of Jimmy Choo or Christian Louboutin heels. It was called Tuol Sleng Shoes. I'd ordered a "medium" cow from him a while back to surprise my Harley-riding best friend, Ann, with a pair of chaps when she visited. His shop stood diagonally across from S-21, the Tuol Sleng Genocide Museum.

I'd visited Tuol Sleng once, years before, with Ann. It had been a Monday in August 1996, the same year three foreigners were killed in the south of the country, and western backpackers like us traveling to Cambodia still felt edgy and wild. The owner of the guest house where I was staying told me to knock on the metal gate at Tuol Sleng, then slip a few dollars into the guard's hand and he'd let us through and this is what happened because Cambodia was a country where ethics for many people were a privilege, whereas poverty was a fate.

I was just two months out of grad school on that first trip to Cambodia. I'd studied fiction, but then got my first publication for a nonfiction essay in a women's magazine called *Mademoiselle* and realized immediately that nonfiction provided far more paying opportunities for writers. Over the course of that first summer, I threw myself into nonfiction, learning journalism as I went. I wrote a series on youth soccer teams in the suburbs, and a piece on the hazards of Canadian geese. I wrote about growing a garden in one's apartment and one about lipstick. That 1996 trip with Ann was my first concerted effort to actually cover the expense of my travels with my writing. We would end up publishing a piece about a Vietnamese refugee supporting her entire village outside of Dalat through her suburban Illinois restaurant, and another one about a group of Cambodians trying to create awareness about women's portrayal in local media—most often as victims of sexual or domestic violence. And another on the numerous landmines still buried around the country. But on that Monday, we had no real plan other than to try to bribe our way into Tuol Sleng.

The buildings were whitewashed, the lawn patchy. Inside, crude cells cobbled from splintering wood and brick made up the bulk of the first two floors, along with a small museum of photos and information about the 1975–79 genocide. As many as twenty thousand Cambodians were tortured and killed there in that brief four-year period, with seven known survivors. I could just as easily say ten thousand, or five hundred thousand, so abstract are the numbers when I try to imagine them. In those days, there was still a map of Cambodia made from yellowing human skulls on the wall, but the map was later moved to the outskirts of the city where it hangs today at the most well-known killing field, one of many. There are killing fields in far reaches of the countryside, partially cleared for villagers to use the land. There are probably killing fields still undiscovered, just as there are Angkorian temples overgrown with jungle, and other smaller temple structures from this same period— roughly the ninth to the fifteenth centuries—known and rarely visited.

The top floor of Tuol Sleng was closed to the public. I did not know why. Later, my neighbors would tell me it was because the top floor was "thick with ghosts."

On that day, Ann and I walked through a particular kind of treacherous silence. There was no electricity, and the monsoons carried clouds down to earth. It was dark inside the cells, and smelled of tropical rot. Or maybe the smell was from Shit River. Perhaps back then, seventeen years after the last death at Tuol Sleng, the dark stains *were* still blood. There was that map of yellowed skulls. And dust and dirt covered everything. Hundreds of black-and-white photos of victims hung on wheeled display boards. (Today, those photos have been enlarged and span several rooms.) At some point, Ann moved on from the first to the second floor, and when I turned she was gone. I felt that kind of panic where the whisper of your own voice petrifies you. A terror both familiar and ancient.

When I found Ann again one floor up, I realized I'd been holding my breath. I did not leave her side again. I was ashamed of my fear and kept it to myself. I knew nothing of ghosts then, or of how the spirit world in Cambodia exists parallel to the world of the living. I believed my fear stemmed from moving through a physical space where evil had lived for so long.

Almost seven years to the day later, in 2003, I would move to this very neighborhood in Cambodia, and I would learn that the Khmer believe ghosts come to those who are alone. Perhaps this explains my vulnerability the day, many years later, when a ghost came to me, the fact of my brief isolation. I point to this afternoon with Ann as one of the moments when I began to understand that in order to appear brave, I needed braver people beside me. Tuol Sleng taught me the limits of my courage.

Our neighborhood, Boeung Keng Kang III, had a wig shop, an alligator farm three doors down, that cobbler around the corner. Tuol Sleng was the only reason anyone who didn't already live there ever came. Its molding white walls and makeshift cells represented the worst act humanity can inflict on itself. It had once been a school for middle-class Khmer kids, a French lycée. And then it was the center of a cruelty most of us must stretch to imagine. And once we've imagined, we must work to forget. Tens of thousands of people were killed at Tuol Sleng, after enduring electric shocks, starvation, interrogation. They were beaten on the bottoms of their feet and on the sides of their heads. They were chained together in shackles. They must have been as confused as they were terrified. What had happened to their country? What had happened to their lives? They had marched out of Phnom Penh in April 1975 because they'd been told the Americans were coming to bomb their city. We'd already bombed the border they shared with Vietnam and lied to the world about it. Why *wouldn't* they believe our bombs were imminent?

IN THE DOZEN years since I'd gone on Semester at Sea and then finished college and graduate school, travel had come to define my life. Ann and I met immediately after undergrad, when I moved into an apartment in Oak Park, Illinois, in a building she managed. The year I went to sea, she'd traveled around the world with her then-boyfriend, Don. The two of them had lived in Japan. (When it was time for her to cook her hosts a typical American meal, she slapped together peanut butter and jelly sandwiches. Her culinary skills have only marginally improved since.) By the time I met Ann, she and Don had broken up, but they remained best friends.

Ann was the first person I ever encountered who made community service a pillar of her life, an inheritance from her mother. She began the first recycling program in Oak Park. She worked at a community organization addressing decades of racial housing injustice on Chicago's west side. Until I met her, I'd never heard of redlining or blockbusting. She talked about the Fair Housing Act, about racial equity; she'd been the first white person to move into her forty-two-unit building. Part of her job entailed convincing whites like me that Black neighborhoods were safe, that people from different racial backgrounds could form community. This was how, in 1992, I'd come to live in a place for the first time ever where white suburbanites were not the majority. Eventually, Ann would get me a job managing a building just like hers, in which I would be the third white resident in a thirty-two-unit building just around the corner from hers. On paper my job was to clean the building, show apartments, sweep dirt from the alleyways, and shovel snow from the sidewalks. But the unwritten part of the job was the one that mattered: create community among disparate groups, Blacks and whites, young and old, middle-class and poor. During the six years I had that job, I dealt with fires and floods, domestic violence and drug addiction, racism and ageism. I learned more about race and community, class and economics from those years than I'd ever learned from my formal education.

The author with Ann in Siem Reap, Cambodia, 1996.

When I first met her, Ann had a pet rat and wore flowy cotton pants from India. She had no squeamishness when it came to disposing of rodents or spraying for roaches. She read voraciously and had earned a full scholarship to the University of Chicago school of social work for grad school. Our first trip together, in 1994, was to Mexico, Belize, Guatemala, and Honduras. Like most backpackers, we found ourselves in situations so odd they were impossible to capture for people back home: the time we slept in hammocks in a chicken shed and woke up to a cow grazing under us. The time we snorkeled through an underwater cave and wound up in a skiff in eight-foot waves, convinced we would drown. The time I walked full speed into a pole in Havana, the resulting bruise a colorful month-long marker of our journey. The time we got lost in the jungle and I kept recording (instead of wild bird calls, we heard ourselves: "Didn't we pass this tree? Weren't we here earlier?"). The time we got altitude sickness in Tibet, staying awake in a hysteria for days.

Where I seemed always to be searching for a place to belong, for some kind of intentional and chosen family, Ann was both independent and deeply close to her family. Once I met her parents, I could see the ways in which they had shaped her, her intellectual drive, her wisdom, her unparalleled humor. Her father, a blue-collar worker, celebrated his educated wife and her master's degree; he was raucous, cracking jokes so full of good will he'd be forgiven any impolite gaffe. When I visited, he'd shout, "Hi, Rachel!" in a tone reserved for a child who'd been away too long. Her mother, a devout Catholic, had recycled even in the 1960s when it was relegated to hippies and poor people, simply because it seemed to her to be a better way to live. One year Ann and I invited them to join us at my aunt Greta and uncle Wes's house in Pittsburgh. Her dad walked in with a half-empty jug of red wine and went around hugging everyone as if he'd known them his whole life. Eventually her parents moved to Indiana and we saw them often. They kept a picture of me on their refrigerator beside Ann's. Her parents became my surrogates.

The second trip Ann and I took was to Vietnam and Cambodia, where we visited Tuol Sleng, sleeping in a hostel on the shore of Boeung Kak Lake in the north of Phnom Penh. (Several years later, after I moved to Phnom Penh, the lake was filled in to make way for high-end residences.) Through our years in graduate school—me in Boston, Ann in Chicago—and beyond, a map became both our guide and our bond; country by country we built our lives around the idea of where we'd go next. Partners in travel—the local newspaper even ran a few articles on us, showing us in the back of a tuk-tuk in Rajasthan, in a shared rickshaw in Hue, at the walls of the Potala Palace in Lhasa. Travel in this way demands an unusual level of mutual care in remote places. The vomiting, the strange fevers and occasional hallucinations from malaria medicine or lack of sleep or punishing heat. We nursed each other through it all. It isn't just what you learn of the world from travel; it's what you learn of yourself and your people.

Ann had learned photography from Don (who'd taught himself) on their year-long trip around the world, and so as I began to get story assignments for us from the *Chicago Tribune*, *Seventeen*, *Jane*, *Glamour*, *American Heritage*, and other publications, Ann became a de facto photographer. I'd used the same tactic from my White Lie days ("Ann, what's a portfolio and how soon can you put one together?"): We'd choose a destination and I'd research potential stories for months, selling pitches to newspapers and magazines. We'd work like crazy—two or three jobs was our norm, though I once had as many as four—and we'd save as much money as we could. Then off we'd go, spending a month, or two or three, away. We went to Tibet, Nepal, India, Honduras, Guatemala, Mexico, Laos, Cuba, Belize, Romania. Ann made my life more intentional than it had ever been. She made me dream bigger, push myself harder, feel deeper. One trip after another, we met people who had survived unimaginable horror, endured beyond what seemed humanly capable. Slowly, I was learning of the bottomless capacity for both human cruelty and human survival.

WE PUBLISHED THE story of a child bride in Rajasthan. The story of a pair of orphaned brothers whose father stabbed their mother to death in Bucharest, a group of Romanian street kids who stayed warm by living underground in the sewer system. We met students in Honduras rebuilding their country after a devastating hurricane and subsequent mudslides left their neighborhoods in ruins at the bottom of a mountain range; kids in Cuba living under the U.S. blockade in poverty, showering with buckets, playing soccer in flip-flops. Women in Cambodia who'd been gang-raped for vengeance or for sport.

The year we went to Lhasa, there had been increased reports of bombings by the Chinese in the country, and streams of refugees were walking—a monthlong journey—across the Himalayas to Kathmandu before making their way to Dharamsala, where the Dalai Lama lived. At the same time, India and Nepal were conducting nuclear tests, and the world was on alert. We published a series of stories on the bombings, the refugees, the nuclear threat. We interviewed the Dalai Lama the day after Bill Clinton admitted to having had an improper relationship with Monica Lewinsky and I stumbled through an awkward apology on "behalf of all Americans" to him, which made him laugh raucously. We met a Tibetan couple who'd walked from Lhasa to Kathmandu, and then onward to Dharamsala to give birth to their child in freedom. We met a woman who had carried her boyfriend for the last five days of their journey over the Himalayas, after he lost his legs to frostbite.

We met women in prisons and women in poverty, women controlled by men and cast out by men. Women whose lives and aspirations had been stolen; we met mothers who'd buried their daughters far too young, and daughters who'd watched their mothers burn. A child bride in

Romania who, at twelve, sat surrounded by her family as they carefully monitored the questions I asked, and the answers she gave. A woman whose life was eclipsed by caring for her husband, a war veteran who'd fought with the South Vietnamese Army and who now suffered from post-traumatic stress, alcoholism, and what seemed to be bipolar disorder. To calm himself, he would paint. Or he would beat her. One afternoon on the outskirts of Bucharest, we met a woman who had been forced to have five children. Now, at thirty-two, she was a grandmother. I didn't intentionally gravitate toward stories of women; I was interested in human rights, which often boiled down to this question: Who was winning and who was losing? And over and over again, country after country, story after story, it was the men who were winning and the women who were losing. Not always. Not everywhere. But most often, and by a wide, wide margin.

IN 2002, CAMBODIA announced it was going to be starting the war crimes tribunal—finally—against the Khmer Rouge. When Ann and I had visited there in 1996, the country was still under martial law, land-mines were scattered around the rural areas, and new killing fields were found often. Evidence of the genocide was everywhere. The most famous killing fields still had bits of bone, patches of cloth, and kitchen utensils embedded in the dirt as we walked around. I remember bending down to look more closely at what I eventually realized were the tiny hooks of a bra, the rest of the fabric still half-buried. I had seen browned teeth, most with roots attached. Soldiers with AK-47s stood guard in Phnom Penh on street corners, all along the riverside, and near the royal palace. The roads were unpaved, the electricity grid sporadic. Information about the geno-cide wouldn't even make it into standard high school textbooks until 2005. Just months after we visited, civil unrest erupted across the country and a grenade thrown into a Phnom Penh protest killed seventeen people.

Cambodia had haunted me since Ann and I had visited. Tuol Sleng seemed to burn its way into my very neurology. For years I tried to describe in my journals that empty place of ghosts. The stained floors, the manacles and crude wooden cells. There was a hand-painted sign that was allegedly a list of Pol Pot's rules, though by the time I moved there, in 2003, the list had been professionally printed (some scholars believe the list was created and installed by the Vietnamese, after the invasion of 1979). They included this: *While getting lashes or electrification you must not cry at all.*

I THINK I was slower than most journalists to recognize not only the privilege of being able to flit in and out of places, but also the limitations of stories told through my particular western lens. It would be years still before I would glimpse my own white privilege and it would take longer still to define it. But even early on I recognized that landing somewhere and staying for a month or two meant I could only burrow so deep into any place or story. For nearly a year, I pondered how to address this, because it felt to me like a serious and growing limitation. I could get a magazine story out of it, but what good was a magazine story if it didn't compel change? Was a single story enough? Perhaps I should quit writing altogether, I thought. I wondered what it would be like to work at the State Department. Or go to law school.

As a freelance writer, I was eternally broke, though the *broke* of my adulthood in no way mirrored the *broke* of my teenage years. Broke then meant I might not eat; broke now meant I paid only the minimum on my credit card. Once, my boyfriend found me curled up like a snail atop a bed, sobbing because I was going through a particularly thin financial stretch, and I told him in one long sentence how I should have gone to law school, but that also maybe aid work would be cool, though I had no idea how one went about such a career, and the worst part about any of these possibilities was how they took me from the thing I loved most, the thing I had come to rely on to make sense of the world: my writing. He said the equivalent of "there, there" and reminded me we had a monkey to catch.*

---

* Macgyver was a monkey with an infected tail who lived in my friend Sue's Honduran island home, along with eight dogs and a deer named Cometa who believed herself a dog. Twice a year, Sue flew in a vet from the mainland, and the locals would bring their animals to get fixed or vaccinated or checked. I was acting as the physician's assistant's barely competent assistant. We were wrangling the animals for surgery on her dining room table. Dogs lay throughout the house in varying stages of anesthesia. Macgyver was a right asshole, but I loved him and fed him peanuts while he lay on my stomach with his bandaged tail.

When the tribunals in Cambodia were announced, I knew I had to cover them.

My boyfriend, Paul, worked then for a British company called Centurion that trained journalists and aid workers going to hostile environments. Paul had retired from the British military, the Army Commando unit. Every other month he taught the course in Virginia, and I'd fly there to see him. Or he'd fly to Chicago, where I lived. I took dozens of trips to England, and then down to Dorset where he lived. I was shocked when, after several weeks of consideration, he said he'd quit his job and move to Cambodia with me—a place he'd never even been. We arrived in late summer 2003. He was the first boyfriend I'd ever lived with. I was thirty-four when we moved to Cambodia. We planned to stay for one year if we hated it, and two years if we loved it. We were there for six.

Twenty-Nine

House addresses in Phnom Penh were chosen by owners based on what they believed were their lucky numbers. We were House Fifty-Five on Street 350. One of six house number fifty-fives along a two-block stretch. When we described *which* house number fifty-five was ours, we would say "closest to the alligator farm on the corner of Street Ninety-Five" (by the time we moved, it was a nightclub named Martini's). The alligator farm was not, so far as I could tell, an actual working farm, despite the handful of dusty alligators I'd seen there in various stages of laziness.

After we moved in, our landlord's dog, a tall, skinny thing reminiscent of a German Shepherd, had a litter of puppies. One day, while the puppies were only a couple of weeks old, another puppy—this one black and white and herself only a few weeks old—wandered in. This was considered a good-luck omen, because dogs can see spirits, and sometimes spirits can inhabit the bodies of dogs. We believed she came from a house across from Shit River and joked that she'd been a street dog for seven arduous minutes. This little dog fed off the mother right along with her own litter of puppies. The landlord said he had too many dogs and if we wanted a puppy, we could have one. Or two. Or three. Our landlord was a kind man who worked at the port of Sihanoukville, a five-hour drive. He'd stay all week there, and then come back to his family in Phnom Penh. All weekend he'd go shirtless, with a checked sarong wrapped around his waist, his smooth belly protruding from the cloth. He and his wife had been married in one of the Khmer Rouge arranged marriages, where ceremonies would be held for as many as two hundred people at once. Her mother lived with them but spoke very little. When I'd go downstairs, I'd see her hanging squid over their fence to dry, or putting out wet laundry, and she'd offer a betel-nut-red smile, most of her teeth outlined in black. Their nephew, Pousith, who also lived with them, was our main point of contact because he spoke excellent English.

One day, we heard a dog frantically yelping and walked out of our apartment to find the landlord's nephew—a boy of fourteen—kicking the little black and white dog down the stairs. She tumbled in a ball because her legs were too little to navigate them. I found Pousith, and said, "We *will* take one of these puppies after all." I pointed to the black and white one. "That one." Loung Ung, who happened to be visiting Cambodia and staying with us, said we should name her Khmow. Loung had lost her parents and several siblings in the genocide, a story she recounts in her memoir *First They Killed My Father*. We had met a decade earlier after my first trip to Cambodia. Loung told us Khmow means black or black spirit (and is probably more accurately spelled Kmau). We turned Khmow over and could not tell if she was a boy or girl dog. Her paws slipped on our tile floor as she tried to sniff her way around this new environment. We took her to a vet, asked if he knew what kind of dog she was. He nodded.

"Well?" we asked.

"This's a Cambodian dog."

I HAD LIVED in Cambodia for just a few months by the time we got Khmow, the tribunals regularly delayed by questions of funding, jurisprudence, location. In the meantime, I found other stories. Cambodia was the only developing country in the world then that was trying to create an entire garment industry that was sweatshop-free. They'd built it up throughout the 1990s with help from a trade deal under the Clinton administration. By the time I moved there, it accounted for 90 percent of the country's exports. Garment workers got vacation and maternity leave paid, they were given breast-feeding breaks and were free to join unions. But now Cambodia was poised to join the World Trade Organization, which meant they would lose their most-favored-nation trade status with the United States, and it was anyone's guess whether the industry would survive. My reporting on this, which began as a story for public radio's *This American Life*, would eventually become my first book.

That day we got Khmow, I flew to Niger for three weeks for a story on a group of American urogynecologists who were doing pro bono fistula surgeries at the main hospital in Niamey. A fistula is a hole in the tissue, most often between the vagina and the anus, that forms when contractions go on for days and days. In the west, fistulas are rare because of the availability of c-sections, but in developing countries or poor, rural areas, they can be common, especially among young girls whose bodies are not ready for childbirth. Women with fistulas leak urine or feces if they're not surgically fixed, and often this leads to ostracization. In most fistula cases, the baby dies, so women are not only cast out of their villages, but they've also lost their children, and thus their perceived value to the community. Many dozens of women lived behind the hospital in a makeshift community they called the Fistula Village. Some were as young as thirteen, others as old as sixty.

I watched a dozen surgeries a day in two different operating theaters. Women came from all over the country, walking in droves, to have their fistulas fixed. Some would return home, but others stayed in the Fistula Village, where they were poor but had a measure of autonomy and independence and they cared for one another. Some of the women had been butchered when their local doctors had tried to patch them up. For twelve hours a day I would listen to the doctors call out for needles, ask for sutures, swabs, more light. The operating rooms were dim, the floors dirty, the local surgeons all men and the nurses all women. I wrote this story for *Glamour*, which despite its reputation had covered serious women's issues around the globe for decades, even reporting on things like life for women under the Taliban as far back as 1996. (The rampant sexism in the literary world when it comes to women's magazines has not improved much in the past thirty years, I'm sorry to say.)

It was actually an assignment with *Glamour* magazine in Afghanistan, just after September 11, 2001, that brought Paul into my life. I signed up to take a hostile environment course for journalists before I went to Kabul. He was one of the British instructors, all of them former commandos. He was handsome, a little goofy, did not subscribe to the machismo of most military men, and immediately made the world feel safer. Unlike me, he was exactly who you wanted beside you in an emergency. I told one friend after I met him that I could be hit by a car, I could be shot and left with a sucking chest wound, I could be facing a flood, fire, mudslide, hurricane, tornado, and he would know what to do. I once came upon him in our bedroom with Khmow laid on her back, all four of her paws in the air. Paul was feeling around her groin area with two fingers in a manner I would call "intimate." I stood in the doorway, alarmed, and said, "Uh. What're you doing to our dog?"

He looked up but didn't move his hands from her groin. "Feeling for her femoral artery," he said, "in case we ever need to stanch the flow of blood." Luckily, we have never needed to stanch the flow of our dog's blood.

Paul and I would marry on the south coast of Cambodia atop an elephant we'd paid for in banana trees after a jasmine-water blessing by monks. Khmow would trot me down the grassy aisle to Paul, waiting under a Jewish chuppah made of silk and bamboo and stuck into the sand. Ann would be my sole bridesmaid. Don would come with his new wife, a Cambodian American doctor named Soleak whom I'd met in Phnom Penh and introduced him to. ("You don't even know me," she laughed when I suggested she meet my friend, Don, from Chicago. "I know," I told her. "But I know him.") Our friend Tapley would officiate. And Cambodia would become the place I lived the longest since leaving Pittsburgh more than twenty years earlier. It would also be the place where the darkness of my own past receded.

In part, because I carried inside me the tiny seedling of a girl.

Thirty

One morning, I woke to the sound of monks chanting into a tinny speaker. A large tent spanned our house and continued all the way across the street. For the next week, the road would be impassable for cars. Enormous aluminum pots on open flames held various soups, a dozen tables with chairs were brought in. We smelled incense and noodles. A white alligator flag, the sign of death and mourning, hung outside the tent signaling a funeral week for our neighbor. At dawn, the monk had come and begun his melodic chanting—called a smot—offering prayers to the departed. He sounded almost hypnotic. The Khmer believe that the soul stays in the room with the body at the time of separation, and that the soul will be initially distressed at this separation. The monk's chant was a way to ease the soul's worry on its way to the next life. People came at all hours of the day and evening that week to pay homage. They gave offerings so that his spirit would not be hungry or broke or lacking in his next life. An unsettled soul causes mischief to the living.

The first day of the funeral, Khmow sat in the corner of the living room and looked up toward the ceiling. Hour after hour, she stared into that corner. When I called her, she would turn and look at me for a moment, then go back to her staring. All that day, she seemed to not move. Late in the afternoon, Pousith came up to invite us down to the funeral to eat and pay our respects, and I pointed to Khmow, told him she'd been in that position all day. Staring up at the corner of the wall.

"Yes, of course," he said. He explained to me that Khmow could probably see our neighbor's spirit. Pousith was sitting, as he always did, straight-backed on the edge of our teak couch. The wood was so hard we'd had a long, black cushion made for it in silk and cotton. Here cotton was the splurge at the market. Silk was always cheaper. "He's waiting for you to say goodbye," Pousith told me. "So his spirit can move on."

I SPENT THESE years in what felt to me like a sacred pursuit: to learn as best I could how different lives could be lived, different belief systems understood. Several years into my life in Cambodia, I was sent to Vietnam on assignment with the American military to search for men missing in action from the Vietnam War—or what they often call in Vietnam the American War of Aggression. Sometimes simply the American War. We took a helicopter to the A Shau Valley, near the DMZ just eight kilometers from the border with Laos. At eight hundred meters high on top of the mountain, we hung in a cloud forest in the midst of rainy season. Banana, banyan, and cassia trees surrounded us in verdant shades, the dirt like curried sludge. The jungle wilted in the humidity. Poisonous snakes, leeches, stinging ants, biting centipedes, and disease-carrying mosquitoes abounded. Locusts and birds created a stereophonic orchestra, and the mist was so heavy that the human forms took on a ghostly quality from even just a few meters away. In his short story collection *The Things They Carried*, Tim O'Brien wrote about the spookiness of the A Shau Valley, how voices echo in the darkness and ghost soldiers appear from between the trees. The characters carry a bone-deep fear, the experiential moment overpowering their own cultural beliefs, the kind of enemy that none of their weaponry can vanquish.

On a small, covered platform built of bamboo, several Vietnamese minders smoked. I was there with another journalist. We each had our own assigned "minder," a Vietnamese government official traveling with us to make sure we didn't go outside the bounds of what was sanctioned. The other journalist was generous with her knowledge. She had already given me one excellent piece of advice: "Don't talk so much."

We were searching for one soldier, a Huey helicopter pilot who had been shot down in 1967 along with three of his crew. The other crewmembers had been found and rescued within forty-eight hours. But despite several rescue attempts in the days and weeks afterward, enemy fire had proved too heavy to retrieve him. Along with an American archeologist and ten military personnel on this dig, there were also seventy Vietnamese, who walked two hours up the mountain in flip-flops from their village of Houng Phong. So far on this dig, the group had found a rusted bayonet from an M-16, a whip antenna from a radio, a load-bearing equipment fastener, a number of shell casings, and what's known as a data plate: a metal disk that bore the serial number, make, and model of an aircraft. It matched the downed Huey.

A compass, a survival knife, a boot, and a scattering of globules formed from the melted windshield. Dog tags, the data plate, a wedding ring. The United States spent millions of dollars every year searching for missing soldiers from various twentieth- and twenty-first-century wars. The effort began after World War I. The archeologist in charge of the site told me that not many other cultures go this far to "honor those who died."

But honor is a matter of definition. In Vietnam, hundreds of thousands of soldiers were still missing from the French and American wars—wars that the Vietnamese government estimates killed upwards of three million between 1945 and 1975. The souls of those hundreds of thousands of missing are believed to be wandering the earth, forever unsettled. The government has a department of clairvoyants to help suffering families reunite with the souls of their departed. The mediums will sometimes create two-sided maps of the terrain where a death occurred; one side is for the living to read, and the other for the dead. During the war years, if a death occurred in jungle terrain, the living soldiers would sometimes write the name of their fallen comrade, along with his home village and the date of death, and then seal the tiny paper in wax and place it in the mouth of his corpse in the hope that he might someday be found and buried. Thousands of reunions have happened. Some of the country's most famous mediums have been featured in international news stories channeling these hungry ghosts, offering details and memories to suffering families. In both Vietnam and Cambodia, it's morally crucial for families to make offerings to the dead—fruit, coun-terfeit money, flowers, and incense—to appease and honor their spirits, to settle them in their afterlife. In these hallowed places—a pagoda in Cambodia, an elaborate gravesite in Vietnam—the world of the living and the world of the spirits will meet. Reunifications transform the dead, from unsettled ghosts to spirits that can help the living.

This, I suspect, is in part why Cambodians seemed so rarely to visit Tuol Sleng. It did not have a spiritual component, at least during the years I lived nearby. There was no place to give an offering, no spirit house to provide rambutan, or lychee or longan, no sand-filled bowl in which to light incense and offer prayers. It is a monument not to the dead, but to death; and it offers nothing to the living.

Thirty-One

Before I moved to Cambodia, I wondered how people had moved past the genocide, which is to say, how did the victims live among their former perpetrators in what seemed at least *some* kind of harmony? Once I moved there, I understood that part of the answer was that the older generation said little to nothing about those years of suffering to their children. An historical erasure. For self-salvation, for survival. The grandchildren of survivors tended to be the ones who would draw out the stories of their elders, learn of the horror. This was true of the Holocaust, and had slowly begun in Cambodia, too. By the time I left, class trips would sometimes visit Tuol Sleng. The war crimes tribunal, which finally began in 2007, encouraged survivors to visit.

One morning I interviewed a woman in a province several hours outside of Phnom Penh. We sat on the wood floor of the home on stilts she shared with her daughter and son-in-law and their children. The kitchen was underneath the house. Chickens wandered about; I was warned to watch my ankles because village chickens were aggressive. The woman told me her story of surviving the Khmer Rouge. She lost her husband. She found the body of one of her children bloated and long dead in the river near her hut. She worked in the rice paddies all day every day, on the brink of starvation for years. She smiled as she told the story; it is common for Cambodians to smile, or even laugh, when they are uncomfortable. I was taking notes as she talked, looking up at her every few seconds. When she finished, she pulled a piece of glass from the pocket of her sarong and popped it in her mouth, gumming the smooth side to calm herself. Then, with barely a pause, she launched into the story again, word for word.

It was only after small groups of young people working for a nongovernmental organization went out into the countryside and interviewed village elders, gathered stories of the Khmer Rouge years, that school textbooks included a section on the genocide. People tuned in to the tribunal on their televisions. Only five people were ever charged, including the infamous leader of Tuol Sleng, Kaing Guek Eav, who went by his nickname of Duch and claimed to have become a Christian after the fall of the Khmer Rouge. He said that God would be his judge. It was the closest any of the five of them would come to acknowledging their actions.

One afternoon, I sat with Khmow and a friend of mine at a café across from a park named for Prime Minister Hun Sen (given the lack of rules around pets, we took Khmow everywhere, even building a seat for her atop our motorcycles). In the spring, the flame trees bloomed all along Hun Sen Park. It was one of my favorite views in the city, perched on the second-floor terrace of the café, looking down at an enormous backdrop of red blooms.

I sipped my lime drink and watched the park. All at once a small fire erupted. Someone must be cooking outdoors, I thought. I watched for a few seconds, my mind taking too long to process what I was seeing. That underneath the flames was a man, his charring skin turning a multitude of colors, magenta and ocher and gray. A gas can sat behind him, and beyond the gas can, the Independence Monument. Shaped like a lotus flower and colored crimson, it marked the heart of the city. The man was silhouetted against it. Seconds later, a woman in a sarong threw a bucket of water on him.

My friend and I stood at the balcony. The man toppled forward, bent over, still half in flames. There were no ambulances in Cambodia then. We wondered if his self-immolation was a protest, against corruption, against land-grabbing, against the tribunal. Many people felt the fifty-million-dollar proposed cost of the tribunal would be better spent on alleviating poverty or building infrastructure. Maybe the man was tired of the sex trafficking, the acid attacks, the political killings. Others came and tossed water on him, and then someone covered him with a blanket and put the fire out fully. A van came, and the small crowd scooped him up to be taken to Calmette Hospital.

He lived only a few more hours.

The next day, the newspaper ran a story about him. He hadn't been protesting corruption or politics or human rights violations. His wife had cheated on him, and he had fallen into despair. I began to think this was how trauma seeped out in Cambodia, in public displays of private pain. It lived among and within people all over the country. They were a generation removed from unfathomable tragedy. It had left Cambodians with scars, passed on through blood and through those things of which they dared not speak. The kids in modern Cambodia carry the consequences of mass murder, they carry the distrust, the anger, the apathy. If there is a larger context at all in which to place the burning man, maybe it is this: he lived surrounded by an unutterable pain, among people desperate to fend off their own desperation.

There is a cynical name for a certain kind of travel to places like Tuol Sleng: genocide tourism. You can read academic papers on it. Cambodia is on the list, and all the concentration camps spread across Germany and Poland and beyond, and Rwanda is there as well. There is something that travelers who visit such places are attempting to touch, some deep part of their own humanity, I believe. Maybe there is a solidarity in these places. A way to give one's own story necessary context, not to compare, but to acknowledge an infinite human continuum of despair and grief and, if we're lucky, hope.

It had been rainy season when Ann and I visited Tuol Sleng in 1996. August. And the air was heavy with grit and heat. Patches of green grass were divided by red earth walkways, and the wet colors were luminescent, almost garish. The roads around Tuol Sleng were unpaved; they would not, in fact, be paved until about three years into my stay in the neighborhood. If the rains were too long in coming and the dust rose up, people would take buckets of water and toss them onto the dirt roads.

There were no lights on in the museum, and so the cells were darker than usual. When I ran up those stairs, whisper-yelling Ann's name, I began to feel something beyond myself, something akin perhaps to what my father felt as he stood in the congregation with his arms raised toward the ceiling and prayers on his lips. I would reject what my father believed in—the Christian God, Jesus, the Holy Trinity, salvation, a literal heaven and hell—but on that day and in that place, I had to acknowledge there was something more than what could be explained by my five primary senses.

During my time in Cambodia, something in me began to soften and crumble, a long-held cynicism about spirituality and what might be out there. The mistrust of anyone or anything that spoke about powers beyond human abilities or understanding. The evangelicalism of my youth had turned me off so much that when Ann and I traveled, I would wait outside if she wanted to visit some renowned and beautiful church. In Italy, I waited outside for her as she reverently visited cathedral after cathedral. She went to the Vatican and I stayed in our hotel. She visited churches in Spain. And in Honduras. And in so many other countries. But here, in this place that was wildly foreign to me, I began to seek out pagodas for the quiet, the reverence. I loved the smell of the incense, the cool darkness of the spaces, tiled in ocher or red. Buddhas in a thousand sizes perched on altars with thick, dripping candles the color of marigolds. I began to go on the anniversary of my mother's death. Times when I wanted to be alone, to think, to untangle some question I had about a piece I was writing, or to think through a memory, or a problem.

I am not Buddhist. I am not Christian or Catholic or Muslim or Hindu or Sikh or Mormon. I am at best culturally Jewish—defined at least in part by the loss of something that I no longer fully even remember. The Jewish holidays and food, the Jewish prayers and rituals. Judaism, this thing I know now only very superficially, becomes a stand-in and a symbol for all that my mother was to me, how very much I lost when I lost her. There is something richly unknowable by intellect but felt by the soul in the silence of such a hallowed memory. A death, a birth, a wish, a sorrow. What we believe and what we hold faith in has as much to do with geography, which is to say culture, as much to do with the very fate of our birth, as anything. So I hold no faith of my own. But pagodas become my version of kaddish, the place where my past and my present meet. I go not to pray, but to ponder. And perhaps this foreign place was where I could make peace with what my father believed. Not to accept it or condone it, but to stop judging him for needing it.

There was something else about Tuol Sleng that was important, though, beyond the ghosts and the darkness. At night, after it closed to tourists, it opened as a parking garage. Boeung Keng Kang III was not a neighborhood built for cars, and many homes had nowhere at night to park their cars. It was not unusual to see Camrys and Daelim motorcycles parked for the night in someone's living room. But at Tuol Sleng, for two thousand riel, or fifty cents, you could park from eight o'clock at night until eight in the morning, an hour before the gates opened for tourism. Paul and I each had a motorcycle for the first three years that we lived in Phnom Penh, but eventually I sold mine and we bought a cobbled-together SUV, a Kia Sportage body with a Mitsubishi engine and air-conditioning.

Then we, too, became nighttime patrons of the Tuol Sleng Genocide Museum parking garage. We'd pull in to the gate and hand money to one of several guards hanging out in hammocks as a soccer game played on an old television hooked up to a car battery. At first it was hilarious, and then an odd fact we'd share among our friends, and eventually just part of our daily routine. There was the horror and the memory, there were the ghosts and the darkness, but there was also the absolute utilitarian need to go on.

Thirty-Two

My stateroom is pitch black. I can't see my own hand, but something catches my eye, a darkened shadow moving in my periphery. I am not fully awake. I see in the black air two legs, disembodied, billowing pants. I bolt upright and fall out of bed, a long fall because I am in the top bunk and pain shoots through my ankles as I rush three steps and flip on the light. The shadow is my own pants, hanging from the television, the olive khakis I've been wearing every single day for three weeks now, airing them out as best I can at night, back on at dawn to fly in a helicopter mornings, from the aircraft carrier to what's left of the shores of Aceh, Indonesia.

I have been to the sites of natural disasters in my reporting. This is another scale entirely.

The ocean rendered human cartography obsolete. Killed hundreds of thousands of people across half a dozen countries in mere seconds. Destroyed crops, buildings, homes, forests, beaches, hotels, vehicles, roads. People stand atop island mountains now, stranded by brown, murky water on what was shoreline just a day before, their homes submerged. The tsunami happened the day after Christmas. Body counts trickled in and then spiraled. A hundred, a thousand, ten thousand, a hundred thousand, a quarter of a million. I watched as the news tried to keep up with the numbers of the dead and missing, the inevitable questions: were the Thai islands ruined for tourism? How had the animals known to retreat? Why was there no tsunami warning in place in most of these countries?

My friend Kris, a photographer living in Singapore, called and we arranged to meet as soon as possible in Bangkok, figuring out the rest as we went. I packed two sets of clothing, emergency medical supplies, iodine to purify water, a charcoal mask to keep out the smell of the dead, paper, pens, galoshes, Ziploc bags to use for everything from covering wounds to waterproofing notes to holding soiled laundry, a Swiss Army knife, a compass, twine, gloves, granola bars, a tarp, flashlight and batteries, and a first aid kit.

From Bangkok, we made our way to Pattaya, Thailand, where we boarded the *Abraham Lincoln* along with two dozen other journalists. Kris got stuck with the rest of the male journalists down in the crew racks, where the beds were stacked in threes and privacy was a mere curtain. One other female journalist and I were given a stateroom. But she left after a week, and so I had it all to myself. There was a small TV bolted to the wall. A small sink, a small closet, small bunk beds. Everything in miniature. But compared to Kris I was living large. I hung my pants from the television, washed out my T-shirts and underwear in the six-inch sink.

The helicopters are first come, first served for the journalists, so we rise at four A.M. and line up, sit when we can. The main priority is getting water and food to stranded people on the mountain islands. "Seat" is a euphemism; if there is room among the five-gallon water bottles and boxes of ramen and energy bars, we wedge ourselves, or sometimes just sit atop all of it. The helicopters are flying in ways they were not built to fly, making multiple trips back and forth from dawn till dusk, over-loaded with supplies in the morning and injured people in the after-noon. In Aceh there is nowhere to land, no solid ground. The water has turned everything to sludge. The remnants of foundations are the safest landing zones, but under them it is all slurry now, and the weight buries them and the choppers start to sink, so the pilots max out the engines, keep the revs as high as they'll go, and we push the food and water out as fast as we can, screaming at the villagers who collect the aid to mind the blades lowering as we get sucked into the muck. We land for only seconds at a time, frantically push out food and water, and then we are up, into the sky again. I am here as a journalist, but first as a human being.

Kris and I hop on and off the helicopters like they're public transpor-tation. We interview the commander of the *Abraham Lincoln*, who is from Illinois and asks me if I'm a Democrat or a Republican. When I answer, he shakes his head once and says, "Well, it's all right. You're not bad." I take notes with a fuzzy-topped purple pen. The *New York Times* and the *Washington Post* both have reporters here, men, who eye me with suspicion. Suspicion is not the right word. Disdain? Quiet ridicule? But the pen is a talking point. Kids love it. I carry a half dozen and give them away. I'm writing for the *New Republic*, and for *Slate*.

My first rainy season in Cambodia, the water came pouring through our dining room window, even though we lived on the third floor. I don't mean that it leaked a little, or that it dripped down the walls. I mean that the force of the water coming from the sky shot through and around the window five feet into our dining room as if we weren't inside at all. Paul hollered and ran to get towels, but I laughed and danced around because it was too absurd to believe. "It's raining inside," I cried. *"Inside!"* (This is all anyone would ever need to know about which of us to choose in an emergency.)

Days later, we were on our motorcycle when the monsoons seemed to rush from the sky and within seconds the water was running up to our ankles, then our calves. Brown, slushing water, the rain so hard you had to turn your head sideways or it stung your eyes. Cars stalled and Vespas, with their low engines and tiny tires, were useless. Paul and I looked around, and people were smiling at one another as we sat in traffic. It was like the first snow of winter, when neighbors emerge from their cocooned homes to squint in the glare and kids hurl their bodies into snow piles, wild with laughter. The rain cut the intense heat of hot season, strangers laughing, holding their faces to the onslaught of the water, and we laughed, too. The time of the Mango Rains had begun—announcing the season of the fruit.

KRIS AND I spend an afternoon in a makeshift medical tent. Patients on cots groan from bloodied bodies, or they sleep. Some sit up and talk to family members. A boy, twelve years old, can't find his family. He is not injured, but he wanders around the tent barefoot. I tell him to wait for me here, wait until I return. I catch a helicopter, go back to my stateroom, and return to the boy several hours later, offer my galoshes and my Swiss Army knife.

Aceh, Indonesia.

Thailand and Sri Lanka were also hit, but Aceh, Indonesia, got the worst of it, and when the UN came in with their white SUVs, the roads had been swallowed, and there was nowhere to park their heavy vehicles, so they had to build a parking lot before everything else, and then figure out new maps. We Google to see where the shoreline was before and where it is now. Aid pours in, but it remains in warehouses inland with no way, yet, to get it to the people who need it except by the overworked, overloaded helicopters. Where do you start? The injured need to be evacuated. Food and water need to be delivered urgently. Roads need to be built for that to happen. And it all needs to be done immediately.

My first natural disaster was Hurricane Mitch, in October 1998 in Honduras, when it rained so hard for so long that entire mountains slid into the city of Tegucigalpa below. Ann and I stood on a mound one day and our guide said, "This used to be a highway. We could hear people stuck in their cars, honking wildly for help. And then day by day, the horns faded." I wanted to run away, to flee from the dead in their vehicular graves underneath my feet. But I didn't. I stood. I wrote his story in my notebook. He told me he had lost half his neighborhood.

At dinner one night, Kris and I sit with two navy doctors who talk about the urgency of getting the most seriously injured to medical care. They can't rely on a common language, of course, and there needs to be a way to triage the most serious cases. How to do this from inside the open door of a helicopter hundreds of feet up in the air? They can't call down over the noise, even if they spoke Bahasa Indonesia. They don't want to waste precious space on nonemergent injuries. We are eating around communal tables, buffet style. The doctors say the helicopter pilots are enjoying this moment in the spotlight. Usually only the fighter jets get any attention. *Top Gun*, never *Top Chopper*. Here, the fighter pilots are benched. They tease one another about their uselessness.

The two doctors sit with scratch paper and concoct a rudimentary system using enormous rolls of tape. Red or yellow? Red, I believe. They rush off to go find one of the ship's translators. An X in red tape on a mountain island will signal a casualty who needs immediate evacuation. No X will mean the normal food and water drop. Injuries, maybe, but not life-threatening. It could not be simpler. The two doctors fly in a chopper up and down the coast tossing out enormous rolls of tape with the instructions written in Bahasa Indonesia and by the next afternoon, giant Xes have appeared on some of the mountain islands. Multiple helicopters fly up and down the coast picking up the injured. The messaging saves dozens and dozens of lives, maybe hundreds. Maybe more. Every writer has an untold story that haunts her. These two doctors are mine.

One morning, Kris and I catch a helicopter to the base of operations set up by the United Nations and the World Food Programme, and then inland. A river running perpendicular from the city of Banda Aceh to the sea is now filled to bursting with debris. Broken couches and dining room chairs, furniture frames, waterlogged chunks of foam, pieces of drawers, silverware, baby plates and the bars of cribs, dozens of odd shoes, broken glass and mirrors, clothing, hairbrushes and toys, suitcases and curtains, and atop it all, cats poke their heads down and up, walking and sniffing and chewing, and Kris understands before I do. He gets it, and his eyes close and he turns away from me and bends over. He might have vomited. It's hard for us to talk through our charcoal masks, but I look down at the river more carefully and see. Within the splinters of homes are human limbs, camouflaged in the pale wood. An arm, a leg, what might be part of a shoulder. The cats feast.

The body collectors are parked not far from the river. When they find bodies, they wrap them up in white tarps and gently place them in the back of the truck. Several dozen bodies are already piled up. In thick-soled mud boots, two collectors walk across the sludgy yard of a house with only two walls left, and they return moments later carrying a woman by the arms and legs, her long hair black, stringy, full of grit and hanging across her face. They reach us, gently lay her down on their open tarp. Lying flat you can see. She is pregnant. *Was* pregnant. They wrap her and climb up the truck ladder and lay her with the others. Then they go back for more. I look at Kris and he is crying. He is a tall man, one of the funniest people I know. He's American, but he's lived in Singapore for twenty years. He does not wipe away his tears or try to hide his face, or even look away from me. I look at the pregnant woman, piled atop a dozen other faceless dead victims, and I try to summon sadness, some kind of feeling at all. I look back toward the cats and the river. Nothing. There is no feeling.

WHEN I COVER these stories, I think of my mother, and I think of the ocean as I watched it for hours at sea. These two figures from my past. My mother grew up near the oceanfront in Swampscott. Her mother breathed it in every day. It is not some great discovery that water kills, that water is more powerful than our attempts to control it or contain it or worship it or study it or live atop it or explore it from within. Water that nourished my soul for all those months aboard the ship. Water that took this pregnant woman's life. Beauty and violence converging. There are other natural disasters that happen in the world. Earthquakes and fires. I cover water. Perhaps because it feels most like a rupture to me. How what you love is also what is most deadly.

There is a miracle that happens every year in Cambodia, between the Mekong River and the Tonle Sap (tonle means river in Khmer). The Mango Rains in May give way to monsoon floods, and the Mekong, which starts in Tibet more than three thousand miles north of Vietnam's

Mekong Delta, flows so powerfully down to Phnom Penh that the sheer velocity of it forces the Sap River to reverse course. The Sap River deepens by more than ten meters and fills up the Sap Lake near Siem Reap by thousands of square kilometers. Floating villages dot the area. When Ann and I first visited Siem Reap, the streets were unpaved and there were just two guest houses for backpackers. By the time I live in Cambodia, tourists are so plentiful and the rate of building hotels and infrastructure so intense that the entire water table of Siem Reap lowers every year in a slow-motion environmental catastrophe.

The Mekong River begins to split into the Mekong Delta in southern Vietnam. The delta's small rivers and inlets and swamps feed into the East Vietnam Sea, which feeds into the South China Sea and eventually into the Pacific Ocean. In Phnom Penh when the Mekong hits the southern tail of the Tonle Sap and reverses its flow, it's like a glorious trick of nature. The Water Festival, held every year, celebrates this reversal, a signal of abundance for those whose livelihoods depend on the lake.

That the Mekong and Sap don't annually burst their banks or flood the city or otherwise cause damage and destruction is part of the miracle to me. It's the only place in the world where this happens. "All water has a perfect memory," Toni Morrison wrote, "and is forever trying to get back to where it was."

Thirty-Three

The light in my apartment washes to an intense yellow, a pre-monsoon rain where the atmosphere takes on a mustard hue. It's like no light I've ever seen anywhere else in the world. My apartment is perpetually covered in a thin layer of red dust from the unpaved road outside; a For Sale sign appeared on the gate of the alligator farm a week earlier. I popped in once to see the sweeping dirt courtyard, the dusty palms in red clay pots, and concrete troughs with white peeling paint. Five alligators, babies I think. Many Cambodian fables begin or end with various creatures outsmarted by alligators. They are revered because they can live both on land and in water, and because they have only one predator. Humans.

In the warm afternoon, I sense that I am not alone. *Sense* is not a strong enough word. I know it as surely as I know the shape of my own body. There is a presence in the room that I can't see with my eyes but is nevertheless as real as the passion fruit vines growing outside my living room door.

I know this presence. Fully, without a hint of doubt. Had she come to me earlier, when I lived in Chicago, I would have been fearful. I would have turned on every light in my house, played my stereo full blast, called someone, perhaps even fled. Had this presence come even in the first months after I moved to Cambodia, I wouldn't have believed it. But I have been here for years now. I have heard the stories.

So when she comes to me, I know it is her, and I sit down on the couch in my living room. I see her. I feel her. I *know* her.

The Khmer believe that solitude is foolish; it is asking for trouble. But I crave it.

A print of an Apsara dancer from Angkor Wat hangs on one wall, wood carvings of two praying Buddhas on another. "I won't believe this when you're gone," I tell her. Cementing me to the moment by speaking aloud, my own recording, my own fact checker. *No. This truly happened. You felt her. You heard her.*

"Well, I got your boobs," I say. Size D. Sometimes people crack jokes. Sometimes people offer an appraisal, like it's been invited. Large-breasted women know. "Thanks a lot for that." Those life-giving, sexualized organs; I'd had my first mammogram, holding in tears, at twenty-nine. *Diagnosed at thirty. Dead at thirty-five.* It was a doomsday mantra. It was a curse.

I can sense her single laugh. The bamboo mat under my feet shifts. Geckos climb the walls; moths the size of fists cling to the screens.

I tell my mom that Grandma Erma, her mother, has died. That David and I cleaned out her house and I'd found my mother's French class notebook and a 1940s edition of *Alice in Wonderland*, a gift to her from her father. A literary magazine from her high school with her listed as the editor on the masthead. Pictures of her on dates, homecoming maybe, school functions. I didn't know any of the boys she so casually stood beside.

What to do with all the photos? Who were these people, anyway? What to do with the kitchenware? The items in my grandma's bedside drawer, the makeup table with its half-used tubes of cherry-red lipstick? The white lace gloves she wore when reading the Sunday paper?

I tell her I feel too young for this though I know I'm not. I tell her I've been in dozens of countries where married-off girls are expected to have babies at thirteen and fourteen. I live now in a country that trained children to be soldiers, including my friend Loung. I tell her I've outlived her by two years. I've lived in terror of a moment like this for many years, and now that it's here, I feel no fear at all. I feel, simply, the truth of her presence. *I'm sorry*, she says.

Outside, I hear the calls from various sellers. Men on bicycles loaded down with brooms. The knife-sharpener man. The fruit lady. Fresh-cut papaya, watermelon, pineapple. In the evenings, the noodle seller's banging sticks reverberate off the concrete walls. Here, so much of the city comes to you. The heat thrums through the living room, the air heavy.

I struggle with what more to say to her. Do I tell her stories from my life? Ask questions about where she is now? Do I tell her about my father or my brother? How long do I have with her? How much does she already know?

I thought of all those times when I imagined that having a mother would have infused me with some knowledge, unraveled some feminine mystery. Answered my many questions. Questions about dating, romance, love, relationships, womanhood.

Children. That's the question, the only question I really had now. I might someday regret *not* having had one. A terrible reason to have a child. And when you've lost one parent to death and another to religion, you understand in a gut-deep way that there is no guarantee you'll make it through the pivotal years of your own child's life, so what do you do? This, *this* has to be one of those important moments a mother can help with.

And here was my mother, my actual real mother, and I didn't know how long she'd stay, and so I'd asked her this crucial question, perhaps the most pressing question of any woman facing down the finish line of her reproductive years.

"I wish you were here," I said, "to help me decide if I should have a child."

In her answer, I felt a kind of tremor in my body, some long-held artifice begin to crumble. This was what Ann, and Cindy, and other friends with living mothers had told me for years. That there are no real guidelines. That the answers must come from inside. It seems so obvious now, and yet to *hear* her say it was to disengage from a belief about my own deficits that had guided so much of my life. I had been holding a philosophy that said I was ignorant and would always be ignorant about myself. That I had lost my chance forever to live as a woman shaped by intention rather than loss.

Her answer, then, was a gift. It *was* a roadmap. She had freed me. My story was not hers. My story was mine alone.

This is what she said: *Even if I were, I couldn't help you with that decision.*

Thirty-Four

I was driving up the Dan Ryan Expressway in Chicago one Sunday morning when Marian McPartland played a little-known track off John Coltrane's *Crescent* album. It was 1996 or 1997, after grad school. "The Drum Thing" was seven minutes and made up almost entirely of Elvin Jones's drumming. The song itself is quiet, Jones's drums whispering. The song filtered through my car in that closed, soft space. I'd never heard jazz like this. Jazz that wasn't bebop or frenetic. It transported me the way music had always been able to transport me.

But jazz as an art form was a complete mystery to me. It seemed to me that nothing about it should work, how all the improvisation led not to chaos but to syncopation, to a shared language among players. It was this chaos-into-beauty, I told Paul, who was now my husband, that best symbolized what I felt about children and parents. It was why I wanted to name our daughter Jazz.

My due date was smack in the middle of hot season, and that year dengue was the worst it had been in decades. I slathered myself with a non-DEET liquid recommended by the London School of Hygiene & Tropical Medicine. I stayed mostly inside, prayed that the mosquito-eating geckos scampering up my walls would keep my unborn daughter safe. I had lived in Phnom Penh for nearly five years. I knew my way around, had a tiny Daelim motorbike and Khmow and my garden. We shopped at Lucky Market, drank lemongrass chillers at Java Café, splurged for dinner at Malis or Shiva Shakti, got overpriced organic berries and French cheeses at Veggy's Market. I bought watermelon, papaya, and mango from the seller who came down my street at eleven every morning. To get ice, we'd pop around the corner to the man who sold it by the kilo, carving it into chunks off an enormous block. On weekends, we'd drive down to Kep to swim by the South China Sea, or we'd fly to Vientiane, Singapore, or Ho Chi Minh City, which everyone still called Saigon. I missed blueberries, good Mexican food, and cinnamon gum. I missed closed-toed shoes and sweaters. I missed Ann and Don and Soleak. But I didn't miss much else.

Reluctantly, Paul and I had had to leave our apartment with our beloved landlord and his family. We rented a house that had mango, tamarind, and jackfruit trees in the backyard. We went to a sign maker and invented our own house number, drilling the sign into our wall. House 9, Street 19. We lived several doors down from Ieng Sary's house; he was one of the architects of the Khmer Rouge genocide, and before he died in 2007, he was one of the few who would be put on trial by the Extraordinary Chambers, as the tribunals were called. We'd seen him once or twice when we'd visited nearby friends; he was driving his white Camry into his gated compound, his grandchildren clamoring to greet him.

I was thirty-nine years old. I felt my mother with me every day as I lay on the couch in the evenings, sick with nausea. (I'd told Paul in the early days that since I worked at home my plan to address morning sickness was simply to sleep till noon. He shared the sobering news that morning sickness was not literal. This was definitely a piece of maternal knowledge that had somehow eluded me.) There were now entire streets I had to avoid because the smells were too strong, emanating from piles of discarded fruit and vegetable skins, masses of garbage. I couldn't abide having longan and rambutan in a bowl on the dining room table now because the smell made me gag.

I watched my belly grow with a kind of detachment. I wanted this child, but I also felt terrified. Ann had been trying to get pregnant and had had miscarriage after miscarriage. For five years she tried everything, cycles of in vitro fertilization, an herbal Chinese diet, various medications. We talked by phone often. She'd visited twice so far, and Don came every winter, until I introduced him to Soleak. She now lived with him in Chicago. "You were supposed to get him to move here," I joked with her. "Not the other way round!"

The invention of Skype collapsed our distance. The day I learned I was pregnant, my first thought was: Ann.

The minute I heard her voice, I began to sob into my pillow. I was lying on my bed, phone to my ear. "I have to tell you something," I managed between breaths. The air conditioner hummed through my bedroom.

"You're pregnant," she said, without pause.

She knew. Of course she did. We were soul-braided. We always had been. "I'm so sorry," I whispered, crying. "I'm so, so sorry." My heart was a wolf in my chest.

"No," she said. "Don't be sorry. Your body has no bearing on what mine can't do. I can be happy for you and sad for me at the same time."

ANN AND DON and a few other close friends knew I was pregnant before I told my dad and my stepmom. I wasn't angry with my parents. I spoke to them occasionally, saw them every couple of years. But I lived a life entirely separate from them. My father was funny, still, and he told stories. Sometimes, he'd say things like, "Instances of heart disease are *very* low in China. Why do you suppose that is?" Or, "Why don't they have more cancer in Japan? Is it all the raw fish?"

And I'd say, "You know I don't live in Japan, right? You know I don't live in China?"

My father still held the belief that if you spoke something aloud you could make it come to pass. This explains, to some extent, why he did not divulge what was happening to him and to my stepmother in Naperville while I lived overseas. My father wasn't a fool but he believed foolish things. He once told me the Federal Reserve was owned by eight families in Puerto Rico. He said the entire basis of the U.S. federal tax system was illegal. He believed he could eat ice cream and honey buns and offset the effects of sugar simply by taking supplements like milk thistle and fish oil. He wanted these things to be true. He seemed so often unable to recognize the fake from the real, the charlatan from the authority.

After eighteen years at his house in Naperville, which he borrowed against over and over to invest in his various schemes, he'd stopped paying his mortgage. He claimed he had not been informed that the loan had been sold and that this was illegal. Then, he represented himself in court. The bank foreclosed on the house.

He and my stepmother put their belongings in storage and moved to the International House of Prayer in Kansas City, Missouri. In exchange for subsidized housing, they each took shifts in what evangelicals call intercessory prayer. IHOP, as we dubbed it, had teams twenty-four hours a day, seven days a week, praying for a broken, sinful world. My parents stayed there six months and then moved to Arizona, where my brother John, now in his late twenties, had bought a house. They moved in with John and got minimum-wage part-time jobs driving cars at a dealer's auction. Many of their fellow drivers were felons, newly released from incarceration.

Nearly all of this information came to me at once, while I was ten thousand miles away. My dad was cagey with the details, insistent that the government had wronged him and that he was the victim of feder- ally sanctioned white-collar crime.

But the two of them were evolving in ways that I would only come to see later. My father, whose felonious coworkers became his friends, began to talk about the injustice of mandatory minimum sentencing for drug crimes, particularly marijuana. He bemoaned the lack of working oppor- tunities for ex-cons. "They did their time, right?" he'd ask me rhetori- cally. "Haven't they paid their debt to society?" Once when I visited, my father took me around to the car auction introducing me to everyone, patting various people on shoulders, smiling at everyone. Every single person told me how beloved he was. It reminded me of the day so many years earlier when he'd walked me around the grocery store, sampling food, catching up with all the women.

Once, he told me his neighbor had offered him a pot brownie. The man had a prescription for medical marijuana. My father ate the brownie and waited, but nothing happened. His final critique was less that he'd experienced no mind-altering moment and more that the brownie just hadn't tasted very good. Waste of good chocolate.

My stepmother's evolution was more profound. She told me she no longer believed in heaven and hell, not the literal lake of fire or pearly gates. She believed heaven and hell were a state of mind in the afterlife.

There was *something* out there, something beyond our comprehension, but a forgiving god would not send millions upon millions of people to a literal eternal torment.

MEANWHILE, I SPENT much of my pregnancy watching *The Sopranos* on pirated DVDs from the Russian market and lying on the couch waiting for the nausea to pass. I yearned for authentic Italian spaghetti and New York bagels. My British doctor told me to drink a half pint of Guinness every week to keep my iron up and when I would ask her advice about things like soft cheese and sushi, she'd say, "Do you want the American, the British, the Australian, or the Japanese advice?" Whichever would give me permission to do the thing I wanted to do while pregnant, I'd joke.

"Then don't take the American advice," she said. "Everything's a no."

She told me women in France still ate cheese. Women in Japan still ate sushi. Women in Britain drank half pints of Guinness. Mine was a global pregnancy.

In Cambodia, women told me not to lift my arms above my head or I could dislodge the umbilical cord. They warned me to rise early in the morning before everyone else so I didn't give birth to a lazy baby.

Expat women in the region often gave birth at a World Health Organization–certified hospital in Bangkok called Samitivej. Paul and I had a global health policy that covered me in any country in the world *except* the United States. That's how notorious and expensive our health system is. I could have given birth in the Ivory Coast, in Lichtenstein, in Japan. Literally, *anywhere* but my country of citizenship. So we considered Thailand, Singapore, England, Australia, and Canada. We chose Bangkok.

Thirty-Five

S amitivej Hospital was outfitted with everything an expat might need when giving birth: an office to translate the birth certificate into English; a bilingual administrator who did all the paperwork, including passport photos, for various foreign embassies to issue emergency passports so that we could travel back to whatever country we lived in; a twenty-four-hour lactation consultant; Wi-Fi; and a Starbucks. I was given a choice of aromatherapy during my labor (ylang ylang, please and thank you); Paul was given a fold-out bed in my room, and when they brought in a menu for me to choose my meals each day, they offered him one, too. In the end, I had to have an emergency C-section, and at the end of my five-day stay, the entire bill was $7,500, paid in full and at once by insurance. Why, I wondered, would anyone give birth in America?

When I finally saw her, my tiny daughter with punk-rock hair standing straight up, with her deep blue eyes and her matchstick fingers, she felt like someone I had been communicating with for years, but never seen. Like an intense email relationship. I cried when I held her, and Paul thought I was crying from an unspeakable joy. But that wasn't it, I told him. I was crying because all those stories I'd covered, all the people I'd met over the years—they all came back to me, and I understood immediately that there was no place in the world safe enough for me to keep my daughter from harm.

Many people have a moment, after they have kids, when they begin to understand and empathize with their own parents, when suddenly all the difficult moments make sense. The discipline was all about keeping you safe, about teaching you life lessons.

I saw those terrible years that had culminated in my packing up the blue and maroon Samsonite and leaving my parents' house as newly galling. An aberration. How *could* they send me out into the world? How *could* they have done what they did?

I had spent years apologizing for my behavior to my parents. I lamented the trouble I had caused, the revolt I stirred. I had been a terrible child, I admitted. The drugs, the rebellion, the sneaking out, the violence. Over and over I had apologized and taken what I believed to be my share of the blame. But when I became a parent myself, I understood, finally, the source of my anger. They themselves had never apologized. Not really. On the few occasions over the years when I suggested that they had kicked us out, they always maintained that we had moved out of our own accord after refusing to follow the rules. I didn't challenge this framing until I gave birth to my own daughter. There, in my hospital bed at Samitivej, holding my newborn baby with her giant blue eyes and her punk-rock hair, I thought, "No. *You* were the adults. *I* was the child. Fuck you."

ON THE FIRST anniversary of my mother's death after Jazz was born, Paul and I took her to a pagoda that sat on a spit of land between the Mekong and the Sap. Wat Sampov Treileak, as it's called, is built in the shape of a boat, painted gold and, in the middle of the afternoon, dead silent. I went into the main hall where dozens of Buddhas in different sizes and adorned with saffron cloths sat or lay in repose. Incense burned from several porcelain bowls, and golden wax candles flickered in the still air.

I pulled a meditation cushion from a pile at the back of the hall and knelt down. An elderly woman in white with a shaved head—the signifiers of a widow—lit three sticks of incense and handed them to me, offering me a smile and a single nod. I held the incense between my palms and bowed deeply, forehead to floor. Paul was outside holding Jazz, waiting patiently for me.

It was October 7, 2008. My mother had been gone for thirty-one years. My daughter had been in my life for five months. I placed the incense in the sand beside hundreds of other burned-down stumps. I loved the dark quiet of a pagoda. I held no illusions about being Buddhist, but pagodas also held no dark associations from my past. I wanted to feel my mother's presence as I'd felt years before in my apartment. *Here is your granddaughter*, I wanted to tell her, *come back, Mom. Come back.*

Two months later, I heard about a Jewish expat group in Phnom Penh, and I joined its LISTSERV. There was to be a celebration on the first night of Hanukkah and all were invited on a boat that sailed up and down the rivers. Potted palm trees sat in a row across one side. We passed water buffalo soaking in the muddy water and children jumping off the shores to swim. The latkes went soggy in the humidity, and the overbaked rugalach stuck in my throat. Some of the older children tried to play with dreidels, but the ship's vinyl floor was too sticky. The first candle of the menorah would not stay lit in the breeze. And when it came time to pray and sing songs, I looked around blankly at my fellow Jews, all of whom knew the words, the order of worship, the meaning behind each prayer.

I'd wanted to give my daughter a sense of her heritage, to bring some kind of tradition into her life. To say, *this is who you are. This is where you come from.* But I might as well have been trying to hold a flame.

I had a decision to make. My parents now lived in Arizona. What part would they have in my daughter's life? Our relationship was cordial, warm even. But distant. She was my dad's first biological grandchild.

She would never be spanked. She would never be verbally abused. She would never be told her punishments hurt me more than they hurt her. She would never be made to leave home. I want to be more gracious in my writing here; I want to say that my parents did the best they could under the circumstances and with the resources they had. But I don't think this is true. I don't think they did their best.

Realizing this began to free me not only from any vestiges of guilt I carried, but also from my anger. I had long lived without their beliefs. But now I gave myself the freedom to live with a different historical narrative. And in the strangest way, this lifted my anger. It lifted so much of what I had been holding for so many years, the question of where my fault ended and where theirs began. I'd made jokes about how terrible I'd been, but having Jazz made me understand: these jokes came at the expense of my parents' accountability. And I would no longer carry this burden. They could view our collective past through whatever lens they wanted, but I was going to free myself.

And my daughter? She would know them and form her own relationships and memories with them, and I would do all I could to facilitate this because my life was not hers to bear any more than my mother's short life was mine.

I'd been in Cambodia for nearing six years by then and was itching to leave. I wasn't wedded to returning to the United States. In fact, I was extremely hesitant. In Asia, children are revered, beloved by everyone from elders to teenagers. And Jazz was as easy a baby as they come. She slept through the night at seven weeks. She never once threw herself to the floor in a tantrum. When we traveled, she contemplated hotel ceilings in a quiet, jet-lagged haze while Paul and I slept. We took her to Hanoi and Bali and Tasmania. She eased into these new places and new patterns as if she had been born to ceaseless movement.

But I was tired of the heat in Cambodia. The electricity went off daily, without warning, and was sometimes out for ten or twelve hours at a time, the heat inside growing so intense—once, the thermostat recorded 124 degrees—that I'd have to get in our car and go from parking lot to parking lot just sitting in the air-conditioning, feeding and playing with Jazz, who never once seemed bothered by the state of affairs.

I'd be in the shower, soap in my hair, and suddenly I'd be in darkness, unable to rinse the shampoo. I stored extra breastmilk at a friend's house with a generator. We'd have laundry in the wash, and then we'd lose power and everything would just sit in a tub of soapy water for the rest of the day. Or I'd be in the middle of uploading a radio story to public radio's *Marketplace*, and it would cut out. There were days I just broke down crying. Dengue that year was horrific again. Every mosquito carried with it a terrifying potential. They called dengue the bone-breaker disease because that's what it felt like.

I APPLIED FOR professorships in the United Kingdom, and for one at a university in Singapore, and for another in Switzerland. And then several in the States. In the end, I took a job in Washington, D.C., at American University, because the expats assured me that D.C. was a soft landing, that the people I knew from Cambodia would all wind up there for jobs and conferences and visits. Paul and I packed a forty-foot container with half a dozen years' worth of household goods, including a concrete spirit house painted maroon, maize, and black that now sits in my yard. I light candles for the ill in my spirit house, and Jazz makes tiny clay offerings of fruit. On Pchum Ben, a Cambodian holiday that coincides with my mother's death and that honors one's ancestors, I light a candle for my own strange kaddish and think of her, wherever she is.

Part VI

THE HUNTERS

Thirty-Six

I am cooking at my brother John's house, in Arizona. It is a Saturday, December 2016. John's wife gave birth to their second child prematurely, and the baby is still in the hospital. My dad works at the car auction, still, where he has been for nearly a decade, but he also substitute teaches, and he is so popular that he is requested nearly every day. The kids love him, even though some of them seem barely able to speak English, and my father never does learn any Spanish. As a sub, he is basically left with a movie to show in his classes, and he hates that this is what education in Buckeye public schools means, so sometimes he tries to sneak in a math lesson or two. Some of the older kids will swear, and he tells me, "You would not believe the language coming out of these children." But I would. Of course I would.

I think in a very real way, he has blocked the years when I was between eleven and sixteen. Sometimes, I will ask him, "Do you remember the time I cut my wrists with your fishing knife? Do you remember when I came home drunk and fell down the stairs? Do you remember the boyfriend I had for three weeks who wore leather pants with a chain belt in the summertime?" And he never does.

I don't ask if he remembers the person he was in those days. My dad now is soft and funny, politically conservative, but we stay away from politics for the most part. Later, I will learn he is an aficionado of Alex Jones, and I'll say, "You know your granddaughter has been to Comet Pizza a million times, right? You know that's our local pizza place in D.C.?" An armed man showed up to free the children from a pedophile ring supposedly run from the basement by Hillary Clinton and John Podesta.

And he'll say, "I thought there really was a child pornography ring, though. I thought they found evidence." And I'll tell him there isn't even a basement in Comet. And I feel frustration and anger rise up in me because these conspiracies could someday get my family killed. I live in ground zero for political violence stemming from the endless lies he believes.

I've been in D.C. for eight years now, and by some miracle of luck or fate or love, Ann and her husband, Mike, and their daughter, who is a year younger than Jazz and was adopted from Russia, have moved to D.C. and now live a mile away from me. And then Don and Soleak and their daughter, who is two years younger than Jazz, moved a mile in the other direction. Friends for thirty years now, We raise our only daughters as cousins, as sisters, and we travel together in a pack—to Panama, where Don and I made the group go see the Panama Canal.* We went to Costa Rica, where the girls screamed at the racket of the iguanas on our rooftop. Jazz, Yana, Solaya: these are our girls. They love my stories of travel with Ann since so many of them involve diarrhea, nudity, or ineptitude: the time in Vientiane when Ann didn't realize her wrap-around skirt was lose until it pooled around her ankles. The time she lost a shoe in the muck near the Vinh Moc tunnels in Vietnam and drove her motorcycle barefoot. The time I ate fresh coconut from a vendor in Agra and came down with typhoid. The time Ann took off her glasses to snorkel and swam right up to a squiggly fish that turned out to be a German man peeing naked in the water. Our daughters refer to us as "the OG" (the original gang). Intentional family.

But now, in Arizona, my biological family needs help. My father and my stepmom have struggled financially ever since they'd lost their house in Naperville. My brother John has a preemie and a toddler, and his wife needs someone to drive her back and forth to the hospital while he works during the day. And then there is my stepmom. She is the real reason I have come.

---

* I promised the girls ice cream if they would deadpan, on video, "The Panama Canal is one of the greatest engineering marvels of the world." Just recently, I learned they'd said marbles.

She'd been diagnosed a year earlier with colorectal cancer. She'd gone to the hospital with stomach pain, her first time ever going to the emergency room, and then she'd stayed for weeks. My father had called to tell me on Halloween night. As I stood on the sidewalk listening to him—was Jazz a mermaid that year? Alice in Wonderland?—various decorations growled and snarled in the background. Spider-Man and the Little Mermaid stumbled past. Barb went into emergency surgery, and she woke up with a colostomy bag and burst out crying.

She was home for a little while and then more pain, another surgery, only this time, she went into a coma for more than a week, developed sepsis, and then spent a month in rehab learning to walk again. When my father called me to say they could use some help, I knew it meant they were all barely holding on. So Joshua, who had been living in Korea for years, moved back to the States, and the two of us began tag teaming. Why didn't Barb's older children come? Holly and Aaron? I hadn't seen either of them in more than twenty years. I didn't keep in touch with them. I'd heard things about Holly having a fear of flying, or about her not having the money, but I didn't really know. David, who was also married now and had a son, was even more distant than the rest of us. I myself had only seen him once in ten years.

It was as if that day in 1985 had permanently severed us all. I felt relief to have Holly and Aaron gone from my life, to no longer have to pretend we were anything to each other. But I missed David sometimes. In the beginning, I called and left messages, or occasionally sent him an email, but he never answered. I suspected I was just a symbol of pain from our early years. Because David had been the obedient one. David had once believed in Jesus, had preached the word of God. He had never rebelled, never done drugs, never missed curfew. Slowly, in high school, he began to pull away from his belief in God, but he was still responsible and obedient, a good student. And he left right along with the rest of us. It seemed inevitable that he would blame me at some point. It seemed maybe even like justice.

John's house was a newly built subdivision—the kind in which you chose from two or three different models, along with a shade of taupe for the outside. There was a uniformity to everything, faux Spanish architecture with tiled roofs. Colored stones for front and back lawns. Inside, the house had white walls and beige carpeting, an enormous flat-screen television took up half the living room, and it was on constantly in the background.

My dad and stepmom lived a mile away. When they arrived, I opened the door to see my stepmother dressed for deep winter. She wore my father's extra-large flannel shirts, and oversized, loose cotton pajama bottoms. She'd always been thin, but she'd lost twenty or thirty pounds. She had tubes coming from so many different places I couldn't track them all, but I heard them gently slap against each other. She carried her own pillow.

I'd made a gallon of my father's favorite, mushroom soup. Homemade applesauce, mashed potatoes.

My stepmother couldn't stomach anything but the blandest liquid foods. They had stopped eating out. Her illness had a circumference. A visible pallor that whirled around her. She knew people looked at her, people looked and then looked away, soft and sparing with their words and their movements. She knew they knew they were witnessing the very precipice between alive and not alive. That quiet violence. It silences all of us.

On one of my earlier visits, I'd gotten her out of the house and to a strip mall massage place where she had her first and last ever foot massage. I'd learned to love these in Asia. I figured no other place on her body could tolerate being touched. In her massage chair beside me, she sighed contentedly for half an hour. She'd talked about it ever since as a kind of wonderment. *Why had it felt so good? Why had she never had one before?*

Barb moved through the room slowly, gathering up the tubes in both her palms. She eased herself down onto John's couch, pale leather and plush. Everything in Buckeye was a different shade of brown, outside and in. I ridiculed the shades of beige endlessly. "Now is that a sandy taupe or a beigey taupe? Tawny or tan?"

My stepmom wiped her face with her hands and ran them through her long brown hair. Even though she was sixty-eight now, she had very little gray. When she pulled her hands away, they were filled with hair and I saw her face crumple. She had always had a stillness about her, sitting quietly without speaking. Her expression was drawn and serious all the time now. I'd seen her grimace in pain, her hands moving to cover her face; it would become a familiar gesture. This recoiling. A boil had been growing on her. Ascites, it was called, a side effect of the cancer. A rebellion from her body over the battle being waged inside her. *However did they worm their way in?* My grandfather's poem about my mother's cancer came to me often now.

The ascites felt like fire. Soon, the fluid inside would leak and she would find some relief; she'd been through this before. At one point, she had several of these sacs, all filled with fluid, hard as roasted corn kernels, some small as pebbles and others—like this one—as large as a lipstick tube. From her gesture I knew that the pain was so great it took her to an otherworldly place. I saw the machinery under her skin, the struggling systems of bone and vein, lane markers along the highway. She was receding from the outside in. I have a sense of such pain. It is that moment of hard labor in childbirth, when sheer agony takes you to another realm; there you are utterly and entirely alone, your suffering immeasurable, beyond language.

My father couldn't or wouldn't contemplate Barb's death. He hadn't even revealed her diagnosis to her. Nor had the doctor. She learned it from me, by accident. My brother John had told me after her first emergency room visit that it was colorectal cancer, stage four. I called several hours later, and my dad put me on speakerphone from her hospital room so I could talk to both of them. I asked about the prognosis for her cancer.

"Cancer?" she said, her voice thin and weak. "I have cancer?"

There it was: blatant collusion. Her doctor and my father and my brother John. How could all three of these men know more about what was happening inside her body than she, the patient, knew? Surely it broke medical ethics rules. It reminded me of what she had told me about the early days of her marriage to my dad, when my uncle Jim and my father had decided things for her. When she had felt cowed by them. She had told me once how she'd always felt uncomfortable with my calling her Mom, how she'd never wanted to force that on me. I understand that my father held this diagnosis from her out of love. Love had arguably driven his decisions when I was young, too. But didn't love ultimately mean you let go, let a person decide for herself, even if you disagreed? Even if it killed something in you?

AFTER THAT, I vowed to be her advocate in a way that was different than my father's advocacy. He searched for cures, much as he had done with my mother. My advocacy would be to insist that she know everything when it came to her own body. I would ask nurses, caregivers, and staff everything I could think of asking. I would go to her doctor's appointments if she wanted me there. I would interrogate my dad and report back to her. Was I betraying my father's trust by disclosing what he wouldn't? Maybe. But it was a betrayal that seemed a lot more like loyalty to me. Like a person's right to know.

As she situated the pillow half under her, half beside her, I asked if she wanted to talk about what she was going through.

She waved away my question. "I'm okay, Rache."

She didn't want to burden me. I tried a different tactic. "I mean, I'd like to ask you some questions, if you don't mind. About what you're going through."

She was one of the very few people in the world who called me Rache. "Ask me anything you want," she told me.

I didn't really know what I was going to say before the words came out. How rarely we talk about terminal illness and death. How much we fear even witnessing it. The few times I was in public with her, I'd see how people would make a wide berth when walking past her, how they opened doors for her, but refused eye contact. I understood that my father's inability to voice things, even terrible things that were *actively* happening, like losing his house, or watching his second wife battle cancer, came largely from fear, even if he—if most of us—wanted to have faith in the moment.

I struggled to articulate what I meant. "I want to ask you about what you're really going through. Maybe it's too personal."

"Rache," she said, "you can ask me *anything*." She was looking straight at me, her deep green eyes showing me that in fact she understood exactly what I was saying. Perhaps she understood it better than I did at that moment.

The thermostat in my brother's house was set to eighty degrees, but my stepmom shivered. I got her a blanket and put it over her lap, being careful not to touch any of the tubes that I couldn't see in the volumes of extra-large clothes she was wearing. My father must have known from our tone that we were talking privately. He went out the sliding glass door with the dogs, to my brother's rocky backyard.

I took her at her word, and dove into the first question, the hardest question I imagined. "What does cancer feel like in your body?" Translation? How much will she suffer? And also, maybe, how much did my real mother suffer?

Thirty-Seven

My stepmother was shy. And I suspect she was insecure about being a high school dropout. Maybe she felt she didn't have as much to contribute to a conversation. Once, when I was in Los Angeles visiting friends, I threw a small party, and my parents drove in from Arizona. My father went from person to person, talking to everyone, asking them what they did, how they knew me, who they were. My stepmother sat in a swing chair in the corner of the yard and didn't speak to a soul the entire evening. I remember feeling angry at her, wishing she would make an effort. I wonder why it mattered. What did I care if she talked to my friends?

But now she talked. With that one question—*what does cancer feel like in your body*—the words spilled out. "It's not my body anymore," she said. "It's a different body." This different body was pulling her along, a foreign invader colonizing her former self. She said her old body would never return; she'd have to figure out a way to live in this new body. *Clever chaps.* "Even if I beat this thing"—*beat this thing* was my father's phrase—"this body will never feel the same," she believed. She put her hands underneath her thighs to warm them. She had talked for over an hour when my father quietly came in the room. She glanced up at him. His face looked dark and serious, and the dogs followed him breathlessly.

She said, "I'm so sorry this is happening to you again, Rache. I'm so sorry."

I didn't know how much my dad had heard. He had come in and out several times, giving us our privacy or escaping because it was too much for him to hear. Her putting her disease out in the world, her pain, the looming shadow. But now he stood quietly, open to our conversation.

"I'm sorry it's happening to both of you again," she said. The sun had long disappeared; the soup on the stove had been warming for two hours now. What kind of grace was it to have someone apologize for her possible death? I could see my father holding so much in, the dread, the pain, history so cruelly repeating itself.

"Your mother was so brave, Rachel."

She whispered this. It immediately felt sacred, women whispering to one other from other universes, other realms, other lives. Maybe it was a promise, one mother to another. Maybe it wasn't meant for me at all.

WE RECEIVED WORD that the tumor in her colon had metastasized, and she now had one in a lung and one in her pancreas.

My dad went into every rabbit hole the internet offered to avoid the chemotherapy that he believed had killed my mother. "Methotrexate," he would tell me, "was the culprit and it's *still* the primary drug in chemotherapy. Can you believe they're using the same drugs they used in nineteen seventy-seven?" She'd been over-radiated. She died of her cure. I told him that chemo had made great advances in the past forty years, that he shouldn't dismiss it out of hand. He said he had done the research. He knew. As he had with my mother, my father began to try various different "cures." He brought out the old gray juicer from the '70s for vegetable and fruit juices. He bought some contraption off Craigslist that oxygenated water.

He went on CancerTutor.com regularly. He used lingo I had never heard. He said a healthy person's CET markers (a carcinoembryonic antigen test) are under five. That my stepmom's were at forty-six. That my real mother was probably in the hundreds when she died. That at one point, my stepmom's got down to eight.

He said there are tiny particles inside our bodies that move the cancer around. Not cells; smaller than cells. He said a lot of scientists now believe that it's these tiny particles that make cancer metastasize in the body. That chemo can kill cancer cells, but it's these smaller particles that need to be killed, and that's the tough part. He said my stepmom's doctor had to be trained in how to do this treatment, so he was going to get trained and start treatment on her in the fall. None of this would be covered by Medicare.

MY STEPMOTHER AND I talked regularly, several times a week. For the first time in our lives, we called one another. Sometimes I could hear my father's phrasing in her speech, about faith and about God and just believing more and harder and better. They'd found a doctor who was giving her experimental low-dose chemo. We talked about my marriage to Paul, how I had decided it would no longer work and we had started divorce proceedings; although both my parents generally disapproved of divorce, the more I shared with my stepmom, the more she began to understand. And for the first time ever, she talked, briefly, about her own divorce, when she was so young. His name was Ron, and he had not been a nice man. He had abused her, physically. My father, in comparison, was saintly, she said.

One spring I flew out for a week and went to one of her low-dose chemo sessions held in a strip mall in the Tempe exurbs. By now she was using a wheelchair, her legs as thin as my arms, her knees bulbous. In the small office, several other women were hooked up to their own IV bags. The doctor came out, knelt down, and bowed his head. They prayed together, all of them. The doctor, my parents, a couple of the nurses. The hair on the back of my neck stood up. I thought of Pittsburgh, my father taking my mother to that prayer meeting, my mother's face a dark shadow. She hadn't wanted to go. She hadn't believed in his God. I did not bow my head.

When the prayer finished, my stepmom said to the doctor, "I can see my angel right over your shoulder. He's right there. And Jesus is on the other side." The doctor held her hands, told her he was glad her angel was there. Then she turned and said, "This is Rachel. This is my daughter I told you about." He reached out and took both my hands in his, said it was a blessing to meet me. Maybe it was the prayer. I don't know. But I recoiled. From his overly warm demeanor, the public staging of his prayer, his telling me how special my parents were to him. It all felt calculated. Later, I would Google him and within two minutes, I had found my way to court documents. He'd been sued for wrongful death on behalf of at least one patient, and for malpractice by several. He had not left his previous practice out of altruism, as he'd told my stepmother; he'd been fired. He was, by training, a pediatrician.

I dialed the Arizona Medical Board and filed a complaint on their hotline. No one ever called me back.

In front of my parents, I was as supportive as I could be. I went to my stepmom's appointments with her when I was in town, watching this supposed alternative oncologist "treat" her. I wanted to punch him. Especially when, during one appointment, my father came back from the billing office, pale and grim. They owed the doctor more than eight thousand dollars, the equivalent of four months' salary for my dad. And that was only this one doctor, this one office. There were others. The herbalists. The chiropractors.

"They said they'd put us on a payment plan."

"Should we stop?" Her eyes were wide.

He shook his head. "Don't worry, sweetheart. Don't you worry."

I snuck across the sweltering parking lot to the business office in the next building. I handed over my credit card, told them to put five thousand dollars on it, and then asked them not to tell my father. I knew he'd never want to accept my money, but the debt was only causing her to get sicker, him to have to work more. It is not lost on me, of course, that the reason I have the means is because I managed to do enough things differently than him. Several hours later, as we were leaving, my father emerged once again from the billing office, his face alight.

"Well, sweetheart," he said, "we've had a miracle here today." Magically, mysteriously, their bill had been more than cut in half.

Later that night, when she was in bed and I'd fed her some bone broth soup and was lying on her floor reading *Barkskins* by Annie Proulx, the biggest book I could find that took me as far as possible from a Phoenix summer (all the way back to a winter in the seventeenth-century French Canadian territory), she spoke to the ceiling. "It was you, wasn't it?"

I waited a few moments. I considered lying. "Don't tell Dad," I said.

She promised she wouldn't. Then she whispered, "Thanks, Rache."

* * *

THEY LIVED, THAT year, in the present tense. Did she have her B17 shot? Does she feel up to taking a shower? What does she want to eat? In the face of this kind of illness, I understand that the bigger decisions, and the bigger conversations, are overwhelming and so they take on what they can. I'd been up close to illness with my own mother, but I'd been too young to understand what was happening, kept in the dark by everyone around me.

One afternoon, Barb begins to talk to me about my father. About the kind of husband he's been through all this. Since receiving her diagnosis she's had one setback after another, one complication after another. She's had surgical mishaps, leaking bags, even the flu. An endless conveyer belt of side effects. There was that surgery in which she went into a coma and that month in rehab. She weighs 95.6 pounds. She is five feet six inches tall.

My father never complains, she says. He is patient. He is exhaustive in his care. When he isn't at the car auction or subbing, he is seeking out new research, calling about insurance coverage, about financial help for medical bills, about alternative treatments they haven't yet tried. He takes her to doctors and homeopaths. He picks up medicine and supplies for her. She tells me to promise that she'll be buried with him. That is all she wants. I promise.

Illness offers no respite from itself, no time to tackle the big-picture stuff most of the time—the diagnosis, the chemo, the fight itself—because its complications are endless. Ascites plagued her constantly. She got one infection or another. All these sidetracks that took their focus. Cancer does not behave. Cancer *is* the complication, so far as I can tell. Cancer is like one of those tablecloth magic tricks gone wrong: taking everything down with it as it's yanked, the meal, the china, the crystal. All of it crashing to the floor. This is cancer's real menace: that it attacks and then diverts your gaze. It adapts. It survives because it kills everything around it.

My stepmother holds her face in her hands that night in bed. My father comes in the room. "Hello sweetheart," he says. She shakes her head but does not remove her hands. He bends over her, takes one hand away gently and kisses her on the lips.

"I always loved your lips," she tells him.

* * *

I SPEAK TO Jazz about Grammy being very sick, how she has to be especially kind to Grammy, and sometimes maybe just sit with her. I think of my friend in Cambodia, how she sat with her grandmother's body all night, how she learned that death starts as life. How she learned to not look away. People say they don't want the living to remember them in their illness; they only want to be remembered as whole and healthy. But I want to remember it all, the whole cycle.

We are sharing things we've never shared before. I tell her about my marriage. We talk about sex. About love. She says my father took her breath away the first time she saw him, but he had lost his wife so recently that she didn't talk to him. This must have been the summer before 1979, the summer they met but didn't start dating officially. It seems like my father continued dating Karen Jones while he was writing letters to and calling the woman who would become my stepmother.

Jazz is eight years old. She talks to my parents on FaceTime, so my stepmother's appearance when we arrive is not a surprise, apart from the fact that she's cut all her hair off and now every curve and bend and divot in her skull is visible. She has a port over her collarbone on her right side, into which my father hooks liquid Vitamin C or saline bags from the homeopath.

The sun outside is going down, and her vertical blinds are drawn. I ask if she wants them open, just for a little while, and she says that would be nice. Just then I hear a cricket, so loud that it seems to be in the room. "They get in the shower drains," she says.

I go in the bathroom, but the cricket's not in there. My dad hears it and comes in. He, too, looks first in the shower. We are hunters. Her eyes are open and she is watching us now. I open the blinds, but I see nothing. My dad is looking behind the door. Like everything else in western Phoenix, the crickets are pale, completely camouflaged in the beige carpet and in the desert sand, clever little assholes.

I finally find it between her bed and her nightstand. It jumps underneath the nightstand. The nightstand is heavy, three packed drawers, but I manage to move it a few inches. The cricket jumps, up the wall, off the side of the bed, around the carpet, looking for safety. I am Chaplin, I am Lucy, I am Mo, Larry, and Curly, pouncing, screaming. My father stands in the corner saying, "Did you get it? Did you get it?" It fights for its life;

I fight for its death. "Does this cricket have no respect?" I say, only half laughing. I hold a wadded bunch of toilet paper, holding up the flashlight from my phone. The screeching slows, going quiet to conceal its location. Paul taught me, years ago, when searching for something camouflaged, to look for shine, shape, shadow, movement. The shape. I lunge. I cover and then kill it and I've won.

"Thanks, Rache," she whispers.

"I don't think they're going to get the cancer out of Grammy's body," Jazz says as we drive back to the hotel. I splurged for a place with a giant pool and slide. Interstate 10 is straight and long and the sun is unyielding in its torment, even with the air-conditioning on. It shimmers off the pavement. In parking lots we search for the any hint of shade under dusty mesquite trees.

"I think she is in her last wave of life," Jazz says.

A MAN NAMED Joe in dark blue scrubs is giving my stepmom an antibiotic through her port as she sits, wobbly and leaning, at the kitchen table. He tells her she should not have any side effects. No itching. No rash. No nausea. If she does, she should tell him right away. The antibiotics hit and Joe helps her back to bed; I ask if she wants to lie flat. I ask if she needs water, if she needs a heating pad. If she wants the lights on or off, the shades open or closed. We all want to be useful, but we can't really do the thing we want and need, which is to kill what is killing her.

Joe gathers his supplies in a black cloth briefcase. I thank him for taking care of my mom.

My dad takes my daughter out for an ice cream and a walk around the Walmart Supercenter; I tell Jazz her grandfather never met a big box store he didn't love. When they're gone, I tell my stepmom this: "When I was a teenager, Mom, all I wanted was for you to die. And now all I want is for you to live."

"I know," she says. "I know."

Joshua and I are walking around the Walmart Supercenter. We are looking for a bell, for something to attach to the rail of her hospital bed so she can summon help if she needs it. The previous night, she woke and needed to use the toilet. She called and called my father, who was asleep in the other bedroom. She doesn't have the strength to shout. He never heard, and she urinated in her bed, all over the sheets, and when my father found her, soaking, in the morning, she had dried tears on her cheeks.

We look for one of those old-timey motel desk bells. *Ring for service.* How can a store the size of two city blocks not have one? We find a bell in the pet department that is a bird toy. But the jingle is too quiet. We look in hardware, in housewares. In the toy department, we find a blue horn, like what a clown might attach to a tricycle. When you squeeze the blue rubber end, it lets out an *eee-awwww* sound, like a car horn running out of battery. Joshua and I double over laughing in the aisle. We can't get her a clown horn.

Can we?

We put it back.

I almost piss myself with laughter.

Then we race back and buy it.

Every time we hear it go off after that, we look at each other and laugh. *Eee-awwww*, it goes, and my dad or Joshua or I will run into her bedroom, see what she needs. It works for a little while. Even she smiles when she honks it. But then one day she is too weak to squeeze the rubber top. It's too much anyway. How dare it make such a racket among the living and not-quite-dead. I tell Joshua that it's probably best she can't use it, because it would be a shame to accidentally cause our dad to have a heart attack from a bicycle horn while our mom is busy dying. We laugh and cry.

She is often too tired to talk, but she says she wants us to just hang out in her room. I spend long hours in there, sitting against the wall on the floor, talking to my father while he sits in a chair opposite. I tell him stories from Cambodia. The time our boat got stuck in the mangroves and Paul jumped in in his underwear to rock the boat free. I tell them how we built a seat so Khmow could ride our motorcycles with us, how Khmow walked me down the aisle. How Khmow had never seen squirrels before moving to America. I tell them both about the monsoons, and about how the monks appeared at my wedding just to bless us, but their blessing took so long I snuck into the kitchen and just started serving liquor to my guests while the monks were bent over, praying with their eyes closed. I tell them how we paid for an elephant with two hundred dollars worth of banana trees. I tell them about choosing our own house number. I tell them about the time Ann and I were in Cuba and we borrowed a gas can from Billy Gibbons of ZZ Top, who happened to be staying at our same guest house, and he in turn borrowed our dental floss. "No need to return it!" I had told him, because I was hilarious. I said how once in Havana I'd met Che Guevara's widow and her four dogs and she made me promise not to write about her; and the time Paul Stanley of Kiss made me a sun-dried-tomato frittata while his son took swimming lessons in their pool.

It's the first time I've shared these stories, also the first time they've listened. Sometimes my stepmom sleeps. Sometimes she murmurs something to let us know she is listening. *That's funny, Rache.* Or *Oh, Rachel.* She coughs, sucks on lemon drops. The coughing dries her throat, makes it hard for her to talk. My father offers her coffee, tea, juice, water, broth, applesauce, ice cream, yogurt. He rubs her shins and I give her foot massages with Aquaphor, warming it up in my hands, touching where I remember each pressure point, each toe separately, flexing each foot forward and back to stretch her ankles, bending her matchstick legs back and forth from her hip to try and get the blood flowing. She is so fully skeletal now that the chiropractor comes to the house twice a week to put her joints back in place where they've fallen out. There is so little holding her together.

Thirty-Eight

Two weeks later I am back in Arizona at John's house. My dad rings the doorbell. He is alone and it's so terrifically sad, to see what I presume will be his nearer-than-it-ought-to-be future. Though who's to say any of us are owed any kind of life? Longevity, health, happiness. It's a privilege to expect a long life. The movie *Sing* is on. A porcupine plays an electric guitar. An overworked mother pig sings like Christina Aguilera. The dogs go wild with glee at my father's presence.

"No one talked about Mom," I say, meaning my real mom. We've climbed into his van to drive to the store. The air-conditioning blasts. "I didn't know she died of cancer for years."

He says, "You didn't? But all those trips in and out of the hospital. All that chemo."

"I knew she was sick. But she was sick my whole life. I only ever thought she'd be sick. I didn't know she could die." I tell him maybe David knew. He was older.

My dad says, "I could have communicated better."

"Yes," I tell him. "You could have."

I picture time as a great winged creature, my father wrestling it to the ground. His eternal nemesis.

MY STEPMOTHER IS lying on her bed in her paper underwear, atop the covers with a blue T-shirt on. Her eyes are closed. All the tubes and bandages and bags are visible. Her body is a sapling. Her knees are the size of floodlights.

"I'm sorry I'm naked," she says, without opening her eyes. "But we have the same parts."

I smile. Of nakedness my real mother used to say: "If you haven't seen it before, you won't know what it is, and if you have, it won't bother you." Why do I remember this idiom? What other sayings did she have? I repeat things to my daughter in the hope she'll remember them when she's older. Upon waking: "This day isn't going to live itself!" At bedtime: "Mommy loves you, mommy loves you. You're the very best part of my life."

Cancer is everywhere that summer. My friend Danielle loses her mother to cancer. And then my friend Olga in Bogotá. And my dear colleague's wife. It seems to invade all the women around me, and the women around them. It is a mist, a demon, a hurricane. It has followed me my whole life. I know cancer like other people knew sports. This is how we suffer. This is how we end.

I bend down and hug her, the bones of her shoulder blades like compact disks under her skin, her shoulders knobby and protruding. "I'm glad you're here," she whispers. "I'm so glad you came." She is near tears every time I see her now.

I sit on the edge of her bed. She has another urinary tract infection. They are constant, and so terrifically painful. She is prescribed antibiotics to put in her port, and the medicine hits her like cement dumped into her body, she says. She has to go to the toilet. Can I help her? There is a bedside toilet with a folding frame set up beside her. Slowly, I put one arm behind her spine, the vertebrae like peach pits. I put her legs, one at a time, over the side of the bed. Wait. Breathe. She sits on the edge. Once she's ready, she reaches out her arms, and I lift her, help her onto the toilet. Almost nothing comes out. She asks for a cool washcloth, and then holds it there over her burning genitals. "I'm sorry," she says. "But it feels so good."

I tell her not to apologize, that I wish I could do more.

She leans on one elbow, holding her forehead in her right hand, while her left hand holds the washcloth for several minutes until the cool seeps out of it. I lift her off the toilet, help her pull up the paper underwear.

"They used to do C-sections this way," she says, one hand gesturing vertically. "For Holly and Aaron," she says. "And then when John and

Josh came, they'd changed." The mysteries of medicine, the crosshatched scars on her abdomen.

"Do you have a scar?" she asks me.

I nod, unbutton my jeans and pull them down slightly. My scar is tiny compared to hers. "Wow," she says. "They've gotten better, haven't they?" This is where we meet, women and our bodies.

"My water broke at four A.M.," I tell her. "It was just sort of a drip. I made myself a peanut butter and jelly sandwich and took a bath." I did not wake Paul. I knew not to wake him until my contractions were closer together. In our birthing classes at Samitivej Hospital, I'd been told to bring popsicles or something to suck on because breathing through the contractions would dry my throat out. But I couldn't find any kind of popsicle in Bangkok except red bean paste, which I loved, but which were not exactly thirst-quenching. This, oddly, had stressed me out for days.

My stepmother listens, her legs stretched out in front of her. My father putzes around the kitchen. The day wore on and on, I tell her. There was a cyclone in Myanmar, a woman who'd given birth during the cyclone that I saw on the television. Labor was nothing until early evening. The nursing staff kept taking me from my room to the birthing floor down-stairs to check my vitals and the baby's vitals, and my contractions, but I wasn't dilating at all. I wanted to sit in the pool of water in the dimly lit birthing room. It was calm and beautiful. But I wasn't ready, they said, not yet. Not yet.

"The closest I ever made it to that damn birthing room was across the hall," I say, laughing. She smiles in her bed, offers a slight nod once. I never dilated more than one centimeter. Then I was in hard labor, and screaming, and in so much pain I kept leaning over a pail to vomit, except no vomit ever came. No release from anywhere. "I screamed at Paul to do something, and he was like, 'What can I do'? I don't know what I expected him to do." I smile. "He reminded me to breathe, which it turns out is something you do actually forget to do when you're in that much pain."

"Oh, I know, Rache," she whispers. "Me, too."

I got an infection in my white blood cells, and it passed to Jazz. I had to go on intravenous antibiotics for two hours before they could give me a C-section. During those two hours I screamed, howled, begged for an epidural, begged to get the baby out. I told Paul that I thought I might die. I actually felt okay about dying. I told him I wanted to die, because I could not handle this pain for a minute longer.

Morning must have come. I had lost track of time entirely, I tell her. The pain rippled through every part of my body, and I couldn't stay awake, but I also couldn't sleep through this, and I was too tired to scream now, and all that escaped me were long, slow moans that I am sure reverberated far beyond the walls of this fluorescent room.

Then. The epidural. I stopped mid-scream. I instantly felt nothing. I became myself again. They wheeled me into the operating theater and seconds later, Dr. Sankiat held a tiny blob covered in white and red, paste and blood and god knows what, and said, "Kiss your new baby daughter." To be honest, I tell my stepmom, I sort of didn't want to. It was gross. She smiles with her eyes closed. She knows this newborn goop. But I pursed my lips in the direction of the tiny blur that whizzed past me, I say, and then I was asleep and in recovery and Paul was in a pink cotton robe learning how to bathe our new daughter.

My stepmother is sitting up a little, her legs still splayed atop the covers. "I like that story," she says. My birthing story. The story of my life.

I wish you were here to tell me if I should have a child.

Perhaps she can see something from wherever she is after all. But here, in this room, I have this woman. I have this mother. And she's heard my story. I sink down beside her to my knees, lay my head on her hospital bed beside her hip. She puts her hand on my head.

"JAZZY IS A blessing, and a beauty and a joy," she says. I think about when she was healthy and she would sit on the couch with my daughter and not say much. She, too, was like a shell. What was inside her that she could not let out in those days? Why did I assume she was so little?

I tell my stepmom that I am writing about her, about all of this. I tell her that the one thing she always understood about me was that I wrote the world, my world, in order to explain it to myself. She says she knows this about me. She understands.

Thirty-Nine

Death is both unnervingly quiet and tremendously loud.

When I walk in her room, she is holding a plastic tub and wiping her mouth. Vomit. She had been trying to make herself vomit. She had been bloated all the way up to her ribcage, she said. It was terribly uncomfortable. So a friend brought freshly squeezed grapefruit juice, which she loves, and she drank from a straw and threw up. The liquid is dark green.

My dad empties the tub and while he is gone, I say that I want to ask her something and she doesn't have to answer.

"Go ahead," she says.

"Are you afraid?" I ask her.

She is quiet for a moment. Joshua has gone to the store to buy vegetables. He has become an excellent chef, nurturing us with healthy food. He rises in the morning, sautés vegetables for omelets, makes us salad with homemade oil-and-vinegar dressing. It is a gift, his taking this on, without needing to be asked, without needing instructions.

"I was afraid," she says. "The other night, in the hospital, once I realized where I was, I was afraid. That night, and into the next morning, until the chaplain came and talked to us." She told my dad, no more doctors. No more medicine. No more experimentation. She promised him she could still hope. She still did hope for a miracle. God could take it all away. But in the meantime, with Jaqueline-the-chaplain by her side, she said she felt ready, and she needed my dad to be with her, to say yes, to allow her to go. Her angel had been there in her room all week. She could see him as clearly as she could see me.

As she is speaking, my father has come into the room so silently, so stealthily—socks on carpet—that I don't realize he's standing behind me. When she finishes, he takes a step toward her and puts his hand on her knobby knee. I think of Cambodia, how death is just the end of a life cycle, making space to start all over again.

MY DAD ASKED Joshua and me to find a funeral home, to figure out all the logistics of what comes next. I thought this was because he didn't want to leave her. When we return with our folders and our paperwork, the instructions on the bureaucratic nature of dying, we sit my father at the kitchen table, and his face is so serious that I see again the man he once was when I was young. The stern expression, his jaw working back and forth, his eyes squinting. Only now his stern expression says something else to me. Says he is lost.

I tell my father we can choose an urn, that we need to get as many as twenty copies of her death certificate. It feels appalling to even say these words, while she is still alive and in the next room being bathed by a hospice nurse. When the hospice nurses leave, he sneaks bags of Vitamin C and sugar water through her PICC line. Parts of her bloat, bladders form under her biceps and around her joints, filling with liquid. But I can't tell him to stop. I can't. It is illegal, what he is doing. He could be sued by the hospice company. But who would do such a thing? I cannot say to him, "Stop. You're prolonging her agony."

You'll get her back twenty-four hours after cremation, I tell him. And then, while I'm looking at the folder, I feel the kitchen table shake, and my father has pushed himself up and away in one violent move, and he is stumbling, turning in a circle like a wolf with a broken leg. Joshua and I both catch him before he falls. His whole body is shaking wildly and Joshua and I wrap our arms around him. He is sobbing, wailing, a keening animal. I have seen this before. Once. We hold him until he is steady again.

LATER, HE TELLS me how she asked him a few times if she was going to die. "I didn't like to hear that," he says. Even the sentence was like a lurking evil, listening for an invitation the minute it was spoken aloud.

Clever chaps. However did they worm their way in? What I want to tell him but don't is that this presumes cancer gives a shit. Cancer has no feelings for the lives it claims.

The hope she had when I was here last time seems so audacious now. So arrogant. As if we could hope our way out of death. Death howls with laughter at our little human saplings of hope.

A neighbor comes by with food. We eat, but we have no spirit for it. We lounge, looking at our phones. We are waiting and also not waiting. We are just hanging out together, life suspended. Life holding its breath. I have Ocean Vuong's book with me, *Night Sky with Exit Wounds*. I read a poem called "Head First" to her, and after that she asks me to read it every day: *But only a mother can walk/with the weight/of a second beating heart.* We put on a movie but only get five minutes into it. My stepmom calls my dad on his phone. He disappears into her room for fifteen minutes and then reemerges, says she needed to pee, and she needed hydration.

My phone rings a few minutes later. It is her, calling from the next room. I go in and it's pitch black. I might trip on her toilet chair. Or laundry. Every available surface in their home is covered by something. Her bucket to vomit in is too far for her to reach. I move it closer. She has drinks lined up with straws in them, all labeled. Ginger tea, water, grapefruit juice.

"We never finished our talk," she says. I lean down and hug her as best I can.

She says, "You know that song, 'When a Man Loves a Woman?' I sing that song sometimes," she says. "And I think of your dad. For a long time I didn't know how to let him love me. I'd never been loved like that before. I got so lucky with him. So lucky. So many women marry terrible men," she says. "We have so much to learn, men and women. So much work to do to learn to treat each other right."

I ask her about her first husband. Ron.

She says, "Let's not go there. I don't want to go there."

My father has told me only in recent weeks how Ron had once held a gun to her head. "Wait," I tell her. "It's not that. I don't want to talk about him. I just want to tell you that I didn't know. I didn't know how mean he was." I tell her I have been writing for years about women with partners like him, a book called *No Visible Bruises*, but I never knew she was one of those women. Her eyes are looking intently at me. Her hair is thin, fine as dragonfly wings around her head. She nods. She knows who I mean. The women who've been killed or fear being killed, who fought for survival from people who claimed to love them. I told her I had tried to understand the mechanisms of violence, how one person becomes the perpetrator and another person becomes a victim, and how entrenched these roles become. How I don't believe that a person who is violent is consequently incapable of love.

"*No Visible Bruises*, Mom, is yours," I say. I decide in that moment that I'm going to dedicate it to her. She is one of them, the women who've held these secrets inside them for so long. These women who are survivors of a violence that killed so many others. She squeezes my hand, cries a little.

Then she says, "Can I talk to you about the Lord? I just have to, because He's my life."

I nod.

She tells me Jesus is on her right side at that moment and her guardian angel is on her left and they've been there all week. She can see them. They don't talk, except once to say that everything will be all right. But she can feel them and see them. She says once in the CT scanner, the curved walls tight around her, she looked up and there was Jesus, right above her, inside the machine with her. She just wants me to know she can see them, her angel and her Jesus, that they have come to help her on her journey to wherever and whatever comes next. I think of all the spirits I heard about in Cambodia. The girls in the rafters of the garment factory, the neighbor who came to say goodbye. But most of all my very own mother. Of course I believe my stepmother. Of course I do. We travel with our ghosts. Who better to lead us to what comes next? Our next life, our heaven, the birth of our daughters.

When she is gone, she will go to whatever heaven she believes is waiting for her, while those of us who are left will recount stories of her life. Some will offer prayers in a church. Maybe kaddish. In Cambodia, the monks would pray for a peaceful journey to the next world, and we family who are left would offer fruit and money so she would not want for anything in the spirit world.

I understand, then. She's not telling me a story of Christianity or faith or spirituality. She's not even telling me a story about God. She's just telling me a love story. And I am part of it.

ACKNOWLEDGMENTS

I knew this book had to arrive someday; I carried it inside me for four decades. And so with a heart full of gratitude, I would like to thank: Cindy Wyllie and the Landorf family; Jimmy Riley, Chris Wicklas, Frank Pappalardo, Michelle Thompson, and the White Lie gang; Rick Spencer, Scott Brown, and Alison Rusinow; Myles Lee, Lance Lee, Jeanne Lee, Alyssa Lee, Pete and Linda Gorman, David Jonathan Snyder, Joshua Snyder, John Snyder, and Wes and Barbara Snyder. Thank you to Wynne Cougill, Barbara Cigan, Sophea Seng, Nimol Oum, Kurt Macleod and Kettya Kea.

With extra thanks to a scattered posse: Tayari Jones, Beth Macy, Patrick Radden Keefe, Andre Dubus III, Fontaine Dubus, Danielle Evans, Ayelet Waldman, Michael Chabon, Deborah Copaken, Jeannie Suk Gersen and Jacob Gersen, Peggy Orenstein, Loung Ung, Dick and Jeri Maxwell, Tapley and Mia Jordanwood, and Lt. Gov. Eleni Kounalakis. The island of Spetses will forever be the place I go to restore my soul.

Also thank you to my inspiring colleagues in the literature and journalism departments at American University, with a special shout-out to Linda Voris, Despina Kakoudaki, David Keplinger, Stephanie Grant, Dolen Perkins Valdez, Patricia Park, Sandra Beasley, Melissa Scholes Young, Kyle Dargan, Amy Eisman, Margot Susca, and Peter Starr. A special bow of gratitude to the Red Shoe Team: Masha Gessen, Adrian Nicole LeBlanc, Jess Bruder, Sheri Fink, and Suki Kim. You are hands down the best writing group in the history of all writing groups for all time and in all mediums throughout this galaxy and beyond.

Susan Ramer and I are coming up on thirty years of our partnership and I couldn't do what I do if she didn't do what she did so well. Special gratitude to her, and all her colleagues at Don Congdon Associates, especially Katie Kotchman, Michael Congdon, and Katie Grimm. Gratitude also goes to the Guggenheim Foundation and the DC Commission on the Arts and Humanities for the generous grants that made it possible for me to complete this book. At Lyceum I feel confident that everyone works harder than I deserve, but in particular Hannah Scott and Abigail Parker. At Bloomsbury, the team somehow keeps all the wind perpetually at my back, and I offer boundless thanks to Jillian Ramirez, Rosie Mahorter, Katya Mezhibovskaya, Valentina Rice, Lauren Moseley, Akshaya Iyer, Janet McDonald, and most especially my brilliant editor, Callie Garnett.

And, finally, for my eternal beloved gang—that we should all be so lucky to have one: Ann Maxwell, Don Rutledge, Soleak Sim, Mike Reust, Michelle Rieff, Yana Maxwell, Solaya "Ses" Rutledge, Rohilla Rieff, Violetta Rieff, and, above all, beyond reason and description, for Eliana Jazz, and for Khmow, who made it through the drafting of this book but not the publishing. May her next life bring her as much love as this one did.

Intentional family: The gang in Panama.

A NOTE ON THE AUTHOR

RACHEL LOUISE SNYDER is the author of *Fugitive Denim: A Moving Story of People and Pants in the Borderless World of Global Trade*; the novel *What We've Lost Is Nothing*; and *No Visible Bruises: What We Don't Know About Domestic Violence Can Kill Us*, a *New York Times* Top Ten Book of the Year, winner of the J. Anthony Lukas Work-in-Progress Award, the Hillman Prize, and the Helen Bernstein Book Award, and finalist for the National Book Critics Circle Award, the Los Angeles Times Book Prize, and the Kirkus Prize. Her work has appeared in the *New Yorker*, the *New York Times*, *Slate*, and elsewhere. A 2020–21 Guggenheim Fellow, Snyder is a professor of creative writing and journalism at American University. She lives in Washington, D.C.